THE
INFLUENTIAL
MARKETER

366 Crackin' Copywriting, Marketing & Mindset
Ideas to Skyrocket Your Results One Day at a Time

STEVE PLUMMER

Praise for *The Influential Marketer*

"The Influential Marketer is a power-packed book overflowing with real world ideas that you can immediately apply to connect with your prospects. Steve's straight forward, no fluff advice has set me up for success in my target market by opening up endless opportunities for sales. He really does turn your passion into profit."

Therese Markou – Managing Director, CEO Mission Accomplished

"This guy knows what he's talking about when it comes to marketing and direct marketing in particular. I encourage you to read every word of this valuable resource because you will gain invaluable insights and practical knowledge that you can utilise immediately. Steve Plummer is a "Do as I do" kind of guy, not just a "Do as I say" bloke. I guarantee that what you read in this book is exactly what he does from a practical point of view for himself and his clients. We continuously seek education to improve various aspects of our business. Steve has helped us learn a lot in copywriting, marketing and direct sales for a number of years and the ideas and methods we have implemented, have grown our company immensely. We recently decided to engage him to do much of our marketing for us, taking the strain off us, as our company grows. Just one example, based on the principles in this book, cost us just $500 (one posted letter with product info and offer plus 2 follow up emails) returned sales of $92,000! Steve is a delight to work with, and he is certainly an expert in his field."

Alison & Danny Halupka – Grant Sheds

"When it comes to promoting and building your business – words matter. When you need to sustain and grow your business – sales matter. When I need both, Steve Plummer matters. He is a genius that is genuine. Thank you for all your help and sharing it in this valuable book."

Cory Robertson – Aboriginal Resource Group/Goanna Services

"Having filmed most of the successful businesspeople, coaches and marketing experts in Australia, it gives me a pretty good understanding of who is out there helping people in their businesses. Steve is most definitely one of the best marketing brains I've met. His zeal for life, family, his keen understanding of all things marketing, and copywriting is, in my opinion, unparalleled and this book is an absolute must read. If you don't walk away with a list of things you need to implement from this wealth of knowledge, then you're kidding yourself. I'm so proud of him and thankful to call him a friend! Keep rocking it Steve!"

Dan Steinhauer – Aart House Productions

"Every CEO, business owner, salesperson and marketer wants a competitive advantage over their competition, but not everyone knows how to create and deliver that to the marketplace. Most of the marketing, advertising and sales language is either bland, copied, me-too or a total abject failure and as a direct result, way too many businesspeople go through unnecessary financial hardship, frustration with their marketing, advertising and sales message (no real point of difference). If you have any responsibility for sales or marketing in your organisation, you owe it to yourself to read this book (better still, seek Steve out and have him cast his keen eye and brilliant mind over your projects). There is no secret to the fact that there is an army of competition out there attacking business from every angle, stealing market share and driving prices down, turning products and services into commodities and now more than ever it is imperative that you have a substantial edge. I believe Steve is the cutting edge! He is the difference that makes the difference when it comes down to marketing, sales, cash-flow and profit."

Mark Selbst – Automotive Business Coach

"Imagine being taught to paint by Leonardo Da Vinci. That's how we feel after reading The Influential Marketer as we can now craft our messages to attract more leads than we did before. This is a must read for every business owner."

Naomi Radke and Adam Reeves – Blade Bookkeeping

"I must say I am a little pissed off with this new book! There are so many great ideas and tips, you can just bookmark them, and come back to them again and again. I spent countless hours, read hundreds of Steve's emails, and invested a few grand learning and working with Steve to get access to them - now here they all are! And I use a quite a few of them almost every day – PASPA, starting with the end in mind, and Steve's writing processes (yes, I did edit this a day later). Not to mention some of the topic ideas I have "borrowed" over the years, thanks Steve. They have really helped me and my clients, and if you apply a few of them every month, they will almost certainly work for you too."

David Letizia – Your Business Optimised

"Steve's words have helped me create multi-million-dollar campaigns for my own projects and clients over the past many years. When you combine very well-crafted sales copy with well-designed business growth and marketing systems, you see magic happen. His new book The Influential Marketer is a work of art. Steve has condensed real-life learning, tips, strategies, hints and even some Copywriting Jedi tricks (he normally never teaches), that even if you suck at English, you will be able to increase your sales and conversions by implementing what you read. If you are in any type and size of business or even just starting out, this is one of those books that if you implement just a couple of the strategies Steve talks about you will see a real positive difference. This book should come as standard with every business and certainly one I now recommend in my Business and Marketing Growth workshops worldwide."

Colin Cooper – Business Growth Strategist

The Influential Marketer: 366 Crackin' Copywriting, Marketing & Mindset Ideas to Skyrocket Your Results One Day at a Time © Stephen Plummer 2023

www.symmetrymarketing.com.au

The moral rights of Stephen Plummer to be identified as the author of this work have been asserted in accordance with the Copyright Act 1968.

First published in Australia 2023 by Symmetry Marketing and Publishing.

www.symmetrymarketing.com.au

ISBN 978-0-6487841-2-8

Any opinions expressed in this work are exclusively those of the author and are not necessarily the views held or endorsed by Symmetry Marketing and Publishing.

Disclaimer

Dedication

For Jenny, Eliza, Maddie, Isaac and Nate, the closest people in the world to me…
your unconditional love energises and uplifts me every day …

For Vince, my dad, who instilled in me the love of words,
only wish you were here to see this…

For the gentle soul inside the white ball of fluff, the Lhasa Apso X Moodle,
Tilly, who for 11 years was my muse and constant companion when writing…
RIP little one…

And for business owners and entrepreneurs, your courage to go it alone
and run your own race keeps the country moving
and inspires me every day to help you succeed…

This book is for you.

Foreword

A s a schoolteacher and eventually deputy principal, Steve understood that the difference between being a great teacher and everyone else, was not how well they knew the material, but rather how well they engaged the kids.

Some 30 years later, this core truth plays out in all his marketing strategies.

How well you engage your audience is more important than how good your product is … until they buy. Then your product had better match up.

As a sports journalist, he also understood that the reader only reads the article if the headline grabs their attention. He also quickly discovered he could help an athlete's career simply by writing about them as an interesting brand, rather than just another sports performance to report.

Decades later, this basic truth of headline and hook still feature in all his marketing strategies.

I've known Steve for many years and have watched his marketing intuition and strategic thinking evolve into a sharpened set of real-world skills, that weaponize the ability of any business he works with, to reach their target market, with the right message, in a way that stimulates action.

I've watched him present to audiences of widely disparate businesses and deliver immediately actionable marketing strategies that resonated with each business and their circumstances.

His ability to bring it back to the simple is pure gold.

Born out of his hard-wired desire to teach, Steve works with his clients to deliver marketing strategies that not only engage with and influence the target market, but also to improve the marketing capability and resilience of his clients.

A lot of marketers run campaigns. Steve does too!

But Steve is also invested in building internal strength and belief.

When I read Steve's draft of this book I initially took is as a "strategy a day" that I could draw on - and in that sense that's true.

There is so much in here.

If I want to know about diagnosing the market, it's in here!

Or understanding the psychology of sales, it's in here!

Or how to craft great headlines that grab attention, it's in here!

Or dealing with buyer's remorse, writing winning sales letters, getting attention in a noisy world, opening sales conversations in a letter, authenticity, the three key sales questions, success thinking, copywriting tips, lead magnets that work, how to plan a landing page video, lead generation … and more, it's all in here!

Then I started thinking, what if I read only one chapter per day and then used that to ask myself, **how well do we do that in our business, and what small thing could we change quickly that would make us better at it?**

What would my business be like after that process?

Use the book as you best see fit but whatever you do, make sure you appreciate the superpowers Steve has put into these pages.

Ultimately, superpowers are usually pretty simple concepts, but the wisdom of how you use them is what drives the results.

Simon Bowen
Consultant & Creator of the Models Method

Table of Contents

Introduction

If you're looking for a literary masterpiece, stop now. This book is designed with one purpose in mind: to offer you help each day. And that help comes in the form of tips for writing, tips for writing sales language (aka copywriting), tips for marketing, tips for business, and tips to help you master your mind.

One of the things about many business and marketing books is they can be quite "heavy" in that they require focus and time to read, re-read and fully understand. *The Influential Marketer* is deliberately NOT like that. Organised around a "lesson per day per page" format it's a fast and easy read that follows TWO important TRUTHS:

Important truth #1 – Small hinges swing big doors: in other words, it's often not the big breakthrough that changes things… rather it's the application of small things over time that add up to big results

Important Truth #2 – Focus on fundamentals rather than tactics: if you ignore the fundamentals, you are just one algorithm change or media manipulation away from being stuck… whereas if you learn the fundamentals, you can apply them to any media and adapt them in response to change

My hope is you'll take the principles here and apply them to your life and your work tactically, so your influence grows.

Before we go on, let's be clear what "influence" means.

According to Britannica Dictionary "influence" means… **"the power to change or affect someone or something – OR – the power to cause changes without directly forcing them to happen."**

My humble take: influence is a superpower. In a business context, to me it's clear… if you want to expand your audience, deepen your impact, and grow profits… you must be able to INFLUENCE others. And the most powerful way to do this is with your words.

Every lesson in *The Influential Marketer* is based on my journey in education, journalism, copywriting, marketing, and business over the last 30+ years.

I've written it in a conversational way, similar to how I write sales copy.

Therefore you WILL find grammatical errors. If you're the anal type who looks for such things… be warned!

Each entry is about getting my message across to you, fast. It's not about proving I write gooder than you.

The entries are in no particular order although you will find a bias towards copy, in particular, headlines.

You will also see many different tips for similar topics, like headlines. This illustrates the point, **there are many ways to be right.** There's no point sticking dogmatically to one particular theory or template.

If this book opens your mind to new ideas, gives you a different approach to problems, or helps you feel better at a time when you need it, then it's been worthwhile for me to bring it to you.

My life is a good example of what I consider a truth: having a job is easier, but if you're so inclined, running your own business is way better.

Last thing, I leave you with one of my favorite quotes, from US president Theodore Roosevelt: **"Far better it is to dare mighty things, to win glorious triumphs, even though checkered by failure, than to take rank with those poor spirits who neither enjoy much nor suffer much, because they live in a gray twilight that knows neither victory nor defeat."**

May this book help you grow your influence so you never live in that "gray twilight".

To your success.

Steve Plummer

Let's begin…

But I can't write

"I'm not like you Steve, I wasn't good at English at school, I'm not a good writer," said a business owner to me who wanted to learn more about copywriting so he could boost sales.

Great, you'll be able to do well at copy then! Was my not so sympathetic reply.

What the? Yep, you heard it the first time…

You do NOT have to be good at English to be good at copy.

Here's why…

Great copy is NOT written like a story, it's assembled. There's no, *Once upon a time… the end* linear kind of thing. It's vital you plan out or storyboard your sales message. This makes it easier to see what's missing. The plan can be a one or two page "summary" that has the opening, key points you want to make, the offer, proof, the close and so on. Or it can be a storyboard like I do for shock and awe marketing packs… a 1-page doc that has the headlines of each of the chapters clear and often some bullets about what I intend to include in each section.

The benefits of doing this are…

- Clarity (you know where your sales message is "going")
- Efficiency (you can see where the gaps exist)
- Flexibility (you can write in chunks depending on your mood)

The reality is, writing copy is not easy. My thinking is, if I know what I'm doing because I have a plan or outline, I can manage my energy and time much better.

I start with the offer and close. Write that chunk. Then I go to the headlines.

Hmmm not sure what I will do now… look at my plan… ok, I'll write the bullets that go there.

Next time I sit down at the computer… ok, let's tackle the story of the product development which fits here.

Like I said, great copy is not written like a story in school… it's assembled. It's like putting together a wooden chair the old-fashioned way. Piece by piece. Let the glue dry. Sand it down to smooth the rough bits. Wait awhile. Paint it.

Then, ta-da! Your completed sales copy… er… chair. Same thing.

Remember… copy ain't written, it's assembled.

Go forth and assemble your way to greater influence and profit.

When to get emotional in copy

Pass the tissues, it's time to reveal when we need to get all emotional…

In your copy, **ALL THE TIME.**

You've heard the saying, facts only tell, emotions sell.

What emotions are we talking about?

The main ones us humans have:

Love: of family, of business, of customers etc… if selling kids' birthday party plans for instance, it's not just about the cake and the lollies you provide, it's the joy, the memories, the laughter. Sell these.

Shame: as the great Dan Kennedy says, "No one wants to be in Loserville" so make sure your child's birthday party is the one everyone talks about (to continue our theme). Sell here.

Vanity: of course, you want to be the best parent, not just give kids a cool bag of lollies as they leave, so sell this. Mention the lolly bags as an aside, but not as the main thing. The emotion is the kicker.

Good copy forces people to make a decision about themselves. And this is VERY emotional.

So include emotions and wrap them around an engaging story and you have a winning sales formula.

Jerry Maguire headline Secret

Remember the hit flick from a few years back, *Jerry Maguire* starring Tom Cruise and Renee Zellweger? Yes, the *"Show me the money!"* movie.

There's a vital scene towards the end for any marketer or copywriter or business owner, so listen up, class is in…

The pivotal marketing scene starts with a group of women sitting around in Renee Z's lounge in a quasi but nice "man hating" session. In walks a very solemn Jerry Maguire and tries to cut through the bad fest in progress…

"Hello," he says.

Stunned silence. Sooooo romantic…

Ok, just kidding.

He says…

"Hello. I'm looking for my wife."

As a seeming thousand man-hating eyes watch his every move in the awkward silence… In walks the aforementioned Renee Z who'd all but given up on him and his bad husband, career chasing self…

And he goes into his pitch…

"I'm not letting you get rid of me… The company had a big night tonight, but it wasn't complete without you… We live in a cynical world… You complete me," Blah blah blah.

Nice moment for romantic types. It's ok, I agree on that. Anyways… After Jerry's from the heart speech to the stunned, all female audience, Renee Z says…

"You had me at hello."

Remember that? Well, there IS a big headline lesson here…

Unless you hook them with **huge curiosity** or a **strong WIIFM** (what's in it for me)…

YOU LOSE THEM AT HELLO.

And there's no happy ever after, unlike the movie. So **get them at hello or lose them forever.** Sear this one into your brain because a lot of the copy I critique loses me at hello.

Class dismissed.

What the heck is it?

L et's be 100% clear... copywriting is sales language or the language of sales.

How to use words to move a prospect from their position as a prospect into the position as a paying customer.

You've got to get those foundations right. Often, we think it's a really simple thing but if you're going to be really good with your words you have to know what you are doing because it isn't just a thing off the top of your head that you can turn up and do on a whim. You've got to put more thought into it than that.

Here's your first step...

RESEARCH.

The "R" word gets bandied around in copywriting and marketing, often. Only thing is I'm not 100% convinced even experienced marketers really know how to research.

It comes down to finding out "stuff" about 3 things...

- The buyer (their emotions, where in the buying cycle they are)
- The competitors out there (what has come before you and works now)
- The solution you're selling (so you can talk about the features, benefits, and emotional pay off the buyer gets)

Miss one and quite often the message falls flat.

You have to uncover all this before you write a single word of the sales message.

And of course you go online, dig offline, and talk to your customers to find out all of the above.

Just remember...

You need to uncover details about all three (your prospect, your competitor, your product/service) before a single word of sales copy is written.

Where do you get your ideas from?

Yes, it's a question I get often. So… drum roll please because here's the answer…

They just come to me.

Sorry but it's true. That said, when I deconstruct my idea sources, they do seem to come from a common series of "places". So, if you've ever been stuck for what to write in an email, a blog, or video script, you need this.

Here are 11 sources of ideas for content and quick example of how I've used it…

- Family (I often talk about my kids, aging parents when they were alive, and lessons they give me)
- Pets (how we acquired my "little white ball of fluff" Tilly story still cracks audiences up)
- Your failures (I reveal mistakes I made with my 2nd paying copywriting gig – ouch)
- Your successes (hey c'mon… you want to hear them again? Ok so there was the sales letter last year…)
- Travel (I've told MANY holiday stories, in fact it was this time last year we got back from the US…)
- Your flaws (the *Me, the fat bastard* email with before and after pix was one of my most read emails)
- Hobbies (at the gym with my boys boxing, fishing, reading…)
- Client successes (never stop telling about them, like the $5 million real estate campaign I wrote…)
- Pet peeves (yes, I still hate being called "mate" or "dude" by a 15-year-old shop assistant)
- Your transformation (teacher to top of the tree copywriter is part of what makes me me)
- Celebrity encounters (in my trainings I've shown pix of me with Dan Kennedy, Frank Kern, Rusell Brunson etc etc)

Go ahead, for each of these categories write down 5 story ideas… will take about 10 minutes… not the story itself but the idea. Naturally you come back and flesh these out. But 10 minutes now gives you 55 ideas for sales messages. At worst, that's one per week – a whole year's content. Not a bad return for your time invested.

KEY POINT: the story must be about you. People can spot a fake tale a mile away AND (this is big) the story must be relatable back to the problems of your market. Even though it's about YOU it must become about THEM. In each story, identify the lesson for the reader.

Eg From the hobbies category, I told in an email to my list the story of the power of words scattered around the gym where my boys and I box that inspire hard work and dedication… the message from that email was that words DO matter in your business, so choose them carefully EVERY time you go to market.

Now here's the really cool part… when you do this you trigger that part of your brain called the RAS (reticular activating system) and suddenly story and content ideas pop out of nowhere. You start seeing things and remembering things you had never even contemplated. And… it's kind of fun! Enjoy.

Sales Formula

Those who've been around me long enough know my preference for the simple but effective 5-step sales formula, PASPA.

No, I didn't invent it. And no, it's not new. Nor is it the only sales formula. But it IS proven to work.

And in truth it's been responsible for millions and probably billions in sales in all markets over the last century.

Here it is explained:

P = problem (where you identify a challenge your market faces – *If you're in business and you've ever struggled with sales, then this proven formula is a game changer for you…*)

A = aggravate (where you "twist the knife" or "press the bullet wound" so the prospects feel the pain of inaction – *Too often business owners spend a fortune on useless ads or waste countless hours on new closing techniques only to see their results stay the same or, worse, nosedive…*)

S = solve (where you offer a solution to the pain you've created – *Here is the fastest and easiest way to reverse flatlined sales… apply the PASPA formula to EVERY customer interaction. It's easy to learn and even easier to build a presentation around…*)

P = prove (everyone is sceptical, so you need to offer evidence the solution works – *John Smith from Smith Bros applied this formula and in the first week his sales almost doubled… similar story for Mary Jones, a naturopath, whose client conversions were up 30% in the first month she applied it… are quick examples*)

A = action (where you tell them exactly what they have to do to get it – *To get your own copy of the PASPA formula and how to deploy it in your business, click the "Yes Please" button below now…*)

Ok, the examples are just that to illustrate the point. They aren't samples of "great" copy to swipe and deploy.

The thing is, you need to go into every sales situation, in writing or in person, with a proven system to follow.

Now you have one, PASPA.

To repeat, this isn't the only formula… but it's a proven one.

Security is a myth unless you...

Reminiscing with Jenny about her career in nursing and it brought up a real MYTH about work and life.

You see when we were first married, she worked for a small private hospital. I was a teacher back then. We both had an employee mindset. Won't go into all the parents/Depression/war era programming of *get a good job and enjoy the gold watch at the end* kind of thing. We'd bought into it big time.

Anyways the hospital she was at was bought out by one of the big companies that gave shares to employees. Not long after that she had an offer from a bright entrepreneurial doctor who wanted to go out on his own. It was mild panic stations in our employee mind.

What if he fails? What if he gets hit by a bus? What if he gets sued? What if no one books appointments? On and on it went... the toing and froing both in our minds and verbally between ourselves.

Way too risky to leave the big company, right? We'd even lose the shares! Well, she did leave and here's what happened.

She's been with the entrepreneurial doctor for 22 years and is now the Business Manager of a multi-million-dollar enterprise.

The old hospital?

That's been sold two or three times by the corporates and is now a psychiatric facility.

Security?

Bah!!!

There is none, except...

Except you and your own skills. Which is why you should always invest in yourself and your skillset and NEW ways of doing things.

That is the ONLY security today.

Be really good at what you do, and you will always be in demand, no matter what happens in the big wide world.

Keep learning, growing, and say yes to opportunities... it beats staying in one place.

Why the "who" is more important than the "what"

D on't fish in a shitty pond.

Seems simple enough, but many ignore this guiding principle. You see long dead copywriting genius Ed Mayer theorised that the success of any campaign is determined by 40% the market. 40% the offer. And 20% the copy.

Now I'm not certain if these percentages are totally accurate these days but the lesson is huge:

THE WHO you sell to is MORE IMPORTANT than the WHAT YOU SELL.

Sure, your product or service must be good.

But it can be great and if the market you sell to has no capacity to pay, it's wasted time and effort…

AKA a "shitty pond".

And no, this isn't permission to get slack with your copy or delivery.

But…

Pick the right group of people with a capacity to pay, present them with a well-crafted and tight message and strong "I gotta have this now" offer, and your biz life will be so much easier.

If you're in a shitty pond right now, it's not too late to find deeper and cleaner water.

Obvious but often missed

All good things, they say, come in 3s. Yes, same for bad things, apparently. Where did this obsession with 3s come from?

We can blame religion to an extent I believe. Jesus rose from the dead on the third day. Then there's the Holy Trinity (Father, Son, Spirit). And even the less well-known Wiccan religion has a Law of Three which goes something like...

Whatever energy you put out into the world is returned to you THREEFOLD.

Then we have The Three Wise Men, Three Little Pigs and on it goes. So yeah, 3 is hugely important and deeply ingrained in our subconscious.

The marketing world also uses this principle.

In fact, if you're ever looking for a REASON why your ad/sales message didn't work you only need to look at the "marketing triangle". Hmmm a THREE sided figure which tells us, to be successful, we must present...

The **RIGHT MESSAGE...**

Which is seen by the...

RIGHT MARKET...

Because it's in the **RIGHT MEDIA...**

Miss one, and the "magic 3" ain't there and chances are...

Your marketing fails.

Message – Market – Media is one of those "power of 3" rules to follow, always.

A (justified) rant

W rite this one down… it might be marketing 101 but I'm sick of seeing this…

I was talking to a friend who runs a big business and he was telling me things had slowed a little. He said they'd paid <name removed to cover their guilt> marketing agency to re-do their website.

I had a quick look for him.

The headline was…

Drum roll please…

THE NAME OF THE BUSINESS.

True story.

It was name of business and then a lukewarm quasi benefit driven sub head.

What the?

He told me how much he'd paid the "experts".

Double what the?

Wow.

Here it is, THE rant…

YOUR BUSINESS NAME IS NOT YOUR HEADLINE.

Period. Why? No one cares what you call yourself. Not a lick. Nil. Zilch. Nada. They only care what RESULT you can give them.

When you tell them upfront, the What's In It For Me (WIIFM), you at least give yourself a fighting chance.

Sheesh.

Sadly, this happens too often. And it cheeses me off big time (in case you couldn't tell).

Work hard at your crafting your headline and never use your business name… or suffer the lack of sales consequences.

Rant endeth.

How to combat buyer's remorse

The HARDEST, MOST EXPENSIVE and MOST TIME-CONSUMING thing you do in business is get a NEW client. Why then does just about everyone underestimate the difficulty of the task of selling?

Because it's so tough to get a NEW client, it makes sense then to do everything in your power to make the sale stick.

Buyer's remorse is the ever-present enemy… the dragon that can burn a hole in your profits. And it must be slain with maximum prejudice. Otherwise you face more expense replacing the refunded sale.

How do you do that?

In my book there are 3 things. Let's assume it's a great product. It was pitched at the right market. And it does what it should do and gives them a feeling of value for money.

So here's are the 3 things you can do…

#1 – Include a surprise unannounced bonus (which makes them feel good)

#2 – Send a well-crafted stick letter and/or email (makes them feel loved and important)

#3 – Do BOTH (which closes the sales loop and reduces refunds).

When I craft a stick letter or email, I make sure it has these components…

- Congratulations and thank you
- A reminder of what they invested in
- A brief reminder of the result or benefit
- Proof from people just like them
- A list of what they get
- Future pacing (when they implement it, what they can look forward to…)
- What happens next for them

Go forth make the sale stick, it plugs holes in your sales process.

Recklessness is the answer

Yep, seriously.

You need to be more reckless.

Why? Well, the #1 demon many of us face is SELF- DOUBT.

Here's what I mean…

Whenever we face a decision that voice in our heads pings off questions like, *Shouldn't you wait a little longer? Are you really ready? What if they don't like it? What if it fails and you look silly?*

This demon stops all progress.

Question is, how to defeat it…

Reckon it's a combination of bravery + recklessness + action.

No, I'm not talking about mortgaging the house and betting the lot on red at the roulette table or stupidity like that.

But…

Nothing great was ever achieved without a certain amount of recklessness.

Brendan Burchard, in his book *The Motivation Manifesto* summed it up best…

"Our destiny hinges on a mindset for bold action. We gain power from again and again allowing ourselves to choose the kind of recklessness that allows us to be vulnerable, genuine, and brave in pursuit of our dreams."

Been playing too "safe" lately?

Need bold action to break free?

Important questions for you to answer in your business.

Be "reckless"…

Know them – market diagnosis questions

Want a framework for getting into the head of your market?

Not sure who first created this list of profiling questions (think it was Dan Kennedy or the equally brilliant Gary Halbert, or even someone else), but it's been the go-to staple for decades for anyone who wants to know their market better.

So BEFORE you write a word of copy, answer these questions in as much detail as possible…

1. What keeps them awake at night, their guts churning, their mind replaying over and over again as they stare at the ceiling?
2. What are they afraid of?
3. What are they angry about? Who are they angry at?
4. What are their top 3 daily frustrations?
5. What trends are occurring and will occur in their business or lives?
6. What do they secretly desire the most?
7. Is there a built-in bias to the way they make decisions?
8. Do they have their own language?
9. Who else sells a similar product/service to them that you do?
10. Why would they NOT buy from you?

Only when you have **detailed** answers to these questions should you consider putting fingers to keyboard.

How to get a teen to clean his room

7 cups, 3 towels on the floor, 1 mostly empty bowl with spoon, numerous clothes and single shoes scattered afar…

Such was the state of Yr 10 son's room one Saturday morning. If you've ever had a teen in your house, it's probably a familiar tale of woe.

Key question:

How the heck to get a teenage boy to fix his wicked, slothful ways, and clean up his room?

Asking nicely? The 7 cups suggest ineffective.

Threats (and follow through)? Short term fix only.

Bribes to push the positive? Cereal bowl suggests nah.

At wits end? Kinda. Here's what happened…

Frustrated wife thought bugger this, he doesn't respond to normal human interaction (read verbal communication).

And…

Teen is ALWAYS on an electronic device, so…

Instead of asking/telling/yelling/punishing for no result, wife texts son thus…

"Hi buddy, can you do a quick tidy up of your room please. Thanks. Love mum xxx"

Result…

We walked past his room 15 minutes later and everything was clean and tidy.

No fuss. No fights. No stress.

Yes, what the?

Clear lesson:

Like I said in Entry #9… Reach your MARKET in the MEDIA they use with the right MESSAGE. Only then can you get the results you want.

PROOF – How much is enough?

S hort answer… you can never have too much.

Why? We all buy on emotion and justify with logic, so proof covers both.

To explain…

Every one of us is FEARFUL of being ripped off. It's a raw and strong emotion. You must counter this in your sales message.

Not only that…

We need proof to justify the purchase to the logical side of the brain (and anyone who asks why we bought).

Understand too that before we buy, we do a little value calculation in our heads… *If I give up X dollars, will I get GREAT value?*

If the voice comes back with a "No" then sale over.

So you need lots and lots and lots of proof to beat these anti-sale demons.

How much is enough? Include as much as ad/page/channel will allow!

You can generally divide proof elements into 3 categories…

- Testimonials and case studies from users of the product or service
- A "celebrity" endorsement either paid or implied (includes "as seen in" visuals)
- Product in action (such as before and after shots)

Remember you can never have too much proof. All these are used to make it easier for the person to do that value calculation in their heads.

Include as much proof as you can AND as many varieties as you can.

And as always, test and measure.

Know their PNR

W hat's your customer's PNR?

This is key to the sales process. You need to reverse engineer everything with one simple goal: how can we simply, easily, and with least cost get the customer to the PNR.

To explain…

PNR is a pilot term which stands for "Point of No Return". There is a point during the take-off sequence, when the plane reaches a certain speed and position on the tarmac, the pilot has to go through with the take-off because there's not enough runway to slow down. There's no turning back.

It's similar with your sales process. You need to know what your PNR is, the point where if you get the customer there, there's an 80% to 90% chance they'll buy.

Quick example. The PNR in boating is to get a prospect to take a test drive on the water. If they become "emotionally invested" enough to do this, there is an 80%-90% they are going to buy.

What's your PNR? What is that point, if you get a customer to, they are 80% to 90% chance of buying?

Know it and do EVERYTHING to get them to it.

Sales letter sequence

S tuck for a long form sales message formula? Not sure where this one comes from but it's pretty spot on. Follow this 16-step sequence (based on PASPA) and you'll be on the right track...

1. Pre-head which calls out who it's for
2. Attention Getting Headline (curiosity + BIG Promise)
3. Sub-Head that Explains the Promise
4. Opening/Identify the Problem
5. Agitate the Problem
6. Solve the Problem
7. Prove it works
8. How to - Describe Offer in Detail
9. Bullets of benefits (and feelings these benefits give)
10. Answer Objections
11. Warn of the pain of not acting
12. State Price
13. Risk Reversal Guarantee
14. Scarcity and Urgency - Reason to Act NOW
15. Call to Action – what to do
16. P.S. Reiterate why you need to act NOW, guarantee, offer

There you go... next sales message you craft, follow these 16 steps.

And just in case you were wondering, NO, it's not "THE ONLY" formula (but it's a VERY successful one, there are many others). Nor is it a magic pill. It's a framework to follow.

As always, test and measure.

How to open a sales message #1

O ne area where even experienced marketers stumble is the opening. I use two favourites about 75% of the time… the if/then and "list of pain".

No I didn't invent either but use both regularly.

There's nothing worse than staring at a blank screen when you have a sales message to write, so this helps.

These techniques are similar in that they aggravate a problem and offer immediate relief. But also slightly different in execution.

Here's the if/then…

This is a simple one-two.

If you have X problem and want a solution, then this message is vital to your happiness.

If you've ever sat down to write your sales message but started to panic when words didn't magically flow, then this technique is a quick and easy way to get started.

There you go, a couple of quick examples.

P.S. The opening is <u>not</u> where I start writing. I always start with the offer, call to action, then go the headline – see entry #1.

P.P.S. For the second sample opening see #54

What successful people do on long weekends

S o how "successful" are you?

This could be determined by what you do on your long weekends, at least according to a recent article by Atreyee Chowdhury…

Apparently, here are the 7 things successful people do in their downtime:

#1 – Unplug… no mobiles and laptops

#2 – Exercise… because it relieves stress

#3 – Think about things other than work… to refresh the brain

#4 – Do nothing and enjoy the feeling of being uncommitted, unplanned, unscheduled

#5 – Get outside… unwind outdoors in the sun and fresh air

#6 – Meditate… to relax body and mind

#7 – Stay "up"… meaning they block negative thoughts and feelings that can come over you in quieter times

Food for thought at least… while business can be and often is all-consuming, remember even elite athletes have their day off from training, their downtime… do you?

How to deal with client push back

E ver had a client push back on you?

Maybe a new one. Or a long term one. It happens with both.

Let's take **price** for instance…

You send out a compelling and well thought out offer. You don't get the response you expect. You do some digging and get push back on price.

What's your immediate thought? It's too expensive. Or the copy didn't work (no, it ain't always "the copy"!!!). Or they didn't understand the value. And on it goes.

But is that really it?

Do you dig deep enough with your customers and know them intimately?

Because the "no" you got may not be about price. It could very well be about cashflow for them at a certain time of year.

In a perfect world, we'd all have a steady income stream with no peaks and troughs. Not reality though, is it?

Same for your customers.

It could just be your offer landed on them at a time of low cashflow and that was the reason they didn't buy… it wasn't price per se… it wasn't value they didn't understand… it wasn't the copy…

Right now may have been one of those troughs in cashflow. Which is why it's vital you know the rhythms of your market. And put offers in front of them at times they are more likely to be able to say yes.

Dig deeper. Know them beyond the surface level. And above all…

Don't assume, because ill-informed assumptions cost your business.

Please, don't settle

Oh well, only 8 and half years to go...

So said "Phil", a dear and loyal friend of the past 27 years.

We taught together decades ago and caught up at one of my birthday celebrations.

Naturally the conversation had drifted to work, and I'd asked him how teaching was going. To be sure, "Phil" is a skilled and conscientious teacher. But what he said hit me in the gut.

For a couple of reasons...

One, it could have been me saying this had I stayed in teaching.

And two, that's NO way to live...

Oh well, only 8 and half years to go...

Counting down till you "finish" something that no longer serves you, feeling "trapped" by your circumstances.

"Phil" is not the first I've seen in this situation. You too probably know people who had more to give but due to their own limiting beliefs, settled for less.

In fact, the stuck energy of the "Phils" of this world is one of the reasons I left teaching to run my own business.

There was no way I was going to be "that guy".

Like I said, it's no way to live. It was a real down moment in a magnificent 3-day party that took about 7 days to get over.

So please, no matter where you're "at" right now... don't settle.

You have more to create. More to give. More to do.

And that's where the magic is... you creating and doing and building something.

How was your day, love?

The next thing that's said is often something like, "Not bad". Or "Ok."

Sound familiar?

This is surface level stuff, common to most of us as the first few things we say to our partner at the end of a working day.

It takes a little time for couples to get to how things "really" are.

What cheesed you off in the day. What problems are going on at work and so on.

It's this deeper stuff that really counts because it's the **dominant emotion** playing out in our minds.

And so it is with your market.

You see I was asked about tips for researching and getting into the head of your market. If there's one thing I want to know, it's this… what is said behind closed doors once the mundane, *how was your day* surface stuff is voiced.

What's that painful emotion they have. What's playing on their mind.

This, plus the 10 profiling questions (entry #13), is where I start.

Find the dominant emotion, flesh it out with accurate answers to the 10 profiling questions and you're well on the way to making a sale.

Never wait till you're thirsty

A word of caution about sales and marketing...

"Don't wait until you are thirsty before you start digging the well."

Love that saying. It's a mistake many a business owner makes.

And if I reflect on all the sales calls I've done over the years the, *I really want to work with you, but I won't be ready until February* (or whatever "their" time frame is), is not uncommon.

Don't get me wrong, timing IS important in any business relationship.

But what also holds true is that too many people want all the ducks lined up before they act.

And this can lead to a frustrating and expensive game of catch up.

So yes, market NOW, don't wait till the business gets really thirsty... start digging the well... while there's still time.

Language myth exposed: don't fall for this one

"My market won't like that, it's too salesy!"

So said a client once when I showed her a sample of some copy which has worked in a similar situation in a similar market.

It's one of the frustrations of what I do…

Combating the "but my market is different" false belief.

What this often means is that their marketing efforts to date have not given them the results they wanted.

CUT TO THE CHASE:

The idea that your market is somehow separated from the human race, is devoid of emotion, and only responds to formal or "professional" language is wrong.

Plain wrong.

They and you and me all have fears and wants and needs and desires…

We all get up in the morning, brush our teeth for the day and so on.

So conversational copy which talks directly to the person and their problems will bring better results than "professional" language.

Lots of market tests prove this right.

To assume your market is different is a big error to avoid at all costs.

Never gunna give you up...

R emember Rick Astley's smash hit from the 80s?

Never gunna give you up,

Never gunna let you down,

Never gunna run around and desert you.

Aaah the 80s...

High hair, taffeta, shoulder pads and oooh... remember the lycra and leg warmers?

Don't get me started...

Now I'm not much of a cook. But when I do get in the kitchen, I like a beer in hand and some 80s tunes blaring out. When my kids were teenagers, they'd cringe. Now they're more inclined to sing along.

But...

When I was cooking a roast once and was right into it, belting out...

Never gunna make you cry.

Never gunna say goodbye.

Never gunna tell a lie...

I heard 2 teen voices joining in as they passed through the kitchen.

Hah!

Just shows, quality always wins out. And proves the principle that winners are timeless...

Even if teens don't want to admit it.

Which is a bit like the success principles behind great marketing.

The media may change, but the principles of success work across all media. Invest in learning the fundamentals or principles (like in this book!!), they won't let you down.

A confidence trick

J ab - jab - right… BANG!

So goes the sequence in the boxing gym. I love boxing training. And you may be aware I've watched and written about the sport for years. I've even been a ring announcer. Never done it competitively beyond sparring mind you… but watched and written about it plenty…

I know lots about the subject, have some confidence around it, can speak with authority about it.

But, gotta tell you, between KNOWING and DOING there is a BIG difference!

Case in point: when I first started at the gym they described me as "green" (read: no practical idea). When punching my fist didn't roll… chin was held too high… hands didn't snap out and back.

So old pro Tony got me in the ring: he with hand mitts, me with gloves while I punched and learned under his guidance. After just 6 minutes I was exhausted but – and here's the big but - I'd learned. It took an expert with his eagle eye to guide me in the RIGHT way.

In truth my mind had played a CONFIDENCE TRICK on me…

I thought I knew what I was doing but the TRUTH was, as they politely said, I was "green".

MORE:

I now also know that if I could get just one intense expert session with a pro like Tony every week my skills, stamina, and REAL CONFIDENCE would skyrocket.

What about you?

Do you play a similar "confidence trick" about your ability to write cash-pulling copy for yourself or other people's businesses? Think you know a lot about the subject but don't have the RESULTS to back it up?

If so, or even if you're very good, I urge you to keep learning and growing. Keep drilling down. Put the work in.

It really is the only way forward.

Today, find one new thing to learn about your craft, your industry, your business niche.

If we don't adopt this mindset, well, we don't grow. And if we don't grow, the opposite happens…

Remember the good old days...

R emember the good old days, when life was simpler and easier? Less rushed. Calmer. Nicer. Remember then? Answer: yes, we all can.

Example...

My daughters Eliza and Maddie are born 2 days and 2 years apart and have been best friends since forever. They returned home (from uni in Brisbane) one August weekend and gee it took me back to the days when they were inseparable. They were besties. They did everything together. And even though now they are in their early 20s, for a fleeting moment when they were together it was like they were 2 and 4 in their own world having fun.

Aaaah those were the days...

But were they? At one point we had 4 kids under 5. Life was a blur of meals, nappies, washing, playing with kids, driving them to kindy, parties, sleepovers etc. So good old days? At times yes, but if I think about it enough... nope.

But...

And it's a big but with a marketing lesson... In that instant when the girls were together... I only remembered the good times. It's a human trait. You see we all hark back to often imagined "better times" when we were happier, thinner, had more time, laughed more etc.

And it's often complete BS because for some reason we only remember "good things".

Recent example...

I've been doing some copy for a doctors' surgery. Tough market because they compete with bigger medical centres. But if you're a certain age (read "old") I bet you remember when you were a kid, and you had a family doctor who knew your name and the names of all your family and everyone's medical history. Remember how uncomfortable it was on the odd occasion when you had to see a new doctor? It was horrible. Yes, those were the days, right? Or were they?

Now? Medical centres can be impersonal and you're in and out in a few minutes and no one knows your name. Sound familiar?

So what I did for the traditional doctors' surgery client was...

Take the "old school" surgery's prospects back to the day when they were kids. In the copy I pained past "good" times and used them against the "horrible" current times. Result? They stopped the campaign because they were booked out 2 weeks in advance. So yes, nostalgia works. The challenge to you... how can you use largely imagined good times in your sales messages?

PS Apart from seeing the same doctor all the time... think back... were the old times "that good"? Me thinks not. Modern medicine is way superior to 70s and 80s era medicine... but we hark back to the feeling... that is the key when using nostalgia to sell.

Three VITAL Sales Questions

Q uick tip today to boost response.

This applies whether your sales message is written or spoken and no matter what media it appears in.

Every sales message must provide a clear and compelling answer to these three questions:

- **Why this solution?**
- **Why this solution with you, not a competitor?**
- **Why this solution now?**

If your conversions are down, chances are one or more of these key questions are not answered with enough power in your copy.

This is a great place to start your critique because these three key questions are bubbling away in your prospects' minds.

Are the Social Media warriors wrong?

H ustle. Crush it. Smash it out of the park.

These are all buzz words on social media these days.

Inference being…

Unless you push push push you can't be successful.

But is that really the case?

A clear and calm mind is a much better tool than a tired and stressed one. No, I'm not advocating sloth. There is work to be done.

But 12+ hour days, 6 days a week while you push and hustle every minute?

Not so sure, especially after seeing this from Zach Galifianakis. He's better known for his role as "Alan" from *The Hangover* trilogy… and pretty close to my all-time favourite movie character.

A successful actor, here's what he said:

Destroy the idea that you have to be constantly working or grinding in order to be successful. Embrace the concept that rest, recovery, reflection are essential parts of the progress towards a successful and happy life.

Read that again…

A philosophical twist for today, but worth pondering in your downtime…

Another copywriting "click" that's in our DNA

W hat do you do when you go shopping? What about when you're organising a party? Or how about a busy day at work? If you're like most people, **you make a list.**

Lists are ingrained in us as humans. They are also powerful persuasion tools.

Why?

Well, when we see a list, we are hard-wired to read it. Here's how to turn the humble list into a persuasion tool:

Think of as many reasons why your prospects should do business with you. Make sure you hit their buying buttons in the context of your product or service.

Next, give each a number and tease out the details.

Then create a little segue into the list, for example…

Here are the 6 reasons why lists are powerful persuasion tools.

See, you wanted to find out what the 6 are didn't you?

Why this works:

1. We all love lists
2. They act as a powerful summary
3. They can be read quickly and easily
4. Power is in the specificity 9 reasons… *There's 9 (more is better than less… if there are only three, chances are the reader will believe they know them… when there's 7 or 9 or 10 or more, there's a good chance you don't know them all)*
5. They cut through the clutter and are good for attracting the attention of skim readers
6. We want closure, so good chance we'll read to the end

Lists rock… use them wherever you can.

The importance of asking

Y es. No. Maybe.

They are the ONLY three answers you'll ever get when you ask someone for something. So said my very first copywriting mentor, the legendary Ted Nicholas.

And he's dead right. Case in point…

We've had a very persistent carpet cleaning and pest control telemarketer over the last couple of years. They'd call every few months.

Worn down… we finally said yes to a pest control service because the company we'd been using didn't contact us and ask for the job again. The persistent telemarketer did. So it was a yes. We were happy enough with the work.

A year almost to the day later the phone rang again. Same telemarketer. The call went something like…

"It's been a year since your last pest treatment and we're happy to keep the price for you at $169, not this year's price of $189."

So they got a yes.

Persistently asking got them 2 years' worth of business. The previous company? We still haven't heard from.

Back to the telemarketer call…

"Can we do anything else for you while we're there, clean your carpets or a termite inspection?"

Just so happens there was a pee stain or two on the loungeroom carpet from little Tilly's odd accident.

"We can do that for $79 today, it's usually $99."

So for about 2 minutes' phone work they made $253 (or thereabouts).

The two key things here…

They asked… PLUS… They gave a $$$ incentive to say yes, now.

My challenge to you, do you ask enough? And do you ask with a reason for them to say yes to you now?

Especially your past customers? Time to get on the phone perhaps?

Seinfeld success formula

Not sure about you, but I STILL get a kick out of watching *Seinfeld*.

Recently I've found myself saying to my boys…

That reminds me of the Seinfeld episode where…

And I insert the situation. The line. The wacky antics of Kramer. Or the tricky spot the self-absorbed and loathsome George found himself in.

Reckon George was just about my fav character.

Anyways…

The show ran from 1989 to 1998… across 180 episodes. In the last 5 years it was ranked the #1 or #2 show according to Neilsen ratings. An incredible run by any comparison.

How did the show "about nothing" do so well for so long?

Simple answer, which includes the marketing lesson…

The show did what Robert Collier preached all those years ago… it "entered the conversation in our minds".

In other words, we could relate to and laugh at the life events portrayed in the show.

There was a connection there because the show spoke to us, about us… and put a funny twist on (mostly) everyday situations.

So my message, padawan…

When you go to your market, do you do enough to "enter the conversation" in your prospects' minds?

Or do you push your products or services on them?

If it's the latter, might be time for a re-think and re-jig of your marketing messages.

Research tip

It came up again recently…

The question of research.

It's always some version of…

"Everyone tells you to research but no one shows you how."

Fair enough.

I've taught at my workshops numerous research techniques and shared more than a few with my email list.

But hungry you are so here's another "research tip" you can use immediately…

Just Google your product or niche followed by key phrases like…

"How to"

"What is"

"Best way to"

"Breakthrough"

Example:

Say you sell in the bunion removal market. During your research you'd type in…

"Bunion removal breakthroughs"

And see what comes up.

You'll get articles, university studies, competitors' material and more.

From here you'll see what's going on now. What key terms are used. Social proof. New ideas and on it goes.

Like just about all things marketing this is NOT a magic pill…

But it IS one of those levers that can give you the edge.

So when writing for self or others, they say research is key…

Well, now you have another simple and free technique to add to your arsenal.

On motivation

V exing is one word to describe the human trait of motivation.

It's a bit like sunshine…

Sometimes you have it. Sometimes you don't.

Sure the flakey world of social media would have you believe that everyone all day every day is out there "crushing it".

Pfff.

Chatting to a client in Mexico and he asked me about motivation, so thought I'd share some thoughts with you too.

I'm not pretending to have "the" answer, more to prompt you to think…

I want to preface this too with the acknowledgement it's easier to be more flexible when you are a freelancer or work for yourself. In many professions you have to show up regardless of how you feel. That said, it's an interesting topic is "motivation".

My client commented that sometimes he just couldn't be bothered and really had to force himself to work.

My response…

"Maybe it's during those times you're motivated to rest and re-charge, not work. Maybe it's your body or the Universe or some other intelligence that's wanting you to slow down, at least for a while."

There was silence on the other end followed by a "Hmmm… yeah… " as he mulled it over.

One thing I have come to realise is that my best ideas come to me when I'm still… or at least not rushed and deadline focused. And so I'd encourage you to, the next time you don't feel "motivated", to question what the next best action is for you…

Is it to finish work early and rest?

Is it to halve your to do list and find some stillness in the new time you have?

Is it to change task and focus on a new project?

There's no one answer.

What I will say is if you grind and grind the only thing you'll be "crushing" is your energy and creativity and your effectiveness.

Leave you to ponder how "motivation" shows up or doesn't at various times in your world…

Reading list – fav copywriting books

In no particular order, some of my favourite books on the art of copywriting are:

Breakthrough Advertising by Gene Swartz

The Ultimate Sales Letter by Dan Kennedy

The Copywriter's Handbook by Bob Bly

Making Ads Pay by John Caples

Turn Words into Money by Ted Nicholas

How to Write a Good Advertisement by Victor Schwab

The Architecture of Persuasion by Michael Masterson

Words that Sell and *More Words that Sell* by Richard Bayan

Copy Logic by Michael Masterson & Mike Palmer

Persuasion Secrets of the World's Most Charismatic & Influential Villains by Ben Settle

There are many more. And there are others not on that list which "they" will say should be there.

Yep. Remember, there are many ways to be right.

You might like to pick one from the list you haven't read and get it. Good way to invest in your skills!

Radar up

H ere's a quick but powerful reminder of two things…

#1 - I bang on about the need to have your marketing radar "up" as you go about your day… because it's a great way to get ideas for your business…

#2 - what have you done recently that's special or a thank you to current customers?

Reason I ask, and this illustrates both points…

On the way to the beach for a walk this one morning I caught a glimpse of a sign outside Dominoes. It said…

"Customer Appreciation Week - 50% Off".

There was an asterix * there so it comes with some conditions which as the sign flashed by I didn't get a chance to read.

But it did get me thinking and hopefully you too…

How can you turn "customer appreciation" into a marketing opportunity?

No it doesn't have to mirror Dominoes 50% off.

But how can you use this principle in your business?

Food for thought and if you were searching for a new promo angle, you've just been given one on a silver platter… no charge!

Pain or gain, that is the question

If you want to refresh a campaign losing its effectiveness…

Or

Test a new one right out of the gate…

Then consider the gain Vs pain sequence. Often, the negative has more punch, if delivered emotively.

Here's a quick example.

Say you have a product that helps Yr 12 students get the best ATAR rank possible. Your gain headline would be something like…

"Boost Your ATAR Rank With this Simple Memory Technique"

Or

"Results Driven ATAR Preppers Just Love This Memory Technique"

See… promises a big and clear benefit. Should work, right? Maybe.

Now flip it around from the gain to the pain with something like…

"Mum, I Got Rejected!"

No one likes failure or rejection, so this might bump response.

Food for thought next time you are playing with a headline… explore both the gain and the pain, you might just unearth a winner.

Top 13 subject lines

W hat works these days to get your email opened?

Keep reading my padawan coz ye old Jedi Wordmaster is about to reveal…

The top 13 "headlines" (based on open rates) from my email list recently, as they appeared in the subject line…

failure

weird question

see this – idea generator

none of it works [frank admission]

Frequencies + other woo woo stuff

Boring just went to a mil…

Oooooh the controversy!

Really?

Too busy = poor people talk

What the shrink said about you…

Her yuck dinner conversation

Too cheap?

I'm sorry

Why did these get opened by sometimes 7% to 10% more than others? Curiosity… variety… novelty… are all part of the answer.

Feel free to swipe and deploy and test.

Here is the secret to happiness...

Turns out there IS a secret to happiness. So says a 75-year study by Harvard.

It began in 1938 and followed the lives of 268 undergraduates from all walks of life.

Here you go, have a think about these 6 secrets to happiness and your life today...

#1 Value love above all else

#2 Create meaningful relationships and connections

#3 Don't abuse alcohol (a beer or two on a Friday and/or Saturday IS ok... so says a study, by Steve...)

#4 More money and power do NOT = more happiness (might add, nor does more poverty!!!)

#5 Your IQ does not correlate to your happiness

#6 It's NEVER too late to find happiness (yes, we can all breathe a sigh of relief!! Lol).

There you go, something of an "official happiness formula". Hope it helps to maybe re-calibrate your thinking, even just a smidgen.

Have a happy day.

The humble jellybean wins again

They got 160 new leads inside 2 weeks. Yes, ONE HUNDRED AND SIXTY. Would you like similar?

Here's how: the humble guess the number of jellybeans in the jar competition, with a twist. What happened:

I shared with my email subscribers the results of a Facebook campaign a couple of auto repair businesses were running (BTW, this info comes from the very astute Mark Selbst who coaches husband and wife auto repair teams). He's changing lives, literally, with the work he's doing.

Anyways…

One of his clients took a pic of a jar filled with jellybeans (remember those when you were a kid?) and ran a competition on their Facebook page. Guess the number and you win the jarful. To enter they gave up their contact details. Result was 23 NEW clients for the mechanic in the traditionally slow month of January.

Now…

An auto repair business in regional Queensland ran a meat tray comp… guess the weight of the meat tray in the pic. Same principle, different vehicle. Results: 263 entries. 160 left their name, phone number, email and date of their next car service. Reckon you could do something with that data? Hell yes!!! How can you leverage the humble guess the number of jelly beans in a jar?

Well, let's take that **ancient** concept and marry it to another *ancient* principle of entering the conversation in people's minds (thanks Robert Collier) and…

Tah Dah!!!

Around Easter time for example, why not run a *guess the number of Easter eggs in the jar* competition on Facebook? First prize is the jar of eggs plus an Easter hamper. Second could be 3 Easter bunnies. And so on. Sometimes, the simplest things can be winners.

Why this concept works: people love to win. It's low risk for them. It takes them back to their happy childhood. It entertains them in their otherwise dreary day. It's believable because they can see what they will get. It will be fun for them to share with family and/or friends.

How can the humble "jellybean comp" idea work for you to generate new leads?

Fascinate with bullets

S peed of the read is vital.

It's one of the reasons to include bullets or fascinations in your copy.

They help you get the maximum amount of information across in a short space, fast.

To be effective, bullets must arouse curiosity and desire in your prospects. A successful bullet is all about the TEASE.

Remember, curiosity is a very powerful force. It's one of those things that makes us human. We respond to enticing things we can't have or don't yet understand

And that's *exactly* what drives people to take action.

Bullets should therefore "tease" rather than "tell"

Eg a good bullet is NOT

Discover the #1 secret to selling which is, "entering the conversation going on in the prospects' minds"

BUT a better bullet might be

Discover the #1 secret to selling, so simple you'll be kicking yourself when you see what it is!

See the difference? Don't give away the answer.

And no, this is not new. Legendary copywriter Mel Martin was the first to use the word "fascinations" for his bullets. He wanted to fascinate his reader. And boy, did he do it well.

Here are some of Mel's classics:

- What never... **ever** to eat on an airplane
- Where to hide valuables in a hotel room
- How to buy a house with no down payment
- Sexual side effects – good and bad – of everyday medicine
- The smartest time to file a tax return if you want to avoid an audit
- Two famous cold remedies that can make you sicker if taken together

Remember, tease, don't tell.

I'm lonely

B eing in business can be a VERY isolating experience. Sure, if you're like me and work for yourself, it's literally true. But it can also be true if you are surrounded by employees.

You see, it's one of the top complaints most business owners NEVER speak about.

And even though they think it, hardly anyone mutters those soul shattering words…

I'm lonely.

Why?

Perhaps we think a frank admission like this is a sign of weakness. Or maybe it's just too darn hard to say.

Either way, it's real.

So my question, well, challenge really, to you today is…

If you feel lonely in business, what are you doing to overcome it?

The famous American football coach Lou Holtz said: "In this world you're either growing or you're dying so get in motion and grow."

Isolation cannot be an excuse.

Quick example which is hopefully instructive rather than boastful…

I'm in 2 mastermind groups. I regularly attend live webinars. Recently I paid $40 for an eBook to get one snippet of info which will help me. Plus, I'm always on the lookout for JV partners, either here or overseas.

Point is… I know business is lonely…

So I take ACTIVE steps to educate myself, reach out to people, stay connected and learn learn learn.

Challenge…

Do you do enough of this?

Or do you get "busy" and more and more isolated as a result?

This makes objections history

*Y*ou know one of my recent clients, Alex from Melbourne, was in the exact same position you were just 4 months ago...

So might go the segue you use to deal with objections in a sales conversation.

You tell a story.

TRUTH EXPOSED: the value of story in copy and selling is vastly under-utilised and misunderstood.

So hear ye this vital lesson about story to ease your toil, my padawan.

Yes, there are all types of stories those familiar with the wily art of copy know, understand and use.

Your origin story. A transformation story. A bonding story. And on it goes.

In fact one of the greatest and most successful sales letters of all time "The Wall Street Journal Letter" was 100% story.

But I digress.

Because the point of today...

Is to remind you the EASIEST way to sell is to use a story.

How:

When a customer presents with a problem and or objection...

Have a story at hand to relate how client *Phyllis was in a similar predicament and how we helped her was...*

And just tell the story of how you helped the customer.

Have those real stories up your sleeve ready to deploy when needed.

And watch as your prospect, via the story, emotionally gets one step closer to yes.

You are right, that is a BIG $$$ lesson right there.

Lame birthday presents cheese me off

L ame to lukewarm…

That's how I'd describe the direct mail I receive in the couple of weeks leading to my birthday. Frankly, it left me down, from a marketing point of view.

I only received 4 birthday related marketing pieces in the mail which = opportunity lost.

Depressing. And they ranged from, like I said at the start, lame to lukewarm. Case in point:

- A card with a nice happy birthday message in it but no sales focus… brought a smile but that's all… it was impotent from a marketing standpoint
- One of the banks we use sent a card with a "happy birthday, you're entered into the monthly draw for a $100 gift card, we'll contact you if you win" (hmmmm… me thinks I may never hear from them… opportunity lost…)
- And the best of a sorry bunch was the local surf club… come in for 50% off your meal coz it's your birthday type of message

The last was the ONLY one likely to generate ANY new business. It would have been much stronger with a "free meal because it's your birthday when you purchase a meal for a significant other" type of message… more incentive to come in… and of course we'd buy drinks and maybe more meals if the kids are with us.

Just think about that…

Almost every day of the week, one of your customers is having a birthday… if you're not reaching out to them with gift/encouragement to do more business with you… you're missing 365 marketing opportunities. Yes, this takes time. And systems. And effort… but more business through your door every day of the week? Might be kind of worth it, don't you think?

Plus…

As my birthday experience shows, the competition is virtually non-existent, so it's easy to stand out and wow them.

Lead gen error to avoid

T ruth exposed…

It IS getting harder, in this fast-paced, celebrity obsessed, new shiny object every 5 minutes world to generate leads.

Not impossible, just more of a challenge than, say, 5 to 10 years ago.

And it gets worse when you make this mistake…

I was critiquing a client's sales material recently and started with their lead magnet (can't give exact details because it will reveal the business).

But the mistake was clear and obvious to my trained but also "fresh" eyes.

They went far too quickly into promoting the business.

The ONLY job you have when it comes to lead magnets is to market the "bait".

The lead magnet should be about solving a hot button problem in your market.

And all messaging must be focused on this.

Not on your business and the wider solutions you offer.

Solve a problem they are experiencing NOW for free (or very low cost) and you earn the right to market your business to them.

You can't do both at once because it sniffs of "sales" and people run.

Good lead magnet ideas?

It does depend on your market, but checklists, whitepapers, a special industry report, training video, low cost offers, a book can work well…

Providing they are problem focused.

Anything else is a bridge too far too soon.

What you learn while your mother sleeps

I t happened just about every time I visited her in the nursing home. Despite her constant complaints of not being able to sleep…

9 out of 10 visits to my mum began with me sitting in the quiet watching her snore mouth open, *Reader's Digest* resting precariously on her frail chest as it rose and fell followed by an animal like grunt with each deep intake of air.

So here I was one Sunday morning staring around the room while the snoring raged unabated when my eyes settled on a discarded copy of one of her *Reader's Digest* volumes. I picked it up and started to skim through it. I came to a story about Lee Childs, author of the Jack Reacher novels and others. He's sold several million books and is, by all measure, a very successful guy.

His secret? This may surprise you.

You see I was at a public interview with Wilbur Smith (my favourite author) about 25 years ago and he described his success… he starts each book on the same date every year. He writes from 9am till 7pm, 6 days a week. He accepts no social engagements when he is writing. It's focus, focus, focus.

Known "hard nuts" like Dan Kennedy would applaud. Lee Childs shares **one thing and only one thing** in common with Smith… he has the same start date for each novel, in Lee's case September 1.

Childs' writing process? In the article he said…

"I get up disgracefully late and start working at about 1pm. I have few rules in my life but one strict one is nothing of value is ever achieved in the morning. The way I write is completely disorganised. Everything feels like a high-wire act. Somehow magically, it always comes out all right."

Wow. And it would make every success guru or goal setting maven shake their head in disbelief. The point to all of this?

Know you and what works for you and how you work best. Of course, it's simple to dismiss this with, *easy for someone like Lee Childs who's a millionaire several times over, I can't do that in my business.*

Be careful with such thinking. Because I share this with you to remind you, you don't have to keep doing it the way you always did… not suggesting you neglect your customers or your responsibilities either… but where can you change things up, at least a little and be more like a Lee Childs? You might be surprised with the results of unplanned work that flows just because you didn't follow any rules.

[Postscript: my mum, Veronica Plummer, passed away 4/5/2021… RIP mum…]

Ridiculously stupid errors

H ope you make a few dumb mistakes this week, I really do.

Not because I wish bad things for you.

But because…

If you're making mistakes it means you are making decisions and moving forward.

Was reading an article about Dr Chris Tomshack, a US-based chiropractor, who in the last 13 years has grown his business to nearly 300 clinics that help over 13 million patients.

Solid numbers.

Consider all the moving parts in an operation of that size. Would be a challenge, right?

Here's what he said about making decisions in business:

"I've failed many times and made some ridiculously stupid errors… and I'm going to continue making them because I make decisions… you can't hem and haw… you've got to make decisions."

So yep, this week, make some decisions. Make them as calculated in your favour as you can… but make them and implement… even if you're unsure of the outcome.

From your decision and action you will get a result.

And that result (be it "good" or "bad") will inform your next steps.

Wishing you a day full of "stupid errors"

UCTs – the key to crafting a compelling story

E veryone loves a good story. Done well, it's a very effective influence tool. It's also an area many people struggle with.

Here's what I've learned…

There are a small number of "Universal Connection Themes" (or UCTs) which when used, make your story recognisable and relatable for your audience… makes them WANT to read it.

Connection is a key part of the persuasion equation. The more connected your copy is to your market, the stronger the chance of influencing them to take action.

I've found, when you build a story around one of the UCTs your chances of that deep connection are boosted.

Here are three UCTs…

Kids/family – tell a story about your kids which has relevance or a lesson to your market and done right it builds trust and speaks in a soft "parent to parent" way as opposed to a "salesperson to customer" way.

The beach – everyone (or most people) have a connection with the beach or water; my best estimate is this comes from distant memories of happy family holidays over the summer break.

Travel – everyone loves to get away, so, similar to the beach, this one invokes strong and happy memories for people.

Whenever you can incorporate stories with these themes into your copy, do so, because done right, your words connect and impact on a much deeper level.

Just one more cast...

There's an old saying amongst those who fish...

"JUST ONE MORE CAST"

It's all hope and prayer stuff... one more and I'll land the big one... just one more... one more...

How can this be applied to marketing your business that's not "flick a lure and hope"?

"Just one more channel"

As in where can you add an extra media channel to your marketing mix...

Social media

Email

SMS

Landing page

Google ads

Pre-roll video

VSL

Direct mail

Because just about EVERY study I've seen says a multi-channel approach produces the best results.

Note... I'm not advocating ad hoc or last minute with your last morsel of bait... but strategic additions...

Just one more cast is for fishing...

While "just one more media channel" can make a huge difference to your results.

Leave you to ponder how to strategically add "one more" to what you do...

Dumb business or just same-same

It's been said that business is getting tougher and tougher because the marketplace is a "sea of high-quality sameness".

And when you think about it, that's pretty spot on…

There are a lot of VERY good marketers out there today.

So how do you stand out when you're competing against "high quality"?

Simple but not easy.

Here's a hint…

You need a unique method… a special mechanism… a point of difference that is yours alone… a specific and results-producing "something" that is your "thing".

If you don't have this, well, you really are swimming in that sea of sameness with all the others.

Your own pool where you don't bump elbows with others is a much better place to be.

You get this pool of your own when you nail your "special thing" that gives you something to hang your hat on and stand out.

Others then see you differently to the rest.

Simple, right? But it's not easy to nail it.

How are you or how do you do things differently?

Advanced headline formula

A BIG headline secret is curiosity.

If people are curious and there's an implied benefit, you've got a chance of getting past hello.

Gary Halbert's famous...

Wife of Hollywood Movie Star Swears Under Oath that Her New Perfume Range Does Not Contain Illegal Sexual Stimulants

Is one example.

As is John Carlton's equally lauded...

Amazing Secret Discovered by One-Legged Golfer Adds 50 Yards To Your Drives, Eliminates Hooks and Slices And Can Slash Up To 10 Strokes From Your Game Almost Overnight!

How can you emulate the genius of these copywriting greats?

Try this formula...

Take something **known** to your audience.

Add something **unknown** to it.

Add some **intrigue** to get them excited.

That way you arouse interest, anchor it in something they know and promise an exciting benefit.

Halbert's perfume headline and Carlton's famous one-legged golfer do this brilliantly...

Take something known to your audience: perfume, golf training.

Add something unknown: wife of famous movie star swears under oath, one-legged golfer.

Add some spice: does not contain an illegal sexual stimulant, eliminates hooks and slices, slash 10 strokes almost overnight.

See?

Altostratus clouds and your business

Altostratus clouds are mid-level clouds that cover the whole sky.

They form between 6,000 to 24,000 feet and are usually a blueish grey. Sunlight or moonlight can filter through them, to give a kind of eerie atmosphere here on Earth.

These are not to be confused with the high white cirrus clouds, those wispy streaks in the sky we saw as angels when we were kids.

Thanks for the meteorological lesson, Poindexter, what's this got to do with my business?

Glad you asked...

Nothing and everything.

To explain...

In your busy work day, when was the last time you stopped and marvelled at something in nature, like a cloud pattern... even for a few moments.

If you're like most business owners you don't have time for such idle indulgence. But you should. On a macro level as well as micro.

What does this mean?

Micro... it's GREAT for the mind to take a small mental break by doing something simple like looking at cloud patterns... in such stillness a free mind can deliver answers.

The macro...

Well that's even more important.

You see most business owners are too close to what they do, their head down firmly in the next sale, the staff roster, the slow supplier and on it goes. They are so close, so focused, so myopic they miss opportunities.

Which is why a fresh set of eyes can be so invigorating... so helpful in getting your eyes up and looking beyond what you see all the time.

My challenge to you is to ask yourself, do you need to, on either a micro or macro level, get your head up and "look at the clouds"?

The emergency poncho of headlines

They stared at us like we were aliens. Flashback to London 2009 and our first overseas family holiday.

We'd just left a quaint but warm and dry English pub where I'd sipped the top off a pint of the warmest and foulest tasting beer in the world before I surrendered and left it on the counter. We were walking back to our hotel, 4 kids under 11 in tow, and it started to bucket down London style.

So we did what any normal Aussie family would do, whipped out the emergency poncho to stay dry. Funny thing is, passers-by looked at us in a weird way. A couple even laughed at the 6 of us. Ok, an emergency poncho has its limits but in a time of need, it does the job, right? Which brings me to a question I got recently...

Steve, have you got a headline template that works most of the time? This is marketing my padawan, there are no certainties beyond what we all acknowledge... death and taxes. It really is a how long's a piece of string type question. *Surely you've got one you go to often* he persisted. Not really.

But you can try this came my reply.

So thought I'd share it with you because if you're stuck like we were in the London downpour, it's a reasonable headline starting point. Drum roll please...

How to (result your market wants) **Without** (the thing your market hates).

Examples...

How to Grow Ripe Juicy Tomatoes Without Pesticides or Getting Your Hands Dirty

How to Write Engaging Facebook Ads and Posts Without Hours of Study and Big $ Spent Testing

How to Lose 3kg Per Week Without Eating Rabbit Food or Starving Yourself

And on it goes. Or this:

How to Learn a Secret Headline Strategy Without Years of Studying Copywriting

Couldn't resist. C'mon, that's a little funny.

Like all good copy, this works because it's multi-layered. Your prospect wants the result. Of course, that's Copy 101. But deeper... It taps into the human trait of sloth... we all want something for nothing... which is why Gold Lotto, pokies, scratchies and the like are so big.

There you go, if you're stuck for a headline, you can try the proven 1-2 punch template...

How to get X without Y, it's better than walking through a London downpour being laughed at because you're wearing an emergency poncho!

How to open a sales message #2

The second way to open a sales message (the first was entry #18) is with the "list of pain". It's a version of the if/then problem/solution template.

This is where you start with a short sharp question…

Have you ever been embarrassed by these symptoms?

Or

Which of these conditions worry you?

And then you list the 3 to 5 conditions your research tells you are the "hot" buttons the market is embarrassed by or worried about.

Example:

Which of these skin conditions embarrasses you most?

> *a) Continual, burning itching?*
>
> *b) Redness that gets worse after exercise?*
>
> *c) Scaly, blotchy marks?*
>
> *d) Dried, white circles of dead skin on your hands and feet?*

My name is Paul English. I'm a skin specialist who's been treating everyday Australians who suffer from Reticence Syndrome for the past 6 years using a little-known technique called "ex-scaling". I developed this technique after years of watching people suffer. The great news is, after 6 weeks of this treatment, 96.5% of patients walk away happy with skin they feel they can FINALLY live in.

Here's why this treatment works…

So I've made up the above to illustrate the technique… you list their pain points and offer an immediate solution which they have to read on to get.

There you go… never stare at a blank screen again. At the very least to get you started (you can always come back and change it later) try either the if/then (#18) or list of pain openings.

One and done... NO!

I've only got one shot at this, so I've got to get it right.

So came the words from a client when discussing getting a new prospect over the line recently.

It's a reasonable statement because you want to be "up" for any sales conversation. And you want to have lined your ducks up.

But...

It's also the wrong statement. The truth is, "one shot" rarely works.

Which is why you need a funnel, even a simple one.

For example...

You may have 20 targeted prospects you want to go after.

20 x 1 contact only to each is not going to do it.

Plan out what steps you will take.

Step 1 might be a LinkedIn connection.

Step 2 might be a direct mail piece.

Step 3 might be an email.

Step 4 might be a follow up phone call.

Step 5 might be a shock and awe pack.

And on it goes.

You then rinse and repeat... one of these steps every 2 weeks for your 20 (or whatever number) of identified prospects. Of course, the messaging changes with each contact until you get a yes from them.

And here's another key point: you have to know what that end game is... a meeting, a free trial, a small purchase. So don't think one and done is ever the answer.

Plan your steps/funnel and have at 'em.

When not to talk over your woman

O n a recent (mostly) daily morning walk along Currimundi Lake, Jenny was telling me of a chat her and her workmates were having about this new Netflix show where this "little Japanese woman helps people de-clutter their lives".

Oh that Lisa Kondo lady? came my reply.

And then I impressed her with my knowledge of said theory, all based on having read a free chapter many years ago… lucky she didn't know the celebrated author and guru's first name is Marie (I remembered later).

Anyways…

VERY nonplussed by me stealing the story (hey, it's a couple thing… maybe you can relate?), Jenny forged ahead…

She mentioned the Kondo mantra for chucking stuff out…

If it doesn't spark joy, it has to go.

It's a nice way of looking at things… no joy in you, out it goes. And it got me to thinking about business…

Does it still spark joy for you?

Or do you drag yourself out of bed in the morning?

Maybe it's time for some version of a Marie Kondo your business?

A de-clutter or a "new something"? What "NEW" do you need to bring into your business life… skills, mentor, location, website…

What can you stop doing or delegate? What clients or staff would benefit from a "new opportunity" elsewhere?

Maybe a fresh set of eyes is what is best, because so often we are way too close to things.

Does it spark joy for you, still?

Random writing hacks

A couple more tips I've picked up along the way...

Your next 3 steps:

Before you finish your writing session make a note of the 3 things you will write in your next session. Can be on a Post-It note or written in your diary or on the word-processed page. This sets things up in your subconscious brain so when you start next time you get stuck straight into it.

The sun:

Get outside in the sun. Before you write. When you take a break. After you write. The sun, for some reason, boosts your mood and creativity. It only has to be a few minutes but the sun on your back can be a great tonic and boost if you are stuck.

Try them out.

Is there any point?

Why fight a battle you know you can't win?

Yet I see this often…

Businesses trying to compete where a rival has a distinct advantage.

It may be number of locations. Or mobility of service. Or price.

Just to throw a few at you.

If you know you can't beat them at "X", why bother trying? No point beating yourself up and still losing, is there? What's the answer then?

Know them and know you.

Compete instead against their weaknesses. They will have one or two… every business does.

Let's take a smaller business against a big chain that opens earlier and stays open later because they have two shifts. Can't do that because you're too small? True. So what's their "weakness" in this? Might be lots of staff so you never know who you will get when you go there. Might be lack of follow through because they are so big. Might be the presentation of their products.

If you do your homework, you can find their weakness that might also be your strength.

So then your message revolves around the personalised service you give customers. How they are treated at every interaction you have with them. How you always follow up. Of course, this is just a simple example, so you get the idea.

The fundamental at play here is to know your competitor's weakness and take them on where you have an advantage.

Note the word… fundamental… it's always the fundamentals that count big. Food for thought… take them on where you can win.

Scar tissue

A lot of people these days have "scar tissue" that keeps them cemented in places that do NOT serve them.

Such peeps seem to live in constant fear… of failure, embarrassment, criticism, gossip and more.

A big fear I see from time to time is a fear of new or different ideas that might upset an existing belief.

Their status quo, as painful as it is, is easier to "deal with" than stepping outside their comfort zone.

To be blunt…

Don't be that guy or girl.

I remember reading a statistic a while ago that most millionaires make their money after they turn 50.

Good news, right?

And there is ample evidence to support this…

From Colonel Sanders who started selling what is now KFC when he was in his mid-60s.

To Ray Kroc, the almost burnt out milk shake maker salesman in his 50s… before he wrestled control of McDonalds from the founding brothers.

And even Napoleon Hill in *Think and Grow Rich* says the best money making years of a person's life are between the ages of 41 and 74.

So don't let your own "scar tissue" hold you back.

Keep learning. Keep growing. Keep failing forward.

Your past is not your future results.

Have at it today my friend… and tomorrow… and the day after…

Were my early mentors wrong re: response times?

Some interesting research out of Harvard recently about when you should respond to inquiries.

My early mentors taught me it was bad positioning to respond too quickly to inquiries.

Makes you look needy.

And desperate.

Two qualities GUARANTEED to repel sales.

Remember the awkward, needy guy or girl when you were a teenager, couldn't get away from them fast enough, right?

Same thing in sales.

We can sniff a desperado a mile off. And it's over before hello.

More:

Marketing genius Dan Kennedy has become famous for being unreachable unless by his strict rules: via fax or letter through his office whereby he'll respond in HIS time, usually a week or more.

This has worked brilliantly for him.

But is it right?

Research from a study called "The Short Life of Online Sales Leads" suggest a faster response boosts conversion.

According to the study, companies that contacted a lead within an hour were 7 times more likely to qualify the lead ie talk to a decision maker... and...

The "within the hour" companies were more than 60 times as likely to qualify the lead than those that waited 24 hours or more.

This research suggests, contrary to traditional positioning theory, a fast response is better than a slower one.

Consider too the instant nature of SMS marketing... it's all about speed. And of course, if you are a one person show, the "distance" between you and customers is necessary, more so than bigger companies.

Food for thought for how you do things in your business.

'We to you' reminder

Quick tip today and a reminder…

We/us/I are VERY dangerous words in copy.

Why?

They generally precede some boring monologue about you.

I was critiquing a marketing piece recently and, frankly, it sucked.

Full of *we/us* type statements.

Which really is all about your problems and how you solve them.

Who cares, right?

Good copy immediately addresses your prospects' problems.

Reason…

That's all they care about.

Having their problem solved.

So if you want to avoid turning off your reader *you/your* should replace *we/I.*

Note: *we* can be used sparingly as a positioning tool (*we've solved the stiff joint problems of 1,448 Australians in the last 3 months alone* kind of thing).

That's proof and cred.

But *we've just launched a new website, head on over and check out our new colours…*

No. No. And No.

There is a difference, make sure you are all over it when you write.

Tree

Yep you and your biz are in one of two states, pretty much like a tree. You are either decaying or growing.

I did some work for a big client in the US whose reach extends to four continents. We were putting together some training material for a website which coaches some of the biggest and best business owners in his industry (we're talking world's best).

One of the modules focused on staff. The industry is notorious for high turnover of employees.

And the way my client expressed it was…

The staffing question is a challenge or an opportunity. If done wrong, it leads to decay. Done right, well, naturally it leads to growth.

For him the signs of business decay were the high turnover of staff who leave when it all stops being new, and you have no systems in place for training. You constantly chase your tail.

A growing business?

In his niche they have a commitment to education on every aspect of their business operations, and even life skills outside of work his staff find interesting or useful. He is adamant, there are no in-betweens. And this got me thinking…

Are you aware of the signs of decay in you and your business?

Because they can creep up on you… bit like a frog in a pot of slowly heating water… it won't jump out until it's too late…

What do you need to look out for?

Here's a quick go at signs of decay for me… newsletters from a couple of months on the desk unopened and or books I'd bought not read (I've stopped learning)… Few outreaches to prospects, especially new ones in new areas (the pie has stopped expanding)… behind the scenes projects I'm working on that have "stalled" (indicates distraction)… and on it goes.

Hope today's poke in the ribs is useful because it's true… you and me both, we're either decaying or growing… and we definitely don't want it to be the first one, either on a personal or business level.

Is it time to change a thing or two? Leave that up to you.

Sugar on Coco Pops, did you ever?

I never did it but I knew one kid who did, every day.

My boyhood mate, Neil, lived 2 doors down.

And he put sugar on his Coco Pops.

Sure, I used to give the Rice Bubbles a sprinkle.

But not Coco Pops.

C'mon, they were sweet enough, right?

The ol' Rice Bubbles though, well they were a bit bland so a liberal dose of those white granules made brekky much more fun. You do the same when you were a kid?

These types of habits contain a good marketing lesson...

And it's based around the old saying, people buy what they want, not what they need.

Think of people and their hobbies... they spend any amount on new fishing gear, surfboards, shoes etc while their car needs new tyres, the rust cut out of it and more...

So if you're having trouble making sales, maybe you're selling to their need not their want?

Think of sugar on Rice Bubbles...

How can you give what you offer to customers a sprinkle of sugar to make it more tasty to them?

Is it an added bonus? A new twist on a product like removing some part of it and reducing price so it becomes an entry level offering? Maybe it's a whole new and improved version of something? If sales have flatlined, maybe your offer has become stale and needs a sugar hit?

Leave you to ponder that...

Courtroom proof laid bare

There is power in having your "marketing radar up" over the special events like the 4th of July - US Independence Day and Black Friday.

We all get bombarded with "holiday special" offers and copy (like 4th July) which we can easily learn from and leverage in our marketing.

How effective is this?

Glad you asked, Your Honour.

I present my evidence from the 24 hours around 4th July one year recently for the jury to consider...

Exhibit A

One guru banged on about the best marketing book he's read, by Ken McCarthy (considered the founding father of internet marketing). So I jumped up and flicked through my copy to the chapter I wanted, not what said guru spoke about.

RESULT: memory jog for me which I used to help a client the same day regarding the design of their webpage, so it was more user-friendly. BTW... something Ken McCarthy said when I saw him live in US couple years back was how we should get our websites as close as possible to an ATM (click here, next screen, click here get money)... I used this principle to help the client... I may not have thought of this at a deeper level if I'd deleted the 4th of July offer email.

Exhibit B

Took me to an old-time offline ad of the "Dear Abby" variety... humans are voyeuristic and love other people's problems, so the chance of readership is high... This ad was old school but I got a couple of ideas how I might use this concept in an upcoming promo.

Exhibit C

A subscriber from Newcastle forwarded a guru's email about use of adjectives in copy... how some of the best messages in history (10 Commandments, Declaration of Independence, Churchill speeches etc) use VERY few adjectives, which makes the copy stronger and thus, the message clearer... nice reminder to self.

There you go, case closed your honour...

This Judge hereby instructs you to check out all guru emails from the next major special event or promo... you never know what new learnings or powerful reminders you'll get.

It's 10 to 15 minutes of professional development - FREE – which can pay off handsomely.

Trapped Mr or Mrs Busy

F eel the pressure… soooo many things on your plate…

As in no sooner do you start a meaningful task then you are compelled by some unseen force to look at something irrelevant?

Fluffbook. Email. Twitter. Instagram.

This ever happened to you?

If yes, then this may resonate…

"We barely make it through a single day without suffering those long gaps when we are lost in a long chain of clicks and swipes that steal our momentum and leave no trace of our real purpose or accomplishment."

Sound familiar? Ouch, right?

The quote comes from *The Motivation Manifesto* by Brendan Burchard and for me it sums up many of our "busy-ness" problems today.

Anyways, there is a solution. And as Burchard says, it's about choice…

"Our defining moment will come as we either continue to slide into the oblivion of the deep digital stream… drowning in distraction, or take a higher vantage point apart from all the noise and… choose to focus on what really matters in life."

Easier said than done, I'm sure you'll agree.

The key though is to shift your focus from distraction and laser it in on what really matters to you.

A reminder for you, just for today.

When it works, it works, so use it

I got rather pissed at a prospect one day when he said strong direct response marketing doesn't work in B2B.

Just one example…

That same day I received an online newsletter from a B2B marketing agency. Check out the headlines of the articles…

Are you missing a trick? (subject line of the email… leverages curiosity and FOMO)

Article #1 **The complete guide to B2B website personalisation** (sounds like a shock and awe pack title I would write)

Article #2 **New rules for marketing tech companies** (trigger word "new")

Article #3 **Is B2B ready for consumer driven X?** (again, high curiosity)

Article #4 **5 key success factors for your ABM** (numbered list, trigger words key, success, your)

Article #5 **The secrets to running a successful agency** (again, trigger word "secrets")

Need I go on?

Good marketing is based on the fundamentals of great copy… in any market.

Once again… case closed your honour!

Weird word, big impact

Have you ever heard of the word "lagniappe"?

Pronounced "lan-yap".

Does it ring a bell?

If not, listen up because it's crucial to repeat business.

By definition, it means "something given as a bonus or gratuity".

In real terms, it's a small gift or bonus you give a customer when they buy.

It's most powerful when unannounced because it surprises and delights them... and really makes the sale stick because it melts away buyers' remorse.

How can you be angry or regretful when you've just been given a gift?

I know, it's NOT new.

But...

Lagniappe. This weird word is a very good reminder to you about your sales process.

Are you doing enough of this?

Yes, the little things DO matter.

Chew that one over as you head into your day... how can you lagniappe your customers...

Sounds rude, I know, but well worth thinking about.

Which numbers work best these days...

W hat's the BEST number to use in copy when presenting price?

Traditionally it's been any number ending in a 7 or 9... $97, $99, $147, $199 and so on.

More: most traditional split tests also revealed odd numbers worked better than even.

Here's a new trend, according to a BuzzSumo survey... In headlines (yes the magic 7 usually refers to pricing not headlines)... but the number that got the most shares on Facebook...

As in **X Reasons to Avoid Alcohol this Christmas...**

Drum roll again please...

Was...

10.

Followed by 5. Then 15.

With the traditional magic 7 coming 4th.

So 10 Reasons to Avoid Alcohol this Christmas... would have produced more shares than 7 Reasons to Avoid Alcohol this Christmas...

Just shows, pays to keep studying marketing stuff.

To be clear...

Learn the principles FIRST and then adjust them to suit viewer behaviour.

NOTE: many marketers say their price testing software shows, when it comes to sales, numbers ending in a 7 still work best in their niche.

When business gets tough

I t ain't always a bed of roses, this business gig, is it? Takes certain kahunas to stick at it. And yes, no doubt there are times when, even for an instant, we all have that thought occasionally... *"maybe just getting a job will be easier"*.

But only for a second.

It's ok to admit it, promise I won't tell anyone...

So what do you do when these down times hit (which few social media warriors even admit happen)?

Was talking to a client re this very thing. "Everything" he'd tried seemed to "fail". Sales had flatlined. He was pretty down. We discussed some new strategies and came up with a mini plan to get things moving.

But the biggest thing I did was help with his mindset.

And it was interesting how things worked out... the weekend before that call I was going back through old photos and came across some from our family trip to Washington a few years ago... I'd found this gem about a guy in the 1800s which I shared with the client and thought you'd appreciate too...

It was a photo of a plaque I'd snapped somewhere in that beautiful city and had forgotten about. The numbers you see refer to years ie '31 = 1931. Here it is:

Are you easily discouraged?

HERE'S A MAN WHO -

Failed in business '31

Defeated for the Legislature '32

Again failed in business '34

Sweetheart died '35

Had nervous breakdown '36

Defeated in Election '38

Defeated for Congress '43

Defeated for Congress '46

Defeated for Congress '48

Defeated for Senate '55

Defeated for Vice President '56

Defeated for Senate '58

Elected President '60

That man was Abraham Lincoln

Sometimes in business and in life... you just have to keep going.

Have a great, "persistent' day.

Blame game

Hate it when I see media reports of businesses closing, don't you? No one likes seeing people's hard work, livelihood and dreams crash and burn. So when I see it, I get kind of mad, especially when perhaps it could have been prevented.

Like this one…

Was flicking through a local paper one morning over coffee and there was a story of a local clothing retailer closing its doors.

Why? They blamed Council streetscape works for taking up parking spaces, curtailing foot traffic and running the business into the ground. Now I don't know anything about the business or its operations or its marketing. Or what they did to try and ride out the (very real) disruption caused by the roadworks.

They may have done a lot. Or they may have merely waited for things to pick up.

Here's the thing…

Is your business one "event" away from peril?

If it is, what are you doing about it?

Couple of thoughts off the top of my head re what the clothing retailer could have done if they'd had a list of customers they marketed to regularly…

- Because parking spaces were reduced, why not hold a members only after 6pm evening with free X for attendance… access easy… sales could be made to compensate for less daytime traffic
- Hold a street redevelopment sale or promo to give people a REASON to make the effort to come in
- Create a past customers draw - eg "free clothes for a year" - ticket in the draw when you purchase this month. And the "free clothes for a year" might be something as simple as one item off the rack every month for free for the lucky winner… again, a REASON to come into the store

Like I said, these are just off the top of my head. There are many other ways to generate interest and sales. Why not turn the disruption into a marketing opportunity?

Message: build your list so you aren't at the mercy of a temporary "road closure"… and market to that list.

Why would they bother?

L et's be clear… no one wants to buy from you. Or me.

We'd all rather keep our money in our pockets. Except when we want to buy something (or need to).

To explain this contradiction…

You have to understand what part of the buying cycle your prospect is in.

If they are in research mode, they want information.

If they are in buying mode, they want a good deal.

You can present the bestest ever, hottest deal to someone, but if they aren't ready to buy, it won't matter one bit.

And…

If they are ready to buy, the best presented free report, free training, or white paper won't interest them in the least and they'll go to where the best deal is.

Which brings me to queries from prospects about why their website is "not converting".

For starters, the sites they've sent me break rule #1 - your business name is not your headline.

But the bigger issue is…

They have no mechanism to "sell" to people who are in their research phase… ie there was no lead magnet, no way of "capturing" those "just looking".

So make sure your marketing takes into account the various buying phases us humans go through.

If you don't, chances are you're leaving lots of moolah unbanked.

Headline tip that will make you a pro in no time

L oved this "little" marketing tidbit…

Little in that it's only a small thing…

But not so little in its potential impact.

Remember I mentioned a couple of entries ago online content giant BuzzSumo and their survey? Another part of that was they analysed 100 million headlines and came up with…

Yes, 100 million. I know, I know… it's a truckload.

Where was I?

They analysed a 100 million headlines and found a single 3-word phrase that gained more than double the engagements on Facebook.

Drum roll please…

The answer is in the headline for today's entry.

"Will make you"

As in 'This Simple Investing Tip Will Make You a Cool 9% Return in 6 Months"

Or

"The 9 Hard Marketing Truths that Will Make You a Better Businessperson and Recession Proof Your Company"

And on it goes.

Nice one, right?

"Will make you".

Try it out.

Change your mind, change your life

How do we protect our energy and combat negative thoughts like, "I'm just not a natural business owner"?

Denying negative thoughts exist is futile.

We all have that annoying negative "stay safe" voice in our heads.

So instead of fighting a negative thought like "I'm not a natural business owner" try this instead...

When that thought pops up turn that energy around into a neutral thought eg How can I run my business better using the talents I have?

Go ahead...

Say those two thoughts to yourself...

I'm not a natural business owner

and

How can I run my business better using the talents I have?

What did you notice about how you felt after each one?

First one was yuck.

The second...

Anything from neutral to hopeful.

Which do you want your energy to go to... the negative or the neutral (or better)?

Try it next time a mental gremlin sneaks in... change it from a negative thought to a neutral question.

This one action alone changes your energy. And that in turn will change your results.

Why copy doesn't work

Does your copy pass the PUKE test? Not as in vomit but PUKE as in...

Predictable.

Unbelievable.

Know-it-all.

And empty of **E**motion.

PUKE.

I think it was US copywriter Ray Edwards who first shared that acronym but it's a good one to remind you about connection to your market.

To me, the "P" is perhaps most important... people respond to novelty, newness, and interesting stuff because novelty releases small hits of the happy brain chemical dopamine.

And we all want to feel good.

So more effort in making your messages "unpredictable" is a great way to cut through the clutter and get your stuff read... at least then you have a chance at selling... and then you can add in believability, emotion, and connection.

The G-spot, The O-spot

Oooh… let's get a little sexy here…

It's true. They exist, both of them, even if sometimes they are "hard to find". Settle down… I'm talking marketing "G" and "O" spots. What were YOU thinking?

Anyway your copywriting G-spot…

Well that's the "good is good enough" spot. Your copy needs to be **G**ood, not perfect. When it's good let it go forth into the marketplace and multiply. True, if your friends and family think of you as 'anal' this can be hard to do. You want it to be just so, right? Let it go.

Here's the TRUTH…

No copy is ever perfect. And it can always be improved. The thing is it just has to be good enough to work. Notice word choice… Didn't say slack or sloppy. But…

Good. Not perfect. So find that **G**-spot, it does exist.

And your O-spot?

Well, plenty of success stories to prove this too exists. Your "O-spot" is **O**ffline. Do you "hit" it enough? And if you're mainly offline, do you hit YOUR other O-spot… **O**nline? Truth is…

The best, most successful campaigns I've written have included a strategic mix of online and offline.

Both **O**-spots found and hit.

Like the real estate campaign I created which did 7 figures in around 3 weeks.

In today's cluttered market, what new G and O spots can you use to boost response?

Random

This quick 50 second read gives you random observations AND BIG LESSONS from the marketing world recently, with my commentary in brackets...

Dan Kennedy:

"Two different private clients reporting in on monthly calls with me in June each announced million - dollar breakthroughs from specific advice I'd given them... They kindly did not mention the failed ideas I gave them, that produced nothing. We put our heads together and grope." (*no one gets it right ALL the time, even legends*).

Bob Bly:

"It is inevitable that, if you are in freelance copywriting, consulting, or any other service business, you will at times have problems with (difficult) clients" (*yes even when you screen and select them... so much so Bob has created an info product to address the problem*).

Brian Kurtz:

"It was reminded recently (on Facebook of course) that there are folks who think everything we know about marketing today never existed before the Internet. And while technology has sped up everything and made all of our marketing fundamentals easier to implement and more effective in many ways, some good stuff was actually invented before the Internet" (*what makes us buy is timeless, don't dismiss "old" too readily*).

Frank Kern:

"My day of debauchery" – email subject line... (*what's that about getting attention?*).

Mailchimp:

Did a study of 40 million subject lines and the best performing ones were those that described accurately the content of the email (*hmmm interesting and note to self*).

Angelo Dundee, legendary boxing trainer when asked who the hardest working athlete he ever trained was:

"Oh, that's easy. Muhammed Ali. He was head and shoulders above everybody else in work ethic."

(*Reminds me of the biggest sign in the boxing gym where the boys and I train which reads:* **Hard work beats talent when talent doesn't work hard**... *there no shortcuts to success – shoulder to the boulder my padawan and heave!!!*).

There you go, a potpourri of ideas to leverage off today.

Speed wins the day

There's a very true old saying…

"Money loves speed". And certainly the faster you can get your message in front of your prospects and clients, the sooner the till rings, right?

Question is…

How do you achieve speed?

Well, it's a skill I've developed through trial and error.

Proof?

Take this reply from client James re a lead gen letter I knocked up for him…

"I find it incredible that you can put that quality together at such speed. Bloody brilliant!!!"

Thanks James, appreciate the feedback.

One way I do this…

Write in timed blocks with my special concentration music in my earphones.

No multi-tasking.

No emails.

Just focus.

And learning to write with speed also has other benefits, as James went on to say…

"The boss loves the letter. Haven't seen her this excited by my concept ever until now. Great work Steve. Just proves it's all in how you sell it!!!"

Happy to be the creator of marital harmony, James.

Miss this and it fails

You can have the best big idea...

The most eye-popping headline...

The smoothest copy...

The strongest offer...

But if you miss this = failure. What am I talking about?

Execution.

Often marketing efforts fail because of poor execution.

Case in point...

The time I received a "door hanger" flyer from a real estate company. I gave the flyer 4 out of 10 (which is way better than about 90% of real estate marketing I see).

But...

The door hanger was not hung on the door. It was in the middle of a big pile of junk mail. Only reason I saw it was that I dropped the pile on the way to the recycling bin and it nearly blew away in the wind.

So the lesson my friend...

The strategy was solid. The copy (almost) passable. But the execution?

Epic Fail. Reckon 99.9% of these door hangers were missed because of poor execution. Now if the hanger was swinging away on the front doorknob... I see it and I read... then the message had a chance of working. But lost in the clutter of other junk mail...

Execution counts. Big time. So make sure you get it right.

The chance of turning pro – shocking facts

F licking through a magazine and I came across an article about parents and sports rage at their kids' games. Fascinating reading. And a little disturbing.

Having coached kids for 25 years I've seen plenty of the good and bad. Mostly good of great people giving up their time to give kids the benefits of team sport.

Others? Well, it seems they try to live their own (FAILED) sporting dreams through their kids. Sad.

One fact in that article stuck out and get this…

According to a survey conducted recently around 50% of parents believed their child was going to have a pro sporting career. **Yes, seriously. 50%.**

Here's a reality check from the US football (gridiron) scene…

- There are 1,086,627 high school football players
- 6.5% of these go on to play college football
- 1.6% of college players make it to the pro ranks in the NFL

The lesson? Time about 98.4% of parents gave themselves a serious dose of reality.

Same in marketing…

Chances are you may not make the pros and become a world class copywriter. But… And here's the kicker…

To "win" in business you don't have to an "A-List" copywriter, you just have to be better than your competitors. So learn the fundamentals. Practice them. Test them. And learn from your wins and losses. That is the way you "turn pro" in marketing and grow your influence.

Best part… unlike many celebrities, if you master marketing, there's a good chance you'll do very well, without all the baggage that comes with success!

Cost of NO action

E very time you really "want" to do something BECAUSE you know it will be good for you and/or your business, but you don't do it, **there is a cost.**

Any idea what that cost might be?

Here's a little formula for working it out…

Oh, and by the way, I'm not suggesting you chase every shiny object that comes along - and there are plenty. I'm talking about those times when you "feel" it's right, that voice tells you it is right but for some reason you don't act…

And you then play the mind game where you justify your inaction with whatever excuse you used (no time, no money, too busy, too XYZ).

Sound familiar?

If you're anything like me that's a rather loud "YES".

We all do it.

So next time you're presented with an opportunity you KNOW is good for you but you hesitate, this little formula will help clarify your decision…

Start with…

How much $$$ you WANT or SHOULD make every month…

MINUS

How much $$$ you REALLY made last month.

EQUALS how much it's costing you.

And if the offer you're weighing up helps bridge that gap then it's kind of like a no-brainer…

"Yes".

The 3 questions on your prospects' minds

For any sale, your prospect usually has 3 big questions they need to have answered before they say yes.

Remember, everyone underestimates the difficulty of the task of selling. It's true, there is no more expensive or challenging thing than to create enough trust in what you do to compel someone to hand over their hard-earned in exchange for goods or services.

This may help…

When you strip everything away, your prospect is looking for answers to 3 big questions.

Question #1 revolves around authenticity behind the product or service.

That is… YOU. Do you meet their standards of ethical business practices? Have you explained your track record as it applies to them, to others, for example?

Next…

They want proof the product or service works. So their **Question #2 revolves around the credibility** of what you're selling. This can be shown via dramatic demonstration and before and after pix.

And their **Question #3?** Well, it's about them…

Can the thing you're selling **work for them?**

Of the 3, this one is the toughest to prove because you are dealing with their self-doubt, them remembering past failures and so on.

Tip: show how people just like them have benefited.

Only when you've answered these questions will you tip the scales in your favour.

Crafting an offer – steps

More for you to ponder on offers and how to craft them. Follow these principles…

#1 - They buy the offer (so make it strong).

#2 - Weak offer = weak response (so they must be excited by it).

The feeling we want them to have is, "I've got to have it, I'd be nuts to say no" (so you must make it irresistible in terms of the VALUE they receive).

Here are the 5 steps I use when crafting offers:

#1 - Name/Title

Adjective (new, free, advanced, easy, ultimate)

Noun (problem it solves or title eg deal, secret, toolkit, program, code, bundle)

#2 - The result or big win they get

What the customer experiences after they buy (new freedom, confidence) + why it's great ie – saves $X, free etc

#3 - Features and benefits

List these, plus the feelings the benefits give them

#4 – Call to action

Tell them how they get it (click, call, send)

#5 – Create FOMO

Add scarcity and urgency to make it a "now" decision, plus the pain of missing out

Next time you go to craft an offer use this scaffolding.

NOTE: This is usually where I start writing sales copy. Once I've got the offer nailed, I go to the headline/opening or bullets.

The danger of comfort

Warning Will Robinson! Danger! Danger!

Remember that line from the 70s TV classic, *Lost In Space?* If you were born post about 1980 it may be unfamiliar to you…

That was pre-Netflix. No internet. No remote. Black and white picture. 4 Channels. Aaaah the memories!

To the uninitiated the premise of the show was that the Robinson family with a weird "Professor" tag-a-long was marooned on a dangerous distant planet. Their robot, the odd-looking thing with flexi arms and pincers for hands, was their saviour on more than one occasion. His sensors would pick up movement and his electronic voice would bleat…

"Warning! Warning! Danger Will Robinson!"

And just in time the Robinson family would run into their space craft and lock it down. Disaster averted… and a new episode to come…

Remember that? Even if you don't there is still a massive lesson here for us in business. There is a warning for you…

Stop marketing at your peril.

The danger here is, when things are going well, we tend to get "busy". And because there's no dire need, our marketing efforts are the first things that get put on the "tomorrow" list. We all know what happens to things on that list, don't we?

So hear me loud and clear…

Warning Will Robinson! Danger! Danger!

Always be marketing your business… NEVER get too busy to do it. You never know when things will turn, and you might need that next deal or client. Thing is, when you stop, you lose momentum. And like a truck in first gear, it's darn hard to get up to 100 k's quickly. Even worse if you "need" that next client.

Question for you to answer…

What marketing activity have you got planned for this week? What about today?

If your answer is nothing… *Danger Will Robinson!*

Always be marketing. Especially when things are going well.

Productivity secret (it's not about the hustle)

Here's a BIG tip about productivity…

And after now you won't see this word, because productivity is NOT about more "hustle". Yes, that noise is me… *grrrrrr…*

Anyways…

According to the book, *Smarter, Faster, Better* by Charles Duhigg to be more productive (and who doesn't want to be, right?) requires one simple thing.

Will get to it in a sec. First what is productivity?

Not harder work, that's for sure.

Being productive is, to paraphrase the author, *you know what your goals are, and you get closer to those goals without feeling like you're wasting effort and time.*

And…

You feel like you are doing the work that matters to you most at the moment you most want to do it, without having to make huge sacrifices along the way.

Nice, hey?

So that means, what works for you on a Monday, may not work for you on a Thursday, and so on.

The key to you being more productive then?

Expose yourself to the knowledge of alternative ways of thinking. The science reveals most productive people are not that way because they work harder or they're crazy smart. They're more productive because they develop mental habits, that push them to think more deeply about the choices they're making.

So think a little deeper about issues you face. Come at it from a different angle.

The moment you hear yourself saying, "I never thought about it that way" you know you're being productive.

P.S. Another thinking prompt phrase is, "What if I'm wrong?" This one too can open up new avenues of thinking.

Old school Vs hip – a cautionary tale

So are you up to date with the latest and greatest in the marketing world? If not, "they" consider you something of a dinosaur, right? Old school. Ignorant. Boring.

Like the time I was being interviewed by a marketing agency for a podcast and the first question they asked (some prep would have been nice!!??!!) was, "What's the latest app you've got on your phone?"

Uncomfortable pause (while this dinosaur thought long and hard)…

"Whatever my kids had put on there for me. Bubble Explode I think".

Time for *their* uncomfortable pause.

You see I don't use many apps… oh the horror… turn away now…

For a marketing guy, a mortal sin, right? Not so fast.

It's US research but Localytics says 1 in 4 mobile apps are not used ever again after the first use. They cost a bomb to develop so they "should" comprise a "VITAL" piece of your marketing mix? Hmmmm… And no, I'm not "anti-app" or "anti-technology". I am just a stickler for tried and true that's stood the test of time.

More:

Social media is a must, right? So much so that (again US research) Riple analysis shows 55% of small businesses list Facebook as their most important marketing tool.

Counter research…

Mediapost found email to be 6 times likely to generate a direct response.

Ouch. Again, not saying FB doesn't work (I know a couple of very big and successful companies that have been built on social media).

What I am saying is…

Don't chuck out what you KNOW to work for a shiny object which "may" work. Hasten slowly.

Offer tips

W hat's the key to greater influence? Well, of course, a great headline is important. Smooth and interesting copy is vital. But hear this loud and clear, AGAIN...

They buy the offer.

And...

Weak offer = weak response.

So you've got to get this right. Thus went a conversation with a client as we brainstormed ideas. Note to self - none of this is earth-shattering but, and it's a big but, but my client was so caught up in his stuff he'd basically "forgotten" what makes a great offer. Maybe you have too, so here's a quick refresher. To boost response/strengthen your offer think about:

Free shipping or

Free gift with purchase (if ordered before a deadline) or

Discount for 3 days to get rid of old stock before new arrives or

Pre-order discount if you've got something new coming out (order before X) or

A deluxe version which includes A, B, C or

Free trial or

Payment plans and...

A kick arse guarantee.

Nothing brilliantly new and exotic here is there?

But it's VERY handy as a checklist of sorts next time you go to market, to get you thinking about how you can make your offer even stronger. Because the reality is no one really knows how good you are until they buy from you.

Business lesson from a giant of last century

He's considered one of the great leaders of the 20th Century. The man who stared down Hitler and eventually (with an assist from the yanks) defeated him. And he's got a MASSIVE and IMPORTANT business lesson for us all.

I'm talking about Winston Churchill, of course.

If you're under 30 and not sure who he is… Fast history lesson: he was the Prime Minister of England during World War II.

Anyways…

I watched the biopic of his life, *Darkest Hour*. It is the story of his rise to PM up until his epic, "We will fight them on the beaches… we will never surrender" speech to parliament. Where he "mobilised the English language and sent it into battle". Maybe a month in terms of time… but a 2 hour + movie. To be fair, it never reached great heights but was compelling.

Assuming it's historically accurate, the big take away for me was… from one of the greatest leaders in history…

In those dark hours…

Even he, the great leader, was plagued by insecurity and self-doubt… to the point he almost quit. Imagine that.

Boy, would history have been different, because his political opponents wanted to broker a peace deal with Hitler. But it got me thinking… even Sir Winston was plagued by what I see so often in business owners…

SELF DOUBT.

Seems it's a human trait we all battle, sometimes every day of the week. What's the lesson here? If your business is important to you, ride out the self-doubt. It will be your companion whether you like it or not. At the end of the day you have a choice, like Churchill did…

Give up. Or keep going. Granted, the stakes for us may not be the freedom of the world…

But it's the freedom of your world as a business owner. Self-doubt? Yep, it's there in you and me…

Keep going, stare it down. Your business and your freedom are worth it.

Problem or product?

H ear ye this truth…

What should you speaketh of, their pain or your product?

Answer:

Both.

Depending on where in the buying cycle the prospect is.

Listen up, class is in:

You and me both, when we go to buy anything, go through 3 phases.

PHASE 1 - Light bulb: we become "aware" of a problem… need new shoes, a bigger house etc… before the moment of awareness, we are all blissfully happy going about our daily lives. We are not ready to buy. When we become aware of the "problem" we are however ready to hear about the pain we and others experience.

LESSON: to prospects in this phase, speaketh only of their pain, lest they run away coz they are not ready to buy.

PHASE 2 - Research: the next phase we go through is to check out all possible solutions… online searches, talking to friends and more. Here you speaketh of your solution and why it is superior, provide them proof of concept.

LESSON: in this phase of the buying cycle, speaketh of success stories, case studies etc and yes, in this phase it's ok to talk product.

PHASE 3 - Buy: when they are ready, this is where you speaketh your cracking offer…

LESSON: the offer needs to be so "no brainer" good, they think "I'd be crazy not to say yes".

Spend time thinking this through because if you hit them too early, it will be NO right off the bat. Game over.

And remember, no sales = no business.

The power of conviction

Don't get soft.

When you close your sales message, do so with conviction.

Similarly, when you talk about your product or service, make it hit home… explain why NOT using it is harmful to them.

No, you don't have to be cheesy or hypey.

But… if the copy is soft to the point where it doesn't leave them with the feeling that it adds big and immediate value to their lives, how can you expect them to feel it?

And if they don't feel it, it's "no deal".

Put the kid gloves away. Strong copy is needed to sell these days.

Get excited. Get passionate. And get those feelings across to your reader.

There really is no other way.

Help from the Universe

This little tool helps boost your results, so give it a go without judgement. Ok, it may be a little woo woo for you, but it is DEFINITELY worth trying.

It's a process called The Place Mat and it comes from Abraham-Hicks and it's been lifechanging for me.

The tool...

Each day, before you start work, take a piece of paper and rule a line down the middle.

On the left side write at the top **"Things I will do today"**.

On the right side at the top write **"Things I'd like the Universe to do today"**.

Now the word "Universe" is interchangeable. Use whatever aligns with you. God. Spirit. Love. The Angels. Gaia. And so on.

And what you do is, on the left, write things you know you will or want to get to today. It really is your to do list. On the right, write things you'd also want to accomplish but seem too hard or out of reach.

When you have finished writing your lists, let go and get on with your day.

You'll be amazed (like I was) just how many things on the "Universe" side just "happen" without any conscious effort on your part. I've got my theories as to how and why this works but that doesn't really matter.

What does matter is that it works.

When you start your day this way, it's amazing how much you accomplish. How many coincidences happen and work in your favour.

Don't believe me?

Try it out for a week... you'll be glad you did!

Environment always wins

Take a person out into the middle of a desert without food and water. What happens? They are dead within a couple of days.

Why? The environment wins. And it wins all the time.

What's your writing environment like?

My take: writing is a solitary task. It's isolating. So set your environment up to consider this…

Here are ways you can control your writing environment.

1. Write in 33-minute blocks (a-la Gene Swartz or 25-minute blocks a-la pomodoro)
2. Write with flow – no editing as you go
3. Play some baroque background music (eg Mozart Piano Concerto #21)
4. Use 2 screens

This doesn't mean I don't mix it up occasionally and go to a café. Doesn't mean I don't take calls walking around to get energy. And doesn't mean I don't go and sit in the sun at times.

It does mean numbers 1-4 just mentioned are my staple.

Set your environment up to win. Unlike being in the desert, you can create a winning work environment.

What do you need to change about your surroundings?

Landing page video script template

I 've used this over many years (I think it originally came from the great John Carlton, apologies if that's not the case). I like it because it's super simple. And it works.

It has just 4 parts...

1) **Here's Who I am** (credibility building, rapport building)

2) **Here's What I've got For You** (curiosity, future pacing, content)

3) **Here's why it's important** (what they'll get out of it, demonstrating benefits, creating desire for more)

4) **Here's how to get it** (call to action)

Whether it's a shorter video or a longer one matters not. If you're looking for some scaffolding for your next video script, give this a crack. I'm confident you'll love the results.

Way too close

That's what you and me and most of us really are…

Way too close to what we do.

Because our heads are so much down looking into our business, our hands constantly "dirty" with our work, we can miss the obvious. Or the quirky. Or what's needed.

Case in point this book…

I paid eldest daughter Eliza, who was home from uni, to edit this book.

I had a "feeling" a few things weren't quite right… I had looked at it so often however, I couldn't see anything amiss.

Her fresh eyes?

Picked up obvious errors. Found double entries. Offered useful ideas which I couldn't see.

It's the same with every business I go into… I see things they can't… some are obvious, others not so.

Key thing is, fresh eyes…

Need them for your business?

If you answered yes, reach out to aligned people to help… it might cost you short term, but in the long run, they usually pay for themselves many times over.

Gee I hated this at the start

My greatest fear when I began this entrepreneurial journey was... Asking people for money.

I'd get nervous. I'd be uncertain. I'd feel lost. And it's fair to say I avoided "selling", especially when I was feeling down or tired.

Not so much now. It's far easier.

Yes, a lot of that negative stuff came from programming... religion, my upbringing, my teacher job where it was noble to give give give... till it hurt.

But there was another force at play.

And I believe it's what sabotages just about EVERYONE (maybe even you) until you figure it out.

What's the insidious saboteur?

Not knowing your value. Or more specifically not understanding there are 4 pillars to knowing your value AND being able to express these with confidence.

I've said before confidence is key in sales...

But you can only authentically deliver confidence if you "feel" these 4 pillars.

Here's the first one...

Your **BELIEF** in the value of what you do.

This comes from being able to, to use the phrase common these days, stand in your power based on the results you get for your clients.

So my padawan, chalk up "belief value" for today and...

I'll reveal the other 3 soon.

I'm so boring

S tandard responses from business owners early in my dealings with them are one of two extremes…

You don't understand, our business is different.

Or…

We just sell X, the same as everyone else, pretty boring really.

The first response is wrong and/or an excuse for why the business is where it is at right now. And there are methods I use to help a business owner see this truth.

It's the second type of response I want to talk about today, because it's more often than not much more "real" than the first.

Yep, you're boring.

Most businesses are.

They sell mowers. Accounting services. Dental solutions. IT stuff. And on it goes.

How do you stand out in all the sameness out there?

Simple… but not easy…

You take the mundane and make it exciting or curious or entertaining… anything but ordinary.

True, great copy can't sell a turd (it's still a turd at the end of the day and people won't buy it) but you CAN be different.

A couple of ways to make this happen include a great story about the product or founder. A celebrity endorsement (in this celebrity obsessed world). Show product in action videos and photos. And more.

Key point: if YOU can't get excited and interested in your product and WANT to tell prospects about it, how do you expect your customers to?

If you think you're boring, get your thinking cap on… there is GREAT profit in standing out from the sameness of your market.

Size matters

How long should a headline be?

The standard answer to any "size" questions in copywriting is...

Long enough to get the job done.

Great. But what does that really mean?

If you hate the vague and nebulous, try these word count guidelines for your headlines:

Offline:

The great Ted Nicholas, my first copywriting mentor, said that offline you should use a maximum of 17 words. He said he tested longer headlines but response waned with more than 17 words.

Online:

8 to 12 words seems to be a sweet spot. Gary Halbert said if a headline was longer than 12 words, it was too hard for the brain to comprehend in one go.

Socials and emails:

Keep it to 6 or fewer. Speed is vital here.

Yes, you can find examples that break these guidelines. Always. But if you want parameters to work within... the 17, 12, 6 is a good starting point.

Always be...

C losing - so goes the traditional sales in business mantra. Always be closing. Always be closing.

Well, yes. But also no...

I was sitting out the back quieting my mind between writing sessions. It's something I need to get better at mind you because it's amazing the clarity that comes in the stillness. So while I was there just watching I saw a pair of sea eagles wheeling over the water. We can see their nest from our back patio and we watch them often as they make their version of the sale (aka dive into the water for food).

What struck me was this...

For every swoop on the water and attempt to "close" the deal...

They soared. And flew. And watched the water. Most of their time was preparation before they acted. They weren't always swooping and diving. Imagine how exhausting that would be. And maybe even futile.

But there's a lot of real and imagined pressure on business owners to "always be closing"... or "hustling"... or "timid salesmen have skinny kids" and so forth. That advice has its place.

But...

If the majestic sea eagle had a message, I'm betting it would not so much be along the lines of "always be closing" and more along the lines of "always be qualifying".

Watching. Looking. Picking out more of your ideal and more likely prospects.

What would that do to the smoothness of your sales process... your conversion rates... and overall profits?

Always be closing... or... always be qualifying?

The sea eagle may have the answer.

Food for thought.

Writer's block

Ⅰt's crap.

Writer's block does NOT exist. At least for a sales writer.

Here's what I mean…

Sure, I've sat down at the computer and the ideas didn't flow. Yes, I've panicked and felt the despair in the gut. And yes, I've done this over and over again at different times.

And it's all BS.

What "writer's block" really means is…

You haven't done enough research.

Research into the market you're selling to. Research into the product you're selling. Research into the results people get from the product or service.

And, if I'm honest with myself, whenever I've felt blocked it's because I've cut a corner or two.

How to solve…

Interview the owner or a customer.

Write out bullets.

Gather and analyse more testimonials.

Delve into the market even more.

Find research papers about the problem or the solution.

And on it goes.

Writer's block = not enough pre-work by the writer!

The worst thing about clients

I t was the late great Gary Halbert who said often, and he even wore a cap with the words on it…

"Clients suck".

Now apparently, he did it as a repelling/attraction strategy. When you are as good as Halbert was, you can get away with it! I'm not suggesting you treat clients with disdain… in fact you should never lose sight of the fact that your customers do not exist to solve your problems, you exist to solve theirs.

But to a point, Halbert was right. At least in one aspect: clients buy when they want to… not when we, as business owners, want them to. And this can be frustrating.

Take for instance this email conversation I had with an interstate client about the results from a "shock and awe" pack I created for them. They are in the financial services industry. He said…

Steve the shock and awes have been great, but not in the way I first thought they might. As a lead generation tool, they have largely been a failure (not anyone's fault, just reality). Or maybe the way we have marketed them has been a failure. Either way, people just don't know they need or want it, and aren't asking for it in the numbers we first hoped.

But having said that, if someone engages with us in any other way, and then they get the shock and awe, they become a client! Not always straight away, but it is doing all the heavy lifting and planting the seeds in their thinking and it seems to be a rare thing that someone resists and doesn't at least try to get on board with us (we do obviously turn quite a few away).

I have to say I never expected the follow up letters to play much of a role, but they have definitely added to the conversion rate. It is so interesting to realise that just because someone doesn't get on board straight away, that doesn't mean they aren't interested in us, it just isn't yet the right time, but with the various follow ups (letters and otherwise) eventually it is the right time.

Might pay to read that again because this is straight from the trenches, happening now. The big lessons:

- You can't get away with doing only 1 thing and expect sales
- Clients do "suck"… but only because they buy in their time, not ours, so stay in touch
- Follow up is vital, always

Oh, and I might add, the follow up mentioned is dinosaur traditional direct mail I wrote for them as part of the pack, plus email. So remember, they buy in their time… what are you doing to be there at the top of their consciousness… what marketing collateral does the heavy lifting for you… so they say yes WHEN they are ready?

Put some thought into this will you… your conversions will thank you for it!

This is a complete myth

Here is the secret to business success...

Well at least from my perspective.

You see I was asked by a friend about the possibility of them setting up an online store for a "bit of passive income" while they kept working at their day job.

Sure, it can be done.

But...

Business is a serious undertaking. It's a messy kitchen with LOTS going on. And I gave it to him straight...

The 4 hour work week is complete BS.

Even your "side business" online store is not as easy as it sounds... setting it all up, the copy, the tech, driving traffic, fulfilling orders, dealing with refunds/complaints, responding to changes in the market and on it goes.

He got a little discouraged. But better to go into something with eyes open.

I also told him this:

All of the successful people I know (and the list is very long) put in their hours. Succeeding in business is complex. It takes constant work. And sorry, there's no "secret" pill.

Yes, there are certain formulae that work extremely well. But business is not a defined game like sport... known number of players, goal posts that stay still, level field, boundaries.

A crap idea that flops this year may work well next. What flies today may be a dud ad or campaign in 6 months. The business environment is forever on the move. And you have to work to stay with it. Which takes more than 4 hours per week.

Ok, will leave you to it... get to work!

Go sell some stuff and spread your influence.

Long Vs short copy argument solved

L ong copy doesn't work. Ever heard that one before? Of course you have. And usually it's BS.

Case in point…

According to communications executive Gabe Rose, social media sharing is down 50% since 2015. No idea if this is true but it's a solid source (PR Daily News Feed, 31/10/18). Says Rose, "One way to buck this alarming trend is to produce longer pieces, which tend to garner more shares and interactions."

So when someone tells you a "FACT" like long copy doesn't work anymore…

Take it with a grain of salt and ask for solid evidence.

When I was a freelance journo back in the day, in preparation for a story, I asked boxing legend Jeff Fenech to respond to the common wisdom that his fighter would lose his upcoming bout…

His reply…

"Opinions are like arseholes, mate… everyone's got one."

Very elegant Mr Fenech.

But I've never forgotten it.

So just be vigilant…

People will present their opinions like they are indisputable facts, beyond question.

Unless you see evidence, be careful.

The day she "outed" me

I t was the late 1970s and I can still remember the feeling when my mother read it to me. I hated it so much because it exposed my biggest fear, and maybe yours.

What's the biggest fear you and me and your market has? Many would say fear of failure. So in a business context the traditional thinking goes like this…

You present a solution which gives your customer success, rather than them doing nothing and getting the failure they don't want. True, right? I believe… close, but no cigar. There is a deeper fear than this. Brendan Burchard (author of *The Motivation Manifesto* among several other titles), contends what people fear most is…

Embarrassment.

Think about that for a second… which feels worse in your gut… failure or embarrassment? It's why most people rate public speaking as the greatest "trigger" to negative emotion, second only to death. And like I said, I can relate to this, deeply. I'm an introvert by nature. Prefer a small crowd to a big one. Am happy in my own company. And when I was young, I HATED with a passion speaking in front of the class.

Stop looking at me… kind of thing. Maybe you can relate?

Get this… I even had a substitute teacher Mrs S (she can remain anonymous) write on one of my report cards "blushes easily when speaking in front of the class"… like I needed my nosed rubbed in it… what were my parents going to do with that info? It was the late 70s and therapy was NOT fashionable. So why even write that? Anyways, being "outed" like this hurt because, well, it was embarrassing. Hurt more and deeper than any poor grade.

It's ok, I grew out of it… and can speak to big rooms and small for hours at a time these days. In fact, 2,000 is the biggest crowd I've addressed. But this was my kryptonite as a kid… embarrassment. And my very educated guess is, it's VERY close to the top fear your market has too.

Here's a deep little exercise. Pen and paper ready…

What are the top "embarrassments" your market faces? List them.

Next…

How can you use them in your sales messages? Fear of embarrassment is why Caples famous **"They all laughed when I sat down at the piano, but when I started to play!"** headline worked so well and why it's been swiped so much over the decades.

And the Charles Atlas "98-pound weakling kicked sand in my face" ad too. No one wants to be embarrassed. So how can you leverage this in your marketing. Powerful stuff if you take the time to dig deep. Thank me later. And stop looking at me!! Lol.

Dumb tourists power lesson

"Excuse me sir, how do you get to the Sydney Opera House?" Came the rather desperate plea from a lost tourist.

The local answered...

"Practice. Practice. Practice."

And it's the same with copywriting and marketing.

You see most switched on business owners UNDERSTAND the desperate need for good copy and marketing.

Problem for many is twofold...

Limited resources to pay someone like me the coin needed to write for you.

Or...

Limited time to spend the hours needed to learn it yourself so you become self-sufficient.

Which leaves you with a dilemma.

Go it alone and learn it all by yourself – dangerous, time consuming, expensive but not impossible if you have staying power.

Or...

Take the FAST TRACK of short cuts delivered by someone who not only does it every day but...

Also has a PROVEN track record for TEACHING others to do it for themselves.

Seek out mentors who've done what you want to and get to work with them.

This writing secret, do you use it?

One of the keys to selling with the written word is speed of the read. We want our customers to see our sales message FAST, particularly online.

Question is, how do you do this? Simple when you know how.

You must abbreviate your copy.

You must include emotion.

You definitely need rhythm and flow.

And you must eliminate trip words.

These are the killer. They create confusion. Or, as Dan Kennedy says they…

Make your reader feel **vaguely unconsciously uncomfortable.**

Great line that.

What happens when your writing is not "smooth" is the reader will trip or stop on a difficult phrase, an unfamiliar word or sentence that doesn't make sense. They will go back and read it over to try and understand it. And maybe do that a third time.

Trouble is, if your writing is "hard" for them like this where they trip, stop and have to go back over it to make sense of it… it's over. Sale lost. Prospect gone.

To make your copy read fast so you make more money, eliminate those trip words or phrases.

How? Spell and grammar checks help.

So does reading the copy out loud. If you stumble when reading aloud, chances are they will too when reading your sales message. It's a good idea to read copy out loud, pen or highlighter in hand and… whenever you trip up, make a mark on the page and come back at the end and smooth out the copy.

Wordsmith it so it flows better… so they get through your sales message with ease.

Who cares, right?

N o one cares about you. Or your business. Or what troubles you have right now.

All "they" care about is themselves.

And having their problem solved. We know this, don't we…

Your message MUST answer WIIFM (what's in it for me) - been banging on about it for years and you've seen it in these hallowed pages.

Yep, it's common sense and all, BUT…

I still see pages of copy which do NOT follow this golden rule.

Today is a recalibration for you. With a twist.

Try this…

Next time you go to write a sales message, picture in your mind one of your clients reading it.

Just ONE person.

Nothing new in that, I know (banging on about this too for years).

Now here's a deeper thought…

WHAT EMOTIONAL STATE WILL THEY BE IN WHEN THEY READ IT?

Does your message take this into account?

Or is it just a templated same old message with oft-used clicks and phrases?

Reality is, there's a person on the other end reading it, with a whole lot going on in their lives.

Do you consider this when you put fingers to keyboard?

WHAT EMOTIONAL STATE WILL THEY BE IN WHEN THEY READ IT?

Write to them in that state, like you're writing to a favourite relative.

Slay their internal calculator

Y ou have it.

I have it.

We all have it.

That internal calculator that instantly and automatically springs to life whenever we go to buy any good or service. And that calculator goes something like this…

If I want X product or service, I have to pay Y money and time - **is it worth it?**

This kicks into gear at the start of a sales message.

And at crunch time when we decide whether or not to hand over the moolah it pings off like firecrackers in our brains.

My question to you today: do you do enough in your copy to slay this internal calculator?

Reason I ask is I critique copy often and am just as often left with the thought…

So what do I really get?

I'm sure the writer knew what they meant.

But the reader must be 100% crystal clear.

If not, you've made it waaaaaay too easy for that calculator in their heads to say "NO" straight away.

Sale lost.

It starts with the headline. Must be clear in the copy. And the offer must be strong and clearly spelled out.

Every sale you fight to beat this internal calculator.

Make it clear what they get AND what great value it is.

Never assume they will just "get it"… they won't.

And that my friend is a million $ lesson.

Embarrassingly awful

H ave you ever at one point in your life felt "embarrassingly awful" at something?

I know I have.

Today, I want to talk about success, and what it takes.

You see I love this Dan Kennedy quote:

"Everything I've done or do, from which millions of dollars, celebrated reputation or personal satisfaction has come, I started out embarrassingly awful at".

Yes, there is hope.

Your past does NOT determine your future results.

Providing that is…

You do something different.

THE TRUTH:

You can't, if you want to get out of the "embarrassingly awful" stage, keep doing what got you to where you are.

You see being bad at something is ok. We all start there.

Staying bad at it, on the other hand, is a choice.

There is no overnight success… only improvements over time.

Your first email… first sales call… first customer interaction… will probably be some version of awful.

Then you reach that fork on the path that gives you a choice… go left and stay the same… go right and grow and improve.

Remember, your past and how much you sucked at something, is not permanent.

Why they buy

Are you in your market's head enough? Want more info on how to get there? Great, here's a quick analysis of why we buy.

It's based on the famous Maslow's hierarchy of needs.

That is…

We all have 5 basic needs, and these motivate us to take action.

Here they are…

   1. **Physiological needs (food, shelter, sleep, sex)**
   2. **Safety needs (order and stability, freedom from fear)**
   3. **Love and belonging needs (family, friends, work colleagues)**
   4. **Esteem needs (status, achievement, respect)**
   5. **Self-actualisation needs (self-fulfilment, experiences, creative pursuits)**

You've seen this before, right?

So do you target these in your sales message?

This is a timely reminder to be more deliberate in addressing these hidden desires in us all.

KEY POINT: sell to these emotional needs, not your product or service and you've got a much better chance of success.

My take…

The two BIGGEST and MOST POWERFUL needs that motivate us to buy…

Drum roll please…

EASE and HAPPINESS.

In my humble (and accurate) opinion hit these two buttons and you're halfway there.

Sinful spelling mistake

*Y*ou have no credibility…

So said a student of mine many moons ago in one of the first online trainings I ever ran.

What do you mean? I rather nervously asked the student whom we'll call "Trish" (because it's her real name). Trish then said, *Well, on slide #5 you left out the 'U' in the word 'humor'.*

Oh, ok. my bad, thanks for letting me…

And another thing she blurted out in a rather peeved tone…

Your slides are really boring, just black writing on white background, everyone's moved on from that.

So Trish was an unhappy client. I explained the reasons for white background and black print (easiest for communication) and that if she was focussed on one spelling mistake maybe this really wasn't right for her right now. That if her focus was a letter here and there, she might just be missing the big money lesson. You see there are many writers and business owners around the country who've benefited to the tune of big $$$ from my plain old easy communication slides (with the odd mistake here and there). And my copy has made literally millions of dollars over the years for clients.

But Trish?

Well, we agreed she could have a refund and I wished her well. It's ironic because the next lesson in the sequence was about the tone and formality of your sales message. It's a 1-to-1 CONVERSATION. It sure as heck ain't an English essay that gets graded. No, not suggesting sloppiness. But it IS a personal chat between you and your client. And the grading or marketing? Number of sales.

Poor Trish never saw this, her focus was elsewhere, and I suspect her results/career/ business are pretty much where they were when she spotted my spelling mistake back then. So remember, your sales message is about clear 1-on-1 communication, not perfection.

Oh and yeah, Trish will never read this, she was unsubscribed by me a looooooooooong time ago.

Talk to your clients in a way they will understand…

That highlights how you solve their problems at the right price…

That effortlessly leads them to the conclusion we want them to think… *I'd be crazy to say no to this.*

No clocks in Vegas

D id you know…

There are no clocks in most casinos in Las Vegas?

Any idea why?

They want the customer focussed. Not distracted by what time they have to be somewhere else.

The ills of gambling aside, it's a nice piece of sales choreography isn't it?

Do you do enough of this type of sales choreography?

When you get 'em in, are they totally focussed on solving their problem (ie getting your product or service)?

It's why there's an age-old rule of thumb for internet marketing (well, as "age old" as you can get for the internet)…

Only ONE action per page.

Anymore and you run the risk, like the gambler checking the clock, of them being distracted and running out the building.

So break this age-old rule at your peril because if you give too many options you lose them.

How much he spends on himself

A couple of years ago during my lunch break I flicked on the TV and happened on an NFL game between Pittsburgh Steelers and Kansas City Chiefs.

What I heard from the commentator blew me away…

He was talking about linebacker James Harrison. He was 38 and still going strong. For a game like the NFL that sucks in, chews up, and spits out gifted athletes at an alarming and soul-destroying rate (think former NRL player Jarryd Hayne and the movie Concussion)…

Harrison is an anomaly.

Yes, great quarterbacks like Tom Brady and Peyton Manning play to this age and beyond but they are protected and deliberately avoid the rough stuff, unlike our man Harrison.

So how can someone, at 38 and in one of (if not THE) toughest of sports still not just compete but dominate like Harrison did in the game I watched?

Commentator:

"There goes Harrison, a guy well known for spending $350,000 a year on his body to get it right and in tip top condition, everything from chiropractors, to cupping to acupuncture, this guy tries everything to stay in peak physical condition."

Think about that for a sec…

It equates to about $1k per DAY just to stay at the top of his game. Sure, the millions he earns eases the hip pocket pain… But a thousand bucks a day on self…

Wow!!

Begs the question I guess, do you spend (ie invest) enough in yourself to get into or stay at your best in business?

Me… lost count of how much I've invested in courses, travel to events, books, programs, coaching etc etc… but it's well into the multiple 6 figures over the years.

Nothing like Harrison of course but still…

You reading this book is a wise investment in self. The question is, what else will you do to get better at this game?

Shhh... I've got a little secret, listen up

One of the most powerful persuasion forces is our (yours and mine because we are human) belief in secrets.

All of us believe others have answers we don't. We think information is being kept from us. We "know" others have superior or unique powers we aren't privy to.

And we WANT what they've got and what we DON'T have.

NOTE: this crosses all demographics and niches... your market is NOT different. Every human has a belief in secrets hard wired into their DNA.

Simple truth... people say yes to things because of this powerful force.

Here's one way to leverage this force...

Use the word "Secret" in your headline because it's one of those hard-wired into our brains words that instantly grabs us.

Just like these...

"The Secret to Fat Loss Finally Revealed" or

"The Secret to Profitable Stock Picks Which Saw My Last Trade Alerts Yield Quick Profits of 58%" or

"The Secret to a Happy, Fun-Filled Family Holiday Begins with this Checklist – Download Today for FREE!" or

"The 5 Secrets to a Happy Marriage – Which are You Missing?" and so on

Secrets work.

Picasso on pricing

A s the story goes...

The masterful Pablo Picasso is sketching in a park. A woman walks by, recognizes him, and begs for her portrait.

Reluctantly he agrees.

Four and a half minutes later, he hands her the sketch.

Excited, her mind racing about the stories she can tell her friends and in awe at how beautifully it captures the very essence of her character, she asks the all-important question...

"What do I owe you?"

Thinking, because it was a random "social" act, Picasso would come back with a "don't worry, it was nothing really go ahead keep it" type of response. She is shocked at what he said...

"5000 francs, madam."

"What? "How could anything be worth that much when it took less than 5 minutes!?" came the outraged response.

Without missing a beat, Picasso replied...

"No, madam, what you have in your hands took me my whole life to learn."

This, I guess, is the true nature of mastery.

Which begs the question...

What is your time worth?

Do you charge enough for YOUR mastery and the value it brings to your customers?

You, friend or foe to yourself?

W ell, are you your own best friend or…

Something of an enemy to your own success?

More specifically…

Is the "voice" in your head a friend who helps uplift you?

Or

Some kind of saboteur that keeps you stuck?

The first voice gives you confidence. The second saps you of positive energy. We all have both… which is stronger in you?

Here's why…

Back in the 1950s Dr J B Rhine from Duke University in the US conducted experiments proving the effect of this voice. He found that negative suggestions, distractions, and expressions of disbelief on the part of onlookers adversely affected people as they were trying to guess the order of cards in a special deck.

What about positive comments, feelings others were "pulling for" you and encouraging? In every experiment the person hearing the positive comments scored better.

Negative voice = poor result.

Positive voice = better result.

Goes the same for the voice in your head and what it's telling you most of the time.

Here's the thing though…

I believe you must have the positive voice…

But also…

A REASON to feel the positive voice. Confidence must be based on something tangible otherwise it's too easy for the negative voice to win out.

Monitor your thoughts today. Are they mostly positive? If not might need to change some things in your inner world.

When to break the unbreakable rule

I t's been called the unbreakable copywriting rule. It's taught often, and fair enough because it's been responsible for truckloads of sales over the years.

But…

It doesn't always hold true. What is "Mr Unbreakable"?

In your headline always lead with your biggest benefit.

Yes, dazzle them with the transformation they will receive. Good advice for sure. Tied closely to this is another old chestnut to never put the company name in a headline because no one cares. Also true. But it leaves you scratching your head because you see it all the time. Think Coke, Nike, Microsoft etc…

So what's the answer…

To "benefit AND use company name" or not to?

Well here's the thing…

It's ok to lead with your company name or product if you or they have brand name recognition. A benefit really isn't needed, the "branding" does the selling.

To take it one step further…

An ad with a headline like,

"iPads 30% off Today Only"

Will do far better than a "well written" headline like,

"Amazing Time Saving Device that Fits on Your Lap and Eliminates the Need for Your Desktop – 30% Off Today Only"

Ok, so that's not a "great" headline but you get the idea.

When you have a certain brand reach you have to say less to get your message heard. Trouble is, most small, medium and even large businesses do not enjoy the recognition of a Coke or an Apple or a Nike. So you have to do more work with your headlines. The key is to know when and how to weave in a company name.

This hurts...

E verybody has them...

In fact there's not a single business I've seen that doesn't.

Which is not to say it's "ok"...

I'm talking about lost customers.

The economics of losing a customer?

Many experts say it costs 6 times MORE to get a new customer than it does to keep an existing one...

So my sharp little nudge to you today is...

Do you have customer retention strategies in place?

No? Well good chance you're missing opportunities to grow your influence... and they are probably spending money with a competitor.

And here's the next big question (aka nudge in the business ribs)...

Do you have a reactivation strategy?

Again, if no... you're missing out on influence growing, big time.

So as you plough ahead into your day, might pay you to have a think around these two little strategies and what you can do about them... because proven ways to retain and reactivate customers will change the maths in your business, almost overnight.

The most useless word in copy... by far

Here's a cracker of a writing tip...

Give your copy a **"thatectomy"**.

A what?

A that-ectomy... where you remove 80% of the word "that".

Most are NOT needed.

When they go, most of the time your words are easier to read because they flow better.

Example:

Before:

We often find that the day to day operations of a customer's process become so common place that the possibilities of improvements are overlooked.

After:

We often find the daily operations of a customer's process become so common place the possibilities of improvements are overlooked.

See? Smoother. Easier to read. Easier to understand. And isn't that what we want with sales language?

So go ahead... eliminate with extreme prejudice the word "that" wherever you can.

Footnote: sometimes a that is useful for emphasis (eg Yes, the win was that big, it changed the thinking of the entire company), the trick is knowing the difference.

Work interruptions, scary numbers

How productive are you and your staff?

How often do you and they "just check your phone" like it's a life necessity such as breathing?

If you've ever interrupted your work or seen staff with eyes glued to a mobile screen, this will make your toes curl…

- Most people check their phones on average 58 times a day (30 of those during 9-5) - source *Time Rescue App*
- Half of all phone pickups happen within 3 minutes of the previous one - source *Time Rescue App*
- Average time spent on Social Media is 142 minutes a day - source *Digital Information World*
- The average employee spends 2 hours a day recovering from distractions - source *US Bureau of Labour Statistics*
- We lose as much as 40% productive time when we shift between tasks - source *American Psychological Association*

Scary numbers.

And scarier still the implications for the results you get each day from self and staff.

A sobering lesson for you to be vigilant with your time and distractions.

Need to make some changes?

Why brilliant writing never works

Ignore that voice in your head…

The one that says, *"you can't 'write brilliantly', therefore you can't write good sales copy or grow your influence with words."*

Because here's the thing…

Good copy is NEVER about brilliant writing.

It's a conversation you have with another human being which leads them to take an action which will benefit them.

It never need be 100% grammatically correct (talking never is).

It should never be formal English (a 1-to-1 chat never is).

And it should never be flowery or use big words* (we are casual when we chat to each other, always).

You see, thanks to outstanding mentors, I've learned the skill of copywriting, I've taught others how to do it too.

As long as you follow the correct principles (like the ones in this book) you can succeed.

A reminder to let go of the perfection streak… you can write words that influence and sell… especially with a little help from a trusted source, like these pages!

*NOTE: if you sell into a technical market, of course you will use technical terms because that's the way your market speaks.

A powerful lesson from Tay Tay

W as eavesdropping on a conversation as we drove our youngest, Nate, to his soccer game at Rochedale on Brisbane's southside.

In the chat was eldest Eliza and wife Jenny. Nate had earphones in and was staring out the window, uninterested, teenage boy style. I was staring out the front window equally in my own world.

Until the pitch of the convo changed.

They were rather animated because apparently - and this is sooooooooo exciting- at the previous night's Taylor Swift concert in the US (that's Tay Tay to those in the know, like me – an eye roll now is ok…)

Anyways, apparently at the concert, out of the blue, on walks Niall Horan (of 1D boy band fame) for a surprise duet. The crowd went wild.

And it's a thing Ms Swift was doing for this tour… as the audience waits with bated breath, each new venue has a new surprise A-list singer guest for a special performance.

Another night I believe it was Robbie Williams.

So here's the lesson…

Can you be more like my good friend Tay Tay and do more to "surprise and delight" your fans (paying customers)?

At the very least she's got people talking.

The anticipation is palpable… who will it be tonight…

And then, because they are so talented, they rip out a song together and everyone goes home even happier.

What can you do in your business to create a similar buzz… or at least give your paying people a nice little surprise that brings them back to you for more?

Too busy = poor people talk

Ever said those three easy-to-blurt out but self-limiting words...

"I'm too busy"?

I know I have.

And if I'm honest, that's code for excuses.

I believe too many of us wear "too busy" as some kind of badge of honour.

I'm too busy to...

- Stop and take a moment...
- Put my feet up and think...
- Be present with my child or partner...
- Focus on the client fully...
- Take the time to learn new information to keep my saw sharp...

And on it goes.

All of the successful and wealthy people I know have a thirst for more knowledge in their field.

So next time you hear those "I'm too busy" words about to leave your mouth, might pay you to pause, reflect and change the thought.

The best in any field are "busy"... but they also take the time to work on their skills and knowledge.

Wheelie bin marketing secret

Not sure about you but I can never remember which bin goes out which week. Can you?

Here's why this is important to your marketing.

First the context…

Here on the Sunshine Coast we have 3 bin options…

- The green lid bin for garden waste
- The red lid bin for normal household garbage
- The yellow lid bin for recycling

The recycling bin only gets collected every second week. Maybe it's similar to where you live. And as an aside, remember the good old days… When 2 sweat dripping, smelly men clung to the back of a moving truck… When it stopped they hoisted a large metal bin on their shoulder and ran into your yard to empty YOUR metal bin…

They kept doing this until their big metal bin was full when they'd run back to the truck and dump their loads only to run off again and repeat the process. Remember those good old days? How things have changed, right?

Anyway back to my *no idea which bin goes out on which week* and why this is **VITAL to your marketing…**

No, we don't have piles of garbage outside our house. So how do I get it right, EVERY week?

Simple. I follow the crowd…

I see what everyone else in the street is doing and I put my bins out accordingly. You do the same? Which brings me to the marketing point…

I (and probably you too, and most definitely your market) follow the crowd…

So in your marketing you must SHOW others in action using what you sell. We are herd creatures. No one wants to be the only person in the shop. Or the only person to buy the product. So there is great safety in numbers…

Following the crowd makes people feel safe. Makes it "ok" for them to buy from you. Yup, works for me and my weekly bin collection. And it works in marketing too.

Challenge: how can you present your marketing messages to better leverage this human instinct, to show that "everyone" is using your product or service?

Truth about word counts

No way, they are wrong! So said an indignant fan of one *particular* guru. I was in a Facebook group doing some research and came across this interesting discussion about a certain marketing tactic.

More specifically who was "right" about it.

One contributor said guru X was right. And another was adamant guru Y's system was better.

Who was right? Probably both.

Case in point…

Like you, I'm on many emails lists, in dozens of groups, and I've seen lots over the years. Long copy works best. Keep it short. Etc etc etc.

So check this out, here's the word counts in emails from 3 gurus recently…

Guru #1 = 53 words (add in the PS and it jumped to 84)

Guru #2 = 454 words

Guru #3 = 1004

Who's right? Should your copy be X or Y long? These days short copy works better?

Answer: they are ALL right.

All 3 gurus are A-list marketers, exceptional at what they do, and wealthy. So remember this truth about marketing…

THERE ARE MANY WAYS TO BE RIGHT. And you have to test EVERYTHING.

Helps too if you let go of perfection because not everything will work, no matter how much you study or what energy you put into willing it to work.

Relax. Let go. And test. It's the only way forward.

Business yo-yo frustration solution

E ver tried to diet? If yes, you know it goes something like this…

You find something new, get all excited and motivated and it works like magic. Lose those kilos, feel great, bask in the compliments of family and friends.

Then…

The discipline wanes. The kilos creep back on. The compliments stop. And the scales remind you the diet "didn't really work". You have this yo-yo effect going on. Up and down. Up and down.

Similar in business isn't it…

You work your butt off chasing clients (marketing)…

Bask in all the conversions and cash flowing in…

Get busy satisfying clients and then…

Like the diet, you find yourself back where you started… needing new sales.

I've had many discussions with clients about this yo-yo effect and ways to combat it. Would love to say there is a simple magic pill. But like everything in business and in life, there isn't. You can however minimise the business yo-yo to a large extent by…

Planning your marketing by the quarter. And do something EVERY day towards this plan, no matter how busy you are in client satisfying mode. The moment you take the foot off the longer term pedal the closer you are to the danger of waking up one day wondering where all the clients have gone.

And it's back to the yo-yo…

It's what I do when working with the select few in my Private Client Group. We set quarterly goals and I help them work every day towards these. For this small but elite group the yo-yo is firmly tucked away thanks to the structure, strategy and accountability they receive.

So to beat this frustration in your business, focus each day on the longer-term strategy while you also satisfy existing customers.

Out fox the fox

When I asked the now retired, but still considered greatest living copywriter, Gary Bencivenga, a few years back in Connecticut, what the most important thing in copy was…

Must say I was a little surprised by his answer…

Not headline.

Not the offer.

Not flow in your writing.

All are important, sure.

But as far as the great man is concerned, the single biggest thing you need to do in copy is…

Drum roll please…

Add more proof.

Why? Blunt answer…

Our bullshit detector radar is soooooooooooo acutely tuned these days…

One hint of a *"Yeah right, Bozo!"* thought and one of two things happen.

Either:

They turn the page or click off the site.

Or…

They read the copy only so they can play the **"out fox the fox"** game where they go through every sentence with a fine tooth comb looking for where they can expose the flaws in your sales argument.

In either case it's game over. So never make your claims bigger than your proof…

And…

Add, like legendary GB said, more and more proof. Your growing influence and even bank account will thank you for it.

A CEO's success secret

L oved this and wanted to share...

Coz it aligns with what I've been saying about the need to put your feet up and think.

Elaine Jobson, CEO of Jetts Gym (the national 24-hour mob) was asked in a recent interview about the best advice she's been given...

"Spend time thoroughly understanding the problem before you decide on a solution. This advice helped me make the right decisions and not rush into solving the wrong problems, a common error in business."

Read that a couple of times so it sinks in. Clarity of thought is vital to solving business challenges.

The thing is, as entrepreneurs we tend to dive in and fix something. Or just say yes and clean up the mess latter.

This desire for action is hard-wired into most entrepreneurs... but does it always serve you?

As Jobson says, consider **what** problem needs to be solved BEFORE you take action.

Food for thought...

The 3 needs blueprint

Here are the 3 needs for any business success:

You needs strategy…

You needs consistency…

You needs execution…

Reason I bring this up is that in my Private Client Group we do a review every quarter. And this is important for business owners…

We spend so much time looking ahead to the next thing we often don't take time to look back at our achievements.

You see "success" is sexy.

Getting there ain't.

And as I look back with my clients it's, well, kind of boring.

No disrespect intended of course but here's what I mean…

We set the strategy.

We work methodically on it EVERY week.

And we quality assure so the execution is right.

Nothing bold or outrageous or earth shattering… and definitely no shiny objects in sight.

Just a simple 3 step blueprint for success.

Strategy – Consistency – Execution.

Productivity hacks for writers (and everyone else)

A sk and ye shall receive…

I get numerous requests for tips about how to write better. These apply whether you're a copywriter, a business owner who writes copy or someone who pens the occasional email or blog for their business.

Truth… These are not new. I've taught them over many years. But…

You may not have heard them before, or they may be a timely reminder. So if you want to write better, behold these 5 writing "hacks"…

Writing Hack #1 - Music

Listen to something that gets you in the zone or at least zones out other distractions. I've long used Mozart's Piano Concerto #21. Lately I've been experimenting with high frequency music. Google both and try. I remember hearing Perry Marshall say before he writes copy, he plays heavy metal music loud… to pump himself up. Couldn't think of anything worse personally. So try different types and see how you go. Put it on a loop so it plays and plays without you thinking about it.

Writing Hack #2 - Time

The late great Gene Swartz recommended 33 minutes and 33 seconds for each writing session. Put the timer on. Write. When it goes off get up and walk around for a minute or two. Sit down. Timer on. Write. There's also the Pomodoro technique of write for 25 minutes then take 5 minutes off. I've heard others say 45 minutes. Try them. Common denominator: short and limited time. If you try and sit in front of your screen for hours on end you get one result… fatigue. A tired mind can't write well. So work to a timer, your productivity will skyrocket.

Writing Hack #3 - Brain food

Always feed your mind with materials related to your subject. I've got 2 paid newsletters every month and at least 3 marketing type books on the go most months of the year. Sharpen your saw. Keep the brain fresh, the ideas flowing.

Writing Hack #4 - Sunshine

Not sure what it is but time outside, preferably in the sun, works wonders to clear the mind and give you ideas. Just 5 minutes is good. 10 or 15 even better. Fresh air, sunshine and if you can incorporate water (the ocean, a lake or river) better still.

Writing Hack #5 - A clear brain

When you write, write. When you edit, edit. NEVER mix the two. They use different parts of the brain. If you edit as you go what usually happens is the first page (or few paragraphs) are great, the rest, because your brain is confused and/or tired, is ordinary. So write your first draft in one go. Then go back and edit. Push your anal retentiveness to the background and write. Then edit.

There are plenty more. But if you apply these with discipline, you'll love the results you see in a VERY short space of time.

Vanity or sanity + the f bomb in marketing

Want to look good or make money?

To be clear…

Look good = vanity… make money = sanity.

Should be an easy question for entrepreneurs.

It's the money, right?

In fact, it's one of the main reasons why you're in business.

Sometimes though, business owners get too hung up on looking good and appearing nice and "professional".

So they baulk at an emotionally charged headline.

Or they wimp out on a bold guarantee.

Or don't want scarcity and urgency (coz it's "salesy") in their offer.

Strong sales attract criticism. Usually from competitors.

Key to success is to find people interested in what you offer and then present you and your solution in a way that connects to them.

It's not about pleasing everyone.

My favourite Dan Kennedy quote sums this up perfectly…

"Write only to those who are prepared to give you money and let everyone else f*ck off."

Nuff said really.

How many hours a week for you?

I f you do work more than 25 hours a week and you're over 40…

Then a recent study (there's been many prior to this latest one, they all conclude the same BTW) suggests working longer than 25 hours in a week is detrimental to your brain function. In short, the study of 6,500 participants conducted in Melbourne, found the longer you work each week the more it "hurt" you, health-wise.

What do you think? Is 25 hours or less work a week possible or desirable? Maybe for you, the jury is still out. Let's examine some evidence other than the study I just mentioned and the many like it…

Exhibit #1 Your Honour - My experience: I've worked with a lot of gurus and VERY successful business owners and entrepreneurs over the years and very few of them fit into this mode… most work long and hard and enjoy it and the success they create.

Exhibit #2 Your Honour - Contrarians I know personally: they preach a 24/7 system (ie in 7 days you work 24 hours) and they have created very successful businesses and life on this basis.

And…

Friend Adam, who created Australia's only private treasury some years ago, is adamant your output diminishes for every hour you work beyond 24 per week (he told me he only works 15 hours a week these days - it's his sweet spot for happiness and productivity).

Exhibit #3 Your Honour - Business owner's reality: When you are in business for yourself, the buck stops with you. Only issue is, the buck often doesn't want to fit into 25 hours a week, especially because we all know shit happens, right? And you as the business owner is the one who cleans up.

So…

What do you think? Is 25 hours desirable and achievable? Me? I don't have "the" answer, yet. I'm a work in progress.

Today's message is not to preach to you one or the other, I just want to raise awareness and get you thinking… do you work too many hours… if so, what needs to change in your day and week to cut back? Only ACTION will help you get your too long hours down.

You can't read the label...

L ove this saying which is popular in the south of the US...

"You can't read the label while you're sitting inside the jar."

Soooo true right, because we can't always understand what we're too close to.

Like our own business.

It's why I'm a member of mastermind groups and engage a handy (huge understatement) coach or two.

What about you?

Do you feel you're too close to your business, you're too much "inside the jar"?

When we are, our thinking becomes blurred and muddled. We can lose confidence. And when things stop working, we can be paralysed by inertia.

If you "feel" any of these, go find the right group or mentors. One thing I'm certain of, any investment in coaches or mentors pays you back big time.

Time to get outside the jar of your business?

Perspective

Yes business can be tough...

Not enough leads.

Customer cancelled and went to a competitor.

Bloody technology on the blink again.

Staff. BAS. Staff. Customers. Old ads don't work anymore...

Business is hard and getting harder!

Stop for a sec.

How bad are things really?

Two recent reminders that sometimes in business and life we need to pause and take stock of all the GOOD things we have going for us...

Case #1 – at the boxing gym where the boys and I trained for years there was a pro with a young family. His son was born with a rare brain condition – get this – only 4 male babies in the world have it. Imagine waking up to that reality every day?

Case #2 – we know a teenage boy with learning difficulties who's just been admitted to a psych ward... imagine being his parents... you'd wonder about what his future holds...

So, you think you have business problems, and you probably do, but they pale into insignificance when compared to the above real examples.

As you dive into your day, a little nudge about focusing on the good things in your life and business...

Trouble converting

Quick refresher from one of the greats…

What does "great" mean?

Universally regarded as the greatest living copywriter. Oh… that great. Yes.

It was the GREAT Gary Bencivenga, who's now retired, who came up with the 4Us persuasion formula. (Not to be confused with Michael Masterson's 4Us headline test).

Anyways, I was flicking through an old resource and came across the 4Us. Found it a powerful little refresher for me, so thought it may be for you too.

Short version is this…

To persuade effectively, your "sales argument" can only work if you have…

an **URGENT** problem

a **UNIQUE** promise

UNQUESTIONABLE proof

And a…

USER-FRIENDLY proposition

So if you're results are on the slide, it's worth revisiting your copy by applying the great Mr B's persuasion equation.

Lessons from the trenches, Steve style

I love a good client success story/bragging rights like this one.

A client emailed to tell me of the outrageous success of their just completed 4-week campaign

- Total sales = a whopping $894,841.00 (real figure not a typo)
- Yes, awesome, incredible, amazing and every other superlative you could think of
- For privacy purposes, I'm not mentioning names, location, industry
- The SECRET to their success was a very "BORING" 4-step campaign that involved…
- A postcard. Email #1. Email #2. Ad in their mailed newsletter…

And we could add a 5th step: the campaign big idea/offer deadline graphic on every quote sent out.

Now here's where it gets interesting…

There IS a secret sauce to this success which has 5 key parts. Pen and paper ready, school's about to start…

SECRET SAUCE #1 – the list… they have a big list that's been nurtured and cultivated over several years… who are used to receiving communication from them… bi-monthly full colour PRINTED newsletter, emails and other promotions… the list is warm… this was NOT an isolated, 1-off wham bam how bout it ma'am style hit and miss offer.

SECRET SAUCE #2 – reason why for the offer… and this was authentic… beat the price rise for one of the raw materials in the product which everyone in the industry knew was happening. NOTE: this was not BS scarcity, the major supplier had announced the price rise.

SECRET SAUCE #3 – multi-media… postcard, email, newsletter… it was everywhere the company was, VERY hard to miss… important point: we can rarely guess with any accuracy what the favourite media of our market will be at any given time so multi-channel always gives you the best chance of success.

SECRET SAUCE #4 – deadline… that was 100% authentic – created REAL urgency and was splashed everywhere ie "BEAT THE PRICE RISE – Order your new <blank> before Friday 14th October TO SAVE". Remember, this was industry-wide news, so very believable.

SECRET SAUCE #5 – the postcard… yup, old school still works… thing is, not many are mailing postcards (when was the last time you got one?) so it stands out!! And it followed all our "rules" re headline, offer, reason why, call to action.

Plenty there to chew over, wouldn't you agree?

Radar up example

G ood copy is good copy, no matter what media it appears in.

Case in point from a flick through a Sunday newspaper...

Headline #1 from the travel section:

Tokyo's secret streets

(an article about cool but little-known places to visit in Japan's capital... keyword = "secret")

Headline #2 also from the travel section:

What's new in the air

(an article about the latest innovations in plane travel... keyword = "new")

Headline #3: from the health and beauty section

Breakthrough treatment for people over 30 with slow metabolism

(an ad, advertorial style, complete with before and after pix and a strong offer... keyword = "breakthrough" and a clear call out to the target market)

More: these headlines work because they are based on fundamentals matched to the media and the audience. Your market is not too sophisticated, not too "anything" to be above fundamentals, if applied right.

So yeah, always have your radar "up" and look for good examples of great copy in other media.

Your last day on Earth filter

I'm a fireman, I deal with death and destruction every day. I see how random life can be... And how life can change in an instant. And this impacts the way I live each day...

So said my boys' boxing coach, Kim, in conversation with us one time after training. We were speaking with him re them having an exhibition match in the ring soon. And what Kim said really struck a chord with me.

I live each day like it could be my last because you never know when it will be, anything can happen...

And this got me thinking... and maybe you too...

How would we spend our day "IF" it WAS our last one? Would we stress over that unpaid bill? Really worry about the meeting next week? Yell at the kids about their *<insert your issue here - for me it was crap all over their rooms>*?

Does all that "stuff" that occupies our minds really matter?

More:

Do you spend too much time sweating the small stuff? Even sometimes? Would you really spend your last day like that?

Food for thought, isn't it!!!

One of my mantras from now - and no, this doesn't give me license to be slack and not meet deadlines etc...

But one of my mantras is to now see things through this "last day on earth" filter...

And whether I'd want to go out stressed, worried, tired etc etc...

You?

Remember, when things get tense... maybe flip it round to see things through this "LAST DAY ON EARTH" filter..

Might just make a world of difference to your day.

How to stand out

Recent discussions with a client centred around how to be different to his competitors. More specifically, what "little" things he could do to connect more to his customers. And this got me thinking. Now I suspect none of this is terribly new. But... and here's the big but... lately, have you done ANY of the following? If not, then this is timely.

It's a cut down list of "new" ways any business owner can stand out from competitors. And yes, the personal touch is what's emphasised here with these "hello and thank you" ideas. Last thing... you do have to spend some moolah with these, so make sure you know your numbers, your lifetime client value and so forth and make an INFORMED decision about what you can and can't do.

- **Thank long time and/or big customers.** We all know the power of "thanks for doing business with us" messages but what about, to the "big" or "A -list" customers, a hand-written thank you note with a discount on their next order... or a movie or dinner voucher... or (insert something relevant to you)? It's quick and easy to do, and relatively cheap compared to the brownie points gained.
- **Thank new customers.** A short-handwritten note thanking them will be different to what just about everyone else is doing. You could include an incentive to come in/buy from you again although just the thought of the thank you is powerful.
- **A reactivation campaign.** This is often overlooked but can be very valuable. You contact past and dormant customers and give them an incentive to come back.
- **New customers in a geographic area** or a business new to an area, a letter or postcard introducing you and how you solve locals' problems, coupled with a free gift certificate, is very effective. If done right, it gets them in the door the first time which is vital for starting an ongoing relationship.

Keep in mind...

Timing is critical, you have to be on the ball because the gesture falls flat if it's been 6 months since they've done business with you until they get the thank you.

Also, it helps to use multi-media... handwritten note, email, postcard, even your newsletter. Be conversational, energetic and sincere in your thank you note... woo woo moment here... words have vibrations so send out the RIGHT feeling!

How many of these do you do?

Food for thought.

Don't let teenage boys see this...

If you have teenage boys, recommend you DO NOT show this to them...

Saw on Facebook (a media I'm RARELY on) once results of a shocking new study out of England which, if teenage boys discover it, spells doom for households all around the country...

True story!!

What was the study about?

Farting.

Yep, farting.

As if teenage boys need any more encouragement! Apparently, according to the study, farting is good for your health on 2 counts...

When you fart – helps lower risk of cancer, heart attacks and strokes.

When you smell a fart – the main gas, hydrogen sulphate, actually causes your brain to grow stronger and protects from dementia.

Seriously!!!

And yes, someone got PAID to do this research.

Can see it now, all around the country, teenage boys taking even more delight in letting one rip...

And claiming they are doing it for EVERYONE'S benefit!!

Please no...

Just shows... you can find research and proof to support just about any argument these days. It's not lack of resources but resourcefulness that holds some people back.

Information, data, results of research is readily available... do you use enough of it in sales copy?

Why footballers succeed

Ever wondered why football teams win?

I've had my radar up for years for this because, as you are probably aware, I'm a fan of American football, NFL. Yes, I've been to a couple of games, a few years back… in Chicago to watch the Bears lose to Detroit. And in New York to watch the Jets roll the Tom Brady-led Patriots.

Good fun. What's this name dropping got to do with you? Well…

When NFL is in the post season play-offs it's sudden death with teams and fans on a knife edge. I pay particular attention to the post-game interviews. One of the questions that gets asked often, is…

What's your secret to success today?

And it's interesting to observe. In the land of rah rah and high fives and bombast, these multi-millionaire star players are very humble and down to Earth.

The interviewer question invariably goes something like…

"What's been the key for you this season, what has made the difference?"

These superstars don't boast of their talent. They don't mention luck. And they never say, "I don't know".

Their response is usually some version of…

"We turn up to work every day… the players, the coaches, the support staff… and we work hard. We have plans and we stick to them and work towards them every session."

Yep… that's it… boring, right?

But it's also very true… success can be a mechanical repetition of what works. You have to have the discipline to stick at it. Which is why learning what works in the first place is vital to your success, so props to you for reading about the fundamentals here in these pages.

The formula for success, to borrow from the NFL is always… are you prepared to show up, learn the right way, and stick at it long enough to enjoy success?

#1 Mistake Marketers make

J ust one more piece of chocolate… That extra glass of wine… Yes, I'll finish the kids' cheeseburgers…

Ever said (and done!!!) these? It's ok to say yes, no one will hear! And really, no harm in it, right? If you want to lose weight, Houston, we could have a problem.

Case in point… got any idea how many burpees you need to do to get rid of that extra slice of pepperoni pizza?

272.

Yes… to work off 1 slice of pizza means you need to do 272 burpees. Research just in makes it HARD for anyone watching their waistline!!

- 50g chocolate bar = 27 minute run
- Can of Coke = 20 minute run
- Glass of white wine = 28 minute swim
- Pint of beer = 1 hour 4 minute walk

Ouch.

Makes a carrot instead seem mighty attractive right now, doesn't it!!

No, this entry hasn't been hacked by a dieting blog…

The key point…

Eating that bar of chocolate, having that extra stubbie or piece of cake because you'll "walk it off tomorrow" is the same self-delusional talk marketers use.

I'll just run an ad. Just put up a website. Just do X to get more leads.

The result?

Well the marketing equivalent of needing to do more burpees!! The #1 mistake business owners make is UNDERESTIMATING the difficulty of the task of selling today.

You need strategy based on proven fundamentals before you write one word of your marketing piece.

Anything else is akin to eating half a chocolate cake thinking a jog around the block tomorrow will do the job.

Persuasion tool – NOT!

One powerful little tool in your copywriting arsenal is the "not statement".

What this does is SHOW the reader/listener the difference between your solution and a competitor.

The "not statement" frames up the sales argument to say, albeit in subtle way, what you are selling is better than another option.

An example from copy for one of my live trainings:

This is NOT a take home study course that sits in the corner gathering dust… this is real, live, hands-on training. I work WITH you to boost your skills and confidence…

See how it works?

By saying what it's not, you elevate what you sell above the other option.

Try it out and see how you go.

This is NOT a pie in the sky theory, it's a proven persuasion tool.

Sorry, couldn't help myself!

Failure explanation... the "purpose tremor"

E ver tried to thread a needle...

And noticed, for no apparent reason, your hand shaking?

Note: if under 30, Google how to thread a needle... it will explain its purpose and probably there'll be a video.

Back to it...

That shake, like you had a massive hangover or early onset of Parkinson's or something. It appears out of nowhere.

Ever experienced this?

You can be rock solid, steady-handed at all times then go to water under a small amount of pressure. In medical terms this is called a "purpose tremor". It occurs in normal people when they try too hard. Or they are "too careful" in trying to do something.

Similarly, trying too hard when you go to write can affect your copy.

You see my belief is... yep, this is woo woo...

My belief is that words have a "vibration".

If...

And here's the big if...

If you write when you are stressed. Feel under deadline pressure. Or when you're unsure or lack confidence that what you're doing is "right"...

Then you experience a writer's equivalent of a "purpose tremor".

Yes, tension when writing is your enemy. You need to be relaxed. You need confidence to know what you're doing is "right".

Only then will there be "flow" to your words.

Victim of a rising tide... how did it happen?

O n its last visit here, my boys and I sat on Moffat Headland in Caloundra and marvelled as the massive aircraft carrier USS Ronald Reagan left Brisbane for war games off the central Queensland coast.

Boy, was it impressive, a floating city with an airport...

And it got me thinking back to the days of the president after whom the big boat is named.

And in particular one of Reagan's pet sayings to explain the benefits of a strong economy...

"A rising tide lifts all boats." No, he wasn't the first to use the line, but arguably the most famous.

Anyways, it's a reasonably accurate statement about an economy: when it's strong, people benefit. There are more jobs, more opportunity, more money changing hands.

And it's a good thing - for the most part.

Here's where it isn't.

When the tide is "in" business, because of the positives I've just mentioned, is easy. And when things are going well, it's so easy to believe our own crap... that we are somehow invincible... that the current lofty position of the business is, for the most part, due to our genius.

We all do it.

And it's dangerous.

Because if things are not done right, if a business is not built on solid fundamentals like quality marketing assets that can be deployed when needed...

What happens when the tide goes out, which it surely will at some point? Then the blame game starts... it's the economy... the government should do more... and on it goes.

It's one of the things I work hard on for my clients... crafting strategy and creating assets that can be used at high tide... AND when the tide goes out.

Is your business positioned to thrive when the tide goes out?

Leave that with you to ponder...

Headline ideas... have a creative play...

H ere are 7 headline formulas to get the creative juices flowing

"The Truth About XYZ" - (which is curiosity heavy and useful for FOMO type messages)

"Breakthrough for (insert niche)" or "New Method for (result niche wants)" – (shows what's even better NOW or what's old is new)

"Everything taught to you about XYZ is WRONG" (a contrarian or disruptive approach)

"Here's why people like you aren't doing XYZ anymore" (confirms an existing fear the market has)

"Why I stopped using X and started Y instead" (gives a newsworthy angle)

"What to do if ABC happens" (a specific problem-solution angle)

"Get catwalk ready in a weekend!" (a time/result based angle)

These are proven templates... but again... all marketing is situational so don't expect one to be a magic pill or "one and done" solution. They are a good starting point, however.

When your market IS different

““ My market is different,” said one business owner.

“I don’t agree,” responded a second.

And

“Yep, you’re spot on,” said a third.

So went the chat in a group about the age-old feeling many business owners have about themselves, “my market is different”. I often hear that time-worn expression. “But my business is different”. Most responses from the group were in the “you’re spot on” category. But got this one interesting question from one of them…

“Ok, I get it, but can you explain it a little more. I mean you can’t use the same words to sell shoes as you do an investment property.”

True.

So here’s my take on ONE aspect of this debate. Let’s look at the opportunity seeker market Vs an affluent one. And how you might consider different ways of attracting them. When selling to the opportunity market you really want an excited prospect. Not necessarily one that is fully informed.

A trip wire offer (small entry price to get them used to buying) that gives them a taste of what they want generally works well because it feeds that excitement.

But this may not necessarily be the case in the affluent market. You see, while they may respond to tripwires (and it would have to be tested), typically, the more affluent a market is (unlike mass markets) the more well-read they are and info gathering is part of what they do every day.

Lead generation via authority-creating information products that address their needs is what they respond more to. If it’s an offline product (Vs digital) even better.

Next time you’re planning your marketing, consider “who” they are. Yes, they are all human. They all respond based on emotion (and justify with logic). But there are also some nuances you need to be mindful of.

Remember, it always starts with the “WHO”…

And you must know them intimately.

Recommended spiritual/mindset/self-help books

In no particular order, here are some of the BEST books to help shift you from the inside out:

Ask and it is Given – Esther and Jerry Hicks

The Wish – Angela Donovan

The Ringing Cedars Series – Vladimir Megre (all 10 books)

How to Hear Your Angels – Doreen Virtue

You Can Heal Your Life – Louise Hay

The Power is Within You – Louise Hay

The Kryon Series – Lee Carroll

Finding You – Steve Vincent

A Course in Miracles (William T Thetford and Helen Shucman – editors)

Psycho-Cybernetics – Maxwell Maltz

Positive Intelligence – Shirzad Chamine

Letting Go + Power Vs Force – Dr David Hawkins

The Motivation Manifesto – Brendon Burchard

The Go Giver Series – Bob Burgh and John David Mann

The 5 Second Rule – Mel Robbins

Coach Wooden's Greatest Secret – Pat Williams

A New Earth – Eckhart Tolle

I've read them all, they are my favourite non-business books. Pick one, guarantee, you won't be disappointed.

Where the money's really at in writing

What is it that makes good copy really "sing" so it converts like crazy?

The Big Idea behind it?

Yes.

Great headline?

For sure.

Strong offer?

Absolutely.

There is another, not often talked about skill, which makes a world of difference. And it's got nothing to do with the "big 3" I just mentioned. It's not often talked about for the simple reason it's not creative. Or glamorous. Or easy. And it requires work.

Sorry.

What skill am referring to?

Your ability to **critique -- edit -- tweak** your copy so it reads fast.

I've recently compiled, due to a number of requests, a critique checklist. It outlines the 10 steps I go through after writing.

This gives you the edge. It turns average copy into kickin' copy. Go to the resources page to download your copy: **www.theinfluentialmarketer.org/resources**

Your stuff doesn't work in my market

H ave heard that one before. More than once.

What total and utter BS.

Have used "my stuff" for small business. In the corporate space ("they are too busy to read that").

And in the tertiary education space (which is a jargon infested rabbit hole)…

And have made "my stuff" work.

But don't just take my word for it…

My main man in Melbourne, Ron Prasad, who runs an anti-bullying charity for teens riffs thus…

Gotta tell you something exciting - a friend of mine is a medical doctor who has a PhD in medical research. Her colleagues who are very accomplished scientists (academic people) were writing a promo for a presentation on scientific research.

Anyway, she asked me to look at the marketing flyer that was to be sent to many academics. Oh man, it was all about "The research shows this, the research tells us that". There was not even a drop of "WIIFM".

I jazzed it up a little (all thanks to my very enlightening wordsmith mentor - the Legendary Steve Plummer). They were absolutely stunned to see what a massive difference a copywriting perspective can make!

Thank you for all your help mate.

Pleasure is all mine, Ron. And thanks for letting me know.

KEY POINT: Good copy is good copy. As long as it's based on solid principles that are media and market agnostic.

Learn the principles (or hook up with someone who has) and you can pretty much write your own ticket… even if it's in a "boring" space like academia!

When failure gut punches you

N o one is that good, to get it right 100% of the time. Despite what you see on social media. Despite what you hear gurus bragging about. Despite what you perceive as success in marketing and business…

Every single person has their share of misses, failures, and downright disasters. Embarrassing stuff they NEVER tell you about, lest their reputation suffer (gasp!). Truth is, I come up with some pretty good ideas. And some not so good ones that don't work. The good ones make you feel, well, good. The not so good ones make you feel, well, pretty crappy truth be told. Which is why this little tactic, used once a day or once a week, can pay huge dividends.

Case in point, from my email subscribers over a 5-day period, responding to my regular messages:

From Susan: *"All I can commit to at this time is to say, Whoever conceptualized and wrote this copy is brilliant. Well-done, sir. My hat's off to you.* 👒*"*

From Col: *"You are amazing Steve, have amazing gifts and knowledge"*

From Ron: *"This email will stay with me forever! Yes, I sound like a broken record when I say this - you're not just a copywriting genius, you're a very enlightening personal development mentor too. I'm in North East Arnhem Land now, doing some programs for youth. Sending you lots of tropical sunshine brother!!"*

So what's the tactic I'm talking about? Simple. And easy to do. You see business can be lonely. Business can be isolating. And without positive affirmation, in the tougher times, business can get you down.

Sure, collect testimonials to use in your marketing. But just as important, collect testimonials for those times when you need a little pick me up… the down times, the lonely times, the *shit, that didn't work* times.

I have those times. You have them. And even the smiling "successful" faces on social media have them. You can only ignore those **shit that didn't work** feelings for so long. I prefer action. So when I'm feeling down, I go to my file to read messages like I've just shared and watch video testimonials.

They help as a pick me up… help to dust myself off… and help to get me back in the marketing fray. Next time you're feeling bummed out… or have that gnawing failure feeling in the gut that just won't go away… read some testimonials. They will give you a lift, provide perspective and get you back on your way.

Nothing breeds success like a reminder of success. Your success. Hope this helps.

Different twist on the emotions of your market

I t happened again when a rather frustrated new client dropped that old (and sooooo wrong) little nugget…

"But my market is different". If I had a dollar for every time, I've heard that one. My answer is always the same…

"No it's not."

Unless you sell to robots that is. Sure, different markets have certain nuances. There are some things you do differently selling B2B verses B2C.

Remember, all buying decisions are made by HUMANS. And all humans – you and me included, buy on emotion and justify with logic.

In his book *How to Live 365 Days a Year* published in 1954, Dr John Schindler stated every human has 6 basic needs…

1. The need for love
2. The need for security
3. The need for creative expression
4. The need for recognition
5. The need for new experiences
6. The need for self-esteem

If you're going to be successful selling to your market, your message has to hit at least one of these.

Yep, it gets back to the old WIIFM (What's In It For Me).

Does your ad, email, sales letter or blog hit one of these in a new and interesting way? And does it do it in a way to make them want to act?

If your results are less than expected, it might be a good place to go back and rethink.

Instant sales funnel

I f you listen to the doomsayers, email as a marketing channel is on life support. Some studies suggest open rates of 15% to 17% are great. Which is why many are turning to SMS.

Consider:

- SMS blows away email open rates with something like a 98% open rate
- About 90% of SMS's are read within 3 seconds of arrival

Need more proof? Take this self-test…

Think how long it takes between your phone chiming for an incoming text and your hand moving to it. Yep, it's the closest thing to instant available today.

Plus, data out of the US reveals…

- 32% of recipients respond to SMS offers, with texted coupons redeemed 10 times more often than traditional coupons
- 50% of US consumers receiving branded SMS texts go on to make direct purchases
- 29% of SMS marketing recipients click on links in SMS messages they receive, and 47% of those go on to make a purchase (that's nearly 14% conversion!)

Food for thought, right?

Key point: drive your SMS traffic to a dedicated website that's short and simple and shows the result or transformation the prospect can expect.

This works in many B2C markets, even for bricks n mortar.

Boost email response rates – THE key

H ere is a big secret to email success...

Which, it just so happens, is transferable to any media.

The big secret, my padawan, is the first 2 lines...

Your subject line.

And then the first line of the copy.

Because usually this is all the reader sees (especially on a mobile device).

Crap subject line. Delete.

Uninteresting or uninspiring first line. Delete.

Work hardest here because if you miss either or both, it's over.

What's that? You want a couple of tips to help? Greedy are you today, but your wish is my command...

First... use the big C as much as you can.

C = curiosity.

Tease with a strong benefit that draws them into the copy, that compels them to take the next step of reading more.

Second... keep subject lines short and punchy... 4 to 7 words is a sweet spot... although have had success with one word subject lines too, so always test.

Third... keep sentences short and sharp while still maintaining flow so the copy can be read "FAST".

Like I said at the start, all 3 are transferable to other media.

So go forth, my padawan, and apply to your next sales message, you'll love the little bump in response these 3 tips produce.

Old hat or timely?

Prior to one of the live training courses I run I got this question:

"Do you cover Facebook ad funnels?"

My Answer...

Facebook is NOT mentioned once in 12 weeks. Nada. Nil. Not.

The reply: "Ah... this training is old school then... not suited to today's new media?"

Bollocks. The principles are what's important, NOT the media. Get the principles right and you can then adapt them to ANY media.

Here's proof, based on car park gossip...

A friend runs a business in the home services niche.

We were talking in the car park after the boys' soccer game and he was telling me about his frustrations with Facebook ads not converting.

I asked him his demographic and suggested 2 headlines to try.

Long story short - he tried one of the ones I suggested that night plus 5 more of his usual headlines...

He rang me the next day happy that 1 of the 6 he tested worked.

No prizes for guessing which one kicked butt – mine.

Why? Because I know what works, media comes and goes - human buying principles don't.

So learn the fundamentals, they will stand by you as media changes over time.

Scattered thinking kills results

Quick, post on Twitter. Get that Insta up. Get more likes than last week. Try Tik Tok, it rocks.

My point...

Do you really need more?

Isn't one system that works consistently better than a whole lot of other media that only works until they change the algorithm? And yes, here come the modern social media warriors yelling you "have" to be on multiple platforms if you want your business to grow.

But do you? Or does "more" just lead to scattered thinking. And diluted results?

Consistent and persistent... maybe even (gasp) boring... is often better than flitting from one thing to the next. Sure, keep learning and growing, but all these new platforms "they" tell you to be on?

Tread warily.

No I'm not suggesting you doggedly stick to Yellow Pages ads that stopped working 10 years ago.

But as Dan Kennedy says: "... be a true master of a short list and small, rigidly constrained portfolio of media and methods that drive business revenue".

Learn Tik Tok or the next "big" thing? You're probably better off spending the time on going DEEPER into proven success keys...

Know how to write a great headline (a skill that is media agnostic).

Have your writing formula mastered (I use PASPA in about 85% of all sales copy).

Make sure your offer and call to action is clear (eg write it out on a single page for staff... and you!).

Include multiple means of proof (this can be improved in about 90% of clients who come to me).

These, my friend, are the money getters...

Yes, use a multi-channel approach. But also be careful about shiny object chasing... it so often kills results.

The day I became an emotional wreck

I t happened and there was nothing I could do about it.

There I was all comfy and cosy and then… bam!

I became an emotional basket case. Everything I did was governed by emotions… and justified with the logical side of my brain. But the emotions suddenly won.

When was this day?

The day I was born.

And it's the same for you and the peeps you sell to.

Which is why, when we sell, we need to target the emotions of our market. Of course, we back that up with product features and benefits…

But the emotions are KING and QUEEN in all of us.

Here's a quick reminder about the emotions we all have:

1. Fear
2. Pain
3. Guilt
4. Shame
5. Anger
6. Love
7. Passion
8. Joy

The #1 job of your marketing is to identify those which are **most relevant to your target audience right now…** take them to that emotional place and offer relief in the form of your product or service.

And it holds true, the negative emotions (fear, pain, guilt, shame, anger) are easier to stimulate than positive ones.

So next time you go to sell anything, in person or in writing, remember the emotions your listener has going on… and give these a good old poke.

PS Yes, this is one of several entries that talk about emotions and each one gives a slightly different "list"… which one is "right"? They all are. The key is to write to the emotions of your market, however they are defined. The lists I include in this book help to join the dots in your mind.

Easy lead generation

What's the simplest, easiest and fastest way to generate new leads?

Answer...

Ask.

As in for referrals. I believe one survey reveals 91% of people will give referrals but only 11% of sales people ever ask for them.

Wow.

Begs the question...

Are you in that "only 11% who ask"?

If you are, here's a simple template to start with next time you're talking to a customer...

"... ok thanks for that. By the way, Alice, who do you know you'd be happy to introduce me to who could benefit from my service?"

Simple and easy. And free.

My first copywriting mentor, the great Ted Nicholas, was fond of saying...

Always ask because there is only ever **one** *of three possible answers,* **yes, no or maybe.** *So ask.*

Imagine, over the next month you got just two names from every customer you interact with, that's FREE leads, right?

Tip: make sure the ones you ask are "good" customers because in this world, like attracts like.

So today, why not make a commitment to asking for referrals... make a list of "good clients" to approach... and then go ahead and ask.

You might be surprised at the results and increased lead and deal flow over the next 30 days.

Vital headline tactic

What's the easiest way to get someone's attention?

This example comes from one of my favourite copywriters Bob Bly, author of more than 100 books. He sent a promotion recently, "Become a six-figure copywriter at age 50 or older". So what's the headline secret? Think of it this way…

If you saw someone in a crowd and you wanted to get their attention, you'd yell out their name, right?

Hey Steve!

And I'd turn around.

Same in copy.

If you can't use their name, what's the next best? Call out their profession or group they identify with. In Mr Bly's case, it's peeps over 50 who want to have a crack at writing for a living.

This is a time tested and proven headline formula. Call out who you want.

Examples:

Nurses sick of night shift and abusive patients: here's how to use your skills and be paid above award wages

The only way left for business owners to get clients online today

How this New "Mechanism" is Changing the Game for Facebook Advertisers

And on it goes.

These are off the top of my head examples.

But if you follow this principle, your sales message will only speak to the people who are likely to buy. It's an easy way of matching your market to your message and selling more stuff so you help more people.

When you dislike someone...

D o you ever struggle to "like" certain people? You know, when you "have words" with them... You replay the incident over and over in your mind. And frankly it pisses you off. What you SHOULD have said. How you were wronged by them. Why they were totally unjustified in what they said or did. And on it goes.

It might be a customer. Staff member. Family. We punish them and us in our minds in an effort to be "right" and "win". We've all done it. Why?

It's that part of our mind, our ego, talking... trying to keep itself and us "safe". In doing so, our ego is probably doing more harm than good. Because our time here with loved ones, and in business, is finite. Do you spend too much of this precious resource pandering to ego thoughts like...

Fear. Comparison. Judgement. Gossip. Expectation. Anger. Revenge. Haste?

If so, you're not alone... and this poem which I first saw online mid-2018 may help. The message is very powerful because I believe we all waste too much of our time here on shit that doesn't really matter.

Have a read...

Every minute someone leaves this world behind.
Age has nothing to do with it.
We are all in this line without realising it.
We never know how many people are before us. We cannot move to the back of the line.
We cannot step out of the line.
We cannot avoid the line.

So, while we wait in line –

Make moments count. Make a difference. Make the call.
Make priorities. Make the time. Make your gifts known.
Make a 'nobody' feel like a somebody.
Make your voice heard. Make the small things big.
Make someone smile.
Make the change. Make yourself a priority.
Make love. Make up. Make peace.
Make sure to tell your people they are loved.
Make waves. Make sure to have no regrets.
Make sure you are ready.

Just for today, make it count. Quiet that strong ego voice in your head. Think thoughts and do tasks that matter... really matter...

Add value

Want to add value to your offers?

Here are some ideas to get you thinking. You could include a…

- Free interview
- Free demonstration DVD
- Free consult
- Free newsletter
- Free Critique
- Free Trial
- Free software
- Free checklist
- Free sample
- Free upgrade
- Free $X off your next order
- Free email course

And on and on… Hopefully that gets you thinking.

Couple of things about bonuses. They…

- Must have title
- Must have a value (if you don't value it, they won't)
- Must be valuable (if you can't sell it, you can't give it away)
- Must be "sold" the way you would anything else… Outline features/benefits, what result they get, the value of it and so on

Remember, they buy the offer.

Deep Impact on your business

... **W**e *rejoice in what we've been re-given... So now, let us begin...*

So said President Beck in the last scene of the hit 1998 sci-fi movie *Deep Impact* as he tried to inspire humans to start again after the catastrophic comet strike.

Ever watch this?

It's a Spielberg film and stars Robert Duvall and Morgan Freeman and a bevy of "new" stars at the time. It's the story of how the Earth is hit by a huge comet after attempts to nuke it failed. 1 km plus tsunamis resulted and lots of Hollywood type destruction.

Fun stuff.

Luckily for the human race pre-impact preparation meant enough people survived to rebuild civilization.

The film cost about $80 mil to make and grossed over $349 mil. Not bad.

Key thing for business owners though is the premise, as reflected in President Beck's words...

You can, no matter what has occurred, start over in your business and re-build.

There's an old saying which aligns too...

Every master was once a disaster.

Yep, you have to start somewhere if you want to change things in business.

The key is to start. Or start over...

Acid test for your copy

If you're trying to decide if a word or phrase or paragraph or chunk of copy should be included in your sales message, here's the acid test…

Delete it.

That is, get rid of the word, the phrase, paragraph, the chunk of copy… re-read it… and see how it now "lands" on you.

Print out the new version. Read it out loud again.

Is it smoother?

Is it punchier?

Does it work "better" with it gone?

Often the answer is yes.

Here's the thing…

If you have a "feeling" about a word, phrase, chunk of copy, don't ignore it. Trust your gut, it's giving you a red flag that something needs changing.

Elimination of the "red flag" like this is the first thing I do when I edit.

Give it a go.

A fear that paralyses you

Who would have thought a 6 letter word could cause so much stress to us humans...

Proves I guess we are, all of us, as the saying goes, a skin bag of emotions.

What's the dreaded word?

C-H-A-N-G-E.

We hate it. Fear it. Avoid it. You see, it's not just that people fear change. It's also that we believe when we've been doing something a particular way for some time, it *must* be a good way to do things. And the *longer* you've been doing it that way, the better it is.

Kind of makes sense, yes? So change isn't simply about embracing something unknown -- it's about giving up something *old* (and therefore good) for something *new* (and therefore not good). In a 2010 study for example, people who were told acupuncture had been in existence for 2,000 years expressed much more favourable attitudes towards it than those who were told it had existed for just 250 years.

Weird. And something I have personal experience with...

20 years as a teacher made changing careers hard. The "safe" and "easy" thing to do would have been to stay. Something new was risky, right? But... it would have meant staying stuck.

And of course I would never have connected with you!!!

At the time though, I hunted down many sources of inspiration. One of my favourites was the line from the famous poem by Robert Frost...

Two roads diverged in a wood, and I—

I took the one less travelled by,

And that has made all the difference

What about you...

Ever had that urge to change, to do something new, to take the road less travelled?

Do it, trust in yourself and life that everything will work out... whatever happens, it's way better than being stuck.

Why business is like Air Crash Investigators

D amning admission…

I channel flick.

If you're a guy, we are brothers in remote arms.

If you're female, you're probably already cheesed of with me and have turned the page…

Last time I was channel surfing I happened upon Air Crash Investigators.

And it got me thinking…

The miracle that is modern air travel is a lot like business.

As each episode shows, it's usually a series of seemingly random events that leads to the plane going down.

And super smart people get their fine tooth comb out and sift through everything to find out why.

And then, based on the findings, there are law changes. Tweaks in design. New procedures so it doesn't happen again.

It seems it's a constant battle:

Test. Make it work. It's never perfect. So you deal with a problem when it arises (because you simply CANNOT foresee ALL problems).

And gee, isn't that like business…

Fire to put out here. New idea to implement there. An improvement to make with this. Always looking, thinking, refining… never still, never at rest.

It's probably why business owners and entrepreneurs feel run off their feet at times… coz they are! So if you've felt your job is NEVER done…

Relax…

You're normal and so is your business.

What's working now

I get asked often about what colours and styles are working now.

For example…

In the early days of the internet deep red headlines worked best. Add in some yellow highlights (remember those days!!!??!!!) and you bumped response. Then video came along. Then blue headlines.

And now?

Well, red is starting to out-pull blue again in some markets. Trends do come and go but always, the golden rule must be **ease of the read.**

With this in mind, here are 5 pointers to style which I use as a general rule of thumb…

- Limited reverse type (ie white type on dark background… black print on white background is easier to read)
- Sans serif fonts online (letters that have no tail on the end eg Arial, Verdana)
- Serif fonts offline (letters that have the tail eg Georgia, Times New Roman)
- Headlines in biggest font possible without looking "horrible" (a technical term)
- Subheads bold and larger font and maybe even a different font/colour

Are these set in stone? No way. Always you can find exceptions to every rule. Always.

Example: email guru Ben Settle swears by serif fonts for his online sales letters.

And for me it always comes down to overall look and feel… it has to be "right" and give me a "comfortable" feeling (again, both VERY technical terms).

Hope that helps.

Whatever you do, just make sure it's easy to read lest your message get lost or ignored, a horrible sin for any business owner.

Weird contradiction – when nothing is your best strategy

Nothing IS very powerful. And often it's 100% to your advantage to do nothing.

Pardon?

You're in business, it takes the hustle to be successful... do nothing?

Yes.

Especially if you use "nothing" as a deliberate strategy... where you sit and be still and let ideas come to you.

10 mins a day is a good place to start.

Just sit and let your mind wander.

It's amazing what answers come to you when you slow your world down.

Don't confuse the two nothings though...

One doing nothing, like laying in exhaustion in front of the TV, is a by-product of a busy mind, where you just "have" to get away.

The other a deliberate strategy to un-busy your mind and let the ideas flow.

Here's the rub... when you are at your busiest, under deadline pressure, is often the most difficult but most IMPORTANT time to take 10 minutes (or 15) and just sit and do nothing.

Is it really THAT simple?

They turn over in excess of $20 million per year. They have "some" need of marketing help. They are in the "sweet spot" of clients I target. And I booked a second meeting with them. It was easy. And there is a VERY good chance they will get me on-board for a chunk of time and money.

How did this progress so far so fast?

Understand there is a process to selling to companies of that size… it takes several "touches" which I won't go into now. That said, how did I get a meeting with the General Manager to kick things off?

Here's the secret…

I asked.

Pardon?

Yep, we'd had one or two contacts over a month or so. In this instance there was no need to complicate things. So I asked.

It was a version of, "Can I come and see you about how we can solve X problem?".

No multi-step funnels (which do have a place).

No fancy landing page (which is needed at times).

No massive sales force or survey to weed out the likely prospects (which can be useful).

But…

The situation didn't require any of that. Which got me thinking about you…

Do you over complicate things in your sales process? Is there a place to keep it simple and just ask?

Example:

If you run a restaurant - is it as simple as asking current customers back when they pay their bill (eg with a % discount off their next meal?).

Sales is relatively simple… put a good offer in front of the RIGHT prospect…

In our hi-tech, fast-paced world, me thinks at times we've lost sight of a simple but strategically placed "ask for the sale".

Will let you to chew that today. What's the simplest and easiest way to the sale…

Failure

Ever get worried by your marketing failures? You know, this campaign was supposed to bring in X leads.

And didn't.

That ad was supposed to sell Y number of units.

And didn't.

The new launch was going to break industry records.

And didn't.

Ever had that? And got pissed off royally when you didn't get the results you wanted. And said this "marketing crap" doesn't work?

If you've felt this before…

Relax, it means you're moving forward. EVERYONE, and I mean EVERYONE, has failures.

Example from legendary Bob Bly, who writes how humbling the art of copywriting is. He tells story after story of fails, like…

The big name exec who hired a famous copywriter who said, and I'm paraphrasing from memory here, "He (ie big name copywriter) has had more losers for us than I can count".

Or another legend of the game who wrote 7 big promos in a row for a particular company, all of which bombed.

It's not just you. We all produce stuff which doesn't work. You will never succeed at every sale, every campaign, every ad. No one is that good. You WILL fail along the way.

By the way…

"Failure" is necessary to learn the lessons, so it really isn't failure, it's learning what not to do next time.

So relax, keep learning, keep testing, and be a little gentler on yourself.

How to kill off a business

Simple formula: no sales = no business.

Barriers to sales kill businesses.

And I believe there are two BIG barriers we must always work hard to overcome.

The first...

LACK OF PROOF.

I eagerly took note as the greatest living copywriter Gary Bencivenga cautioned thus from stage a few years back:

Your Market has...

NO time

NO interest

NO way to differentiate

NO belief

NO desire to make a decision

Ouch.

So you have to work hard, my padawan, to overcome this apathy and disinterest from buyers.

And you do so with LOADS OF PROOF.

The second barrier?

LACK OF...

Will tell you in the next entry...

How to kill off a biz [Part II]

F rom yesterday's message...

No sales = no business.

And there are TWO big barriers to sales...

#1 revealed yesterday is lack of proof.

And the second BIG barrier to sales today?

LACK OF CONFIDENCE BY THE SELLER.

Confidence comes from two sources...

#1 - the seller's belief in the product

and

#2 - the seller's belief the prospect NEEDS the product

Miss one of these and, well, sales results usually drop.

It's a bullet proof and million $$$ formula right there...

PROOF + CONFIDENCE = sales success.

Chew on that for a while and have a deep think about what needs to change at your sales coalface.

Secret to storytelling

They say, facts only tell, stories sell.

A common complaint about this is, "I'm not a good storyteller".

Remember, I've already told you there exists a number of universal connection points you can build stories around.

Pets/animals

Travel

Family

Water

If you can wrap a story around one of those themes your chances of connection and therefore conversion skyrocket.

Before you write a story, make sure you are very clear about my **PPA formula...**

PURPOSE – be clear why you are telling the story to your audience... is it to sell, connect, get them to register interest?

PLACE – in what media – email, ad, sales letter, FB will the story appear?

ACTION - what do you want them to do when they read the story?

Be 100% clear about all three before you write a word.

Now THAT is a bad day

Think you had a bad day?

Try being in Facebook's shoes on "that" day...

No doubt you heard at the time a few years ago, the stunning numbers reported when Facebook stocks "crashed"...

$123 billion wiped off the business

And

$16 billion gone from Zuck's personal wealth

Now THAT is a bad day!

In fact, future dictionaries, for the definition of "bad day" are likely to say: See Facebook Friday 27 July 2018!

Now I'm not here to crow about anyone's business taking a hit or having the mother of all bad days...

But there is a lesson here which I've been harping on for yonks...

One channel or media to grow your business is VERY dangerous. As you know, stuff happens in this world... companies go bust... laws spring up out of nowhere... algorithms change...

Which is why I teach the **fundamentals** of selling with words.

And not just the **tactic** applicable to X media.

When you understand the principles of great sales language, you can implement them in ANY media.

Which protects you from the proverbial bad day or law change.

It's one of the few ways left these days you can get yourself and your business to safer, higher ground, so your influence grows.

It's all got too hard

S omewhere along the way…

On the journey to online utopia…

Landing pages, upsells, crossells, downsells, one time offers, funnels, click bait and on it goes…

It kind of got all too hard.

At least that's what I hear often when talking marketing and copywriting to clients and prospects.

There's so much to know. So much to master. So much to implement.

Or is there?

My focus with everyone I talk to are the principles of sales language…

Who are you targeting?

What's their pain?

How mature is the market?

What's the value proposition?

What's new and interesting about it?

Why should they believe it?

Why should they act now?

In all honesty, if you can master fundamentals like these in your sales messages the media you use doesn't matter so much. My belief is we have been so caught up in "what shiny object is working now" that many have ignored mastery of the very fundamentals that make a human say yes and buy…

And…

Understanding HOW to communicate them. In your down time might pay to revisit these fundamentals for a little refresher.

How to write copy – the #1 tip

P retty simple really…

Write like you talk

Or more specifically, like your market talks.

Remember this truth: sales is a 1-on-1 conversation with whoever the audience is.

Now you might have a thousand people listening to you, watching you, reading you, but at any one time its only you and one person listening or reading.

So talk directly to them. Use their language.

Your writing/speaking does not need to be 100% grammatically correct. Speaking never is, right? And nor does your sales conversation have to be.

Quick example…

On offer today is a three-day copywriting course where I teach you all of the great wordsmithing techniques that will turn you into an excellent copywriter and boost your earning potential.

Vs

Ok, I've got some really cool tips, skills and strategies to share and I'm going to teach you how to make a 6-figure income from the comfort of home. It's three days with me and 5 other go getters working on ways to turn words into money.

Again, a rough example, but see the difference? The first is perhaps more "correct" but it's also more stifled and boring. The second is chatty but gets the message across in a more exciting and informal way.

Conversational tone… it's vital to all copy success.

Breaking news: How to get attention

There's the answer, in the headline. To get attention, make your copy newsworthy.

In fact, the great ad man David Ogilvy was famous for saying good advertising contained authentic "breaking news".

Example, and consider the power of this…

"Social Media Ad Secret Revealed: How the Top 2% of Marketers Build Million+ Audiences Within 35 days with ZERO Increase in Ad Spend and Without Breaking Any Rules"

So I just made that up, but if you use Social Media to market your business, there's a darn good chance you'll stop and read something like that. Of course, such a claim needs to be backed up by some kind of discovery story and proof.

News "stories" work incredibly well.

CAUTION: If the idea is NOT new or there's not a newsworthy twist to it, then this angle will fall flat.

As with anything in advertising be congruent and authentic.

Our most destructive emotion

C an't believe what they said, and really, I can only put it down to ego and jealousy. Quick backstory…

Stamford, Connecticut was the place. The year was 2014. It was day 3 of Brian Kurtz's outstanding Titans of Direct Response Marketing. What an event. Everywhere you turned there was a legend lurking (and usually smiling, willing to mix and mingle). Joe Sugarman, Dan Kennedy, Gary Bencivenga. Plus, Greg Renker, Ryan Deiss, Parris Lampropolous. The original internet marketer Ken McCarthy, Perry Marshall, Ryan Lee, Jim Kwik and others. Big names who shared their success secrets. Yup, really cool.

And on Day 3 I met copywriter Roy Furr, the guy who wrote the sales copy which filled the room. Heck of a nice bloke. And a darn good copywriter. 300 odd in attendance from all over the world is ample evidence. Here's the thing…When I returned home, I stumbled across an online copywriting forum. Topic for the day was the sales copy for the Titans event. And gee, some "gurus" who weren't at the event were going to town on it. It was this. It was that. It lacked this. It shouldn't have said that. With those names to work with the copy would have written itself. On and on they went poking holes in what Roy wrote. What most of these gurus neglected to mention was…

THE RESULT. Full room. An event that made good money. 2 big lessons here…

No copy is perfect. There is always room for improvement. The result is more important. So let go of the need for perfection. Money loves speed, after all. And the big one… Why were these "gurus" picking apart something that WORKED? Can only put it down to one thing…

JEALOUSY.

"They" didn't get the gig. "They" would have done it differently (read "better"). "They" were more worthy than Roy Furr to write the copy for such big names. What a waste of time and energy on their part.

My humble take… Run your own race. Don't compare yourself to others. Your only competition is you and bettering your result next time. Sure, be market aware. But comparing yourself, your business, your results to others?

MASSIVE waste of energy which blocks your progress.

And it's very interesting how destructive such ego-driven jealousy can be to all parts of your life. Don't want to get all woo woo on you, but the way I see it, negative energy, ego-driven jealousy is the most destructive force any of us can muster.

So remember… Your only competition is internal. Your sole focus needs to be on the result YOU get. Not what she, he or they got. Think about it for a moment…

It's very liberating to let go of all that "stuff" and focus on your next outcome.

Sheer arrogance

W ho is the most arrogant person you've ever met? I bet you can remember them, clearly. Importantly, I bet with more certainty, the memory of that person also sparked a feeling somewhere in you…

A tightening in the gut… a frown… maybe even a slight flush in the face…

The feeling of it, because most of us hate arrogance, will be strong.

Hot on the heels of Entry #76 and the message about taking competitors on at their weakness and your strength (as opposed to trying to beat them when they have an advantage), comes a timely reminder.

Successful companies… small, medium and large… size does NOT matter… but successful businesses very often assume a certain arrogance in some aspect of their operation.

Look for this… because arrogance leads to entitlement… entitlement leads to laziness… laziness leads to weakness…

And that may just be where you can take them on and win.

Where are your competitors arrogant?

Think this through, it might just open a door to more influence and profit.

Beat the pain of rejection – this works all the time

I f you've ever sold anything, you will have experienced the pain of rejection.

Don't know anyone who really likes a "no". I don't. You don't. The Social Media warriors don't (hence their insatiable appetite for "Likes").

Nor does a client I was talking with recently. He asked for some advice about dealing with a sales "no".

We talked about the mechanics of his presentation, made a few minor tweaks. What he wanted most though was skills to deal emotionally with rejection. Get ready for the answer, because this works EVERY time…

Drum roll please…

Learn emotional resourcefulness.

Ta dah!

Sorry to un-impress you but…

Honestly, the ONLY way to deal with a "no" is to pick yourself up, dust yourself off and get set for the next sale. And yes, that all comes with vulnerability.

But you simply have to get used to it. No one closes all the time. No one.

Build what Dan Kennedy calls a "reservoir of resilience"… get back up, smile, and jump back into the fray.

Simple right?

But not always easy to do.

The next "no" you get? Batter up, get back in the game, and take a swing.

More random writing hacks

N ot sure where along my writing journey I picked up these little tips but happy to pass them on for you to test...

Finish each writing block you do mid-sentence

That way when you come to start again the first 3 or 4 words will be easy. And you'll be up and running. No writer's block!

Do a keyword dump

Sometimes mid project you can be stuck for what to write. If this happens grab a blank piece of paper and hand write key words for your market. This can get you back into the groove and re-ignite buried ideas.

Resources Vs resourcefulness – which do you choose?

You have to spend money to make money, right?

Um, well no. Not now at least.

Today you can get started and get moving for little or no cost.

Some examples…

- In terms of a CRM… to market to your list there's Mailchimp and a host of others like Kartra, Keap/Infusionsoft, Ontraport, Funnel Flows
- In terms of books, you can Google just about anything and find a PDF copy for free or low cost
- Screen capture devices? To explain copy and strategy to clients I use Drift, which records my voice/face as well as the text on the screen, so I can "talk them through" what I've done… it's free.. so is Loom
- I mentioned recently apps like Grammarly and Hemingway to make your copy zing
- You can create a LinkedIn profile for free… then there's the slew of Social Media platforms that are no/low cost
- If you need meditation, go to YouTube and search for "Wholetones" and a raft of really cool, peaceful, spiritual type healing music comes up… Hours and hours of everything from Chakra healing to angelic music to specific guided meditations… All for free

And on it goes.

So yeah, when you hear someone mention the BS about "you have to spend money to make money", know it's just limited thinking. Don't buy into it.

Get resourceful… there's plenty out there to help you!

Branding Vs direct response debate

Let's be clear: you need a strong brand to be successful in business. Yes, your logo and colours are important. As is your USP. The flip side of that is, no one ever bought anything because of a logo. Unless you're Apple. Or Coca Cola. Or Fed Ex and the like.

Hey?

And this is where confusion reigns... small business owners get much better return for their buck with direct response marketing... where people buy based on their need to have a problem solved. Not a logo or brand.

The big corporations market for brand awareness, not a direct sale. What they hope to do is move the viewer emotionally. Or entertain them. Or for them to associate their brand with a feeling (Coca Cola = fun, freedom, Apple = innovation and so on).

This takes time and big budgets.

No small business owner or even a medium one for that matter can ever compete with the ad budgets of the big companies, so it's useless to even try. That's why SMEs are far better off using direct response... where the intention is a sale that can be measured... where the brand and logo are secondary.

More:

In the direct response world, the big corporations are referred to by some as "big dumb companies". I reject that outright. You don't get big by being dumb. My experience in the corporate space proves this true.

The leaders here are smart. They are skilled. And they know what they are doing. Sure, they may not be across the ins and outs of direct response... and... there are morons in every industry... but for the main, big = successful not "dumb".

They just go about their marketing differently.

Last point...

I've been able to make direct response marketing work in the corporate world. I'm yet to see where "branding marketing" can be truly profitable in the SME market.

So know what sand pit you're playing in before you spend a cent on marketing... whether you're a big "smart" company or the little guy or girl that's turned their passion into a business.

Cool headline formula, the best ever?

What's the best headline formula?

So came the question during a consultation.

Answer…

I have no idea. Which is "best" that is. There are many that I use…

The "How to" headline (How to Write Headlines So Good they Double Your Response).

Or

The "Who Else" headline (Who Else Wants to Write Headlines So Powerful they Compel Even Disinterested Prospects to Read)

Or

The "Question" headline (Do You Make this Mistake in Your Headlines?).

And on it goes.

Like many things in marketing, there is no one "right" answer. Proven formulae and principles, yes, but never an absolute "right" way. Would be too easy and no fun if it was the opposite!!

One tip… always try and include some sense of novelty in your headline, it's a huge attention-getter.

And you might want to play around with the formula the great John Caples was famous for:

Curiosity + Self-Interest = Compelling Appeal.

Best example of this?

Can't go past David Ogilvy's…

"At 60 miles per hour the loudest noise in this new Rolls-Royce comes from the electric clock"

Bingo… one heck of a headline.

So best headline formula… like I said, no idea, but this gives you plenty to chew over next time you go to write one.

Greatest asset explained

S o when I discovered what my greatest business asset was…

I made a deliberate decision to actively take steps to look after it so it's in peak condition, like a pro athlete would take care of their body.

My GREATEST ASSET = MY MIND.

And taking care of it more has meant…

I'm happier at my work. I'm better at my work. I'm more efficient with my work. I land more deals with my work. And I make more money in my work.

Sound like results you'd like? This thinking is inspired by a guy who ran a billion-dollar company.

Here's how things have changed:

BEFORE: work my arse off so that by mid arvo I was akin to a blithering mess… and then I pushed more to get to get to 5pm or often much later. Toughen up princess, gotta work hard to be successful, right? Respect the hustle…

NOW: I work in 33 or 40-minute blocks… with a 5 to 10 minute brain rest in between… after a couple of these I take a longer period off… stroll on the beach… lay out the back and listen to music… go for a walk… repeat. Key thing is to REST MY BRAIN, so it stays fresh, not pound it into submission. Remember the pro athlete analogy… they have their rest/down times…

BEFORE: try to eat right and exercise but always have a few beers to unwind (mostly weekends).

NOW: eat at least twice a day 2 of the 3 super foods on the planet and tune in to what my body wants with a special technique… result is I drink way less, 2 beers at most, and only 1 coffee a day, and have cut out most junk food and still love the boxing gym… now that I eat the food that fuels my brain my focus is better.

BEFORE: feel guilty when I wasn't going 100 miles an hour and push push push… sorry… hustle…

NOW: relax and understand how it works… the brain, the physical thing in your head needs rest (like any muscle), the mind, that part of the brain no-one can "find" never stops and even when the brain is at rest, it works on my business… way less stress now because my brain isn't fried from hustling all the time. I rest my brain often and stay fresher longer.

Yup, it's pretty cool.

Danger of white space

B ig mistake many make when doing something offline like a flyer, letter box drop, postcard...

And hear this loud and clear...

Blank paper never sold a thing.

You see paper is expensive, printing is cheap.

In other words...

If you've gone to the trouble of crafting a message, printing it, and getting it delivered, you should be using every inch of the printed piece.

A flyer should be double sided.

White space will not sell.

I'm not talking about graphics and layout that makes something readable, although these are important.

I am talking about giving yourself every chance to get the prospect over the line.

But I can say it all in one page **might be your response.**

Doesn't matter... include testimonials, case studies, the guarantee, client list and so on. Just one phrase or line in a testimonial for instance may be enough to get a fence sitting prospect to take action. If there's white space there, you're missing an opportunity.

If you've included a sales device that takes up the blank space, you at least give yourself a chance.

Remember... blank paper never sold a thing.

A quick tip (must see movie)

A s a general rule, I don't like…

Musicals (*The Sound of Music* is an exception).

Or movies that are only loosely based on someone's life (prefer an accurate account).

Or films that are surreal (with different colours for the grass and sky and so forth).

But…

Strong recommendation is to watch *The Greatest Showman* starring Hugh Jackman.

It's all the things I generally don't like in a movie, but the 2 hours whizzed by.

What a show and tribute to the life of a legend, PT Barnum.

One of the things I constantly bang on about is the need to have your "marketing radar up" so you SEE things others miss… and learn from them… so you apply them to your marketing.

And *The Greatest Showman* is chock full of marketing messages.

Plus it's a massive lesson about the Big Idea in business and how to tune into what attracts people.

The music is a delight…

As are the messages about the human spirit and our individuality.

So yeah, lots to love about a movie I should hate.

Do yourself a favour and if you haven't already, give it a go.

Soapbox preaching endeth.

Pen or keyboard? Cool writing tip

If you've ever doodled, you'll take heart from this…

Plus, it's a cool technique for writers and marketers…

MY WRITING TIP…

The pen IS mightier than the keyboard. In most cases.

To explain…

A study at England's University of Plymouth School of Psychology showed that adults who doodled remembered 29% more than non-doodlers.

Interesting.

And…

According to the experts, drawing creates new dendrite connections in neural pathways of the brain, a phenomenon called "use dependent plasticity."

I've also heard it said typing creates 10 neural pathways. Writing with pen and paper creates something like 100.

Bottom line…

Planning your marketing funnel, even writing parts of your copy BY HAND has benefits in terms of creativity and maybe even boosting your "brain power".

And by extension…

What you create.

I do this often. Blank white paper. Blue pen. And away I go. Only then do I go to the keyboard.

Try it for yourself a few times and see if you notice the difference.

Best results = tactics based on fundamentals

How you "show up" when you sit down to write is key to your results. Do you "show up" in your best state?

It really is an individual thing.

Case in point:

As I said earlier, Perry Marshall, from 80/20 marketing fame, says he listens to heavy metal music before he writes, and during. Says it really gets him in an emotional state.

Me?

Couldn't think of anything worse.

I prefer to "show up" well rested with a clear mind.

Then I put my special music on which puts me in an alpha brain wave and away I go.

If you've been to my 2-day event you will know what my "special music" is.

Further proof it's an individual thing:

Shared my special music with a client recently. She tried it but told me she couldn't stand it and preferred street noises in the background. The music annoyed her.

Fair enough.

It IS an individual thing, and you have to work out what's best for you.

That troublesome R word

L ike armpits, it seems everyone has a couple of opinions about how to get to know your market, how to research. And the debate rages.

For example, we all know people buy on emotion.

Which emotions? The greats have left clues.

Robert Collier: love, gain, duty, pride, self-indulgence, self-preservation.

Joe Karbo and his 4 R's: **Reincarnation** (the hope for immortality or life after death - if we don't believe it we want to create some legacy so that at least some part of us will live forever), **Recognition** (respect and admiration of others), **Romance** (sex, love, comfort, companionship, tenderness), **Reward** (material possessions and money).

And Mike Pavlish says it's even simpler because there are two major benefits desired by 98% of peeps... more money and more love.

Does that help to clarify things?

If not, one of my favourite at-a-distance mentors, Bob Bly, uses the BFD formula. **Beliefs - Feelings - Desires**. You research your market by digging into what their beliefs are. Finding out what they feel. And uncovering what it is they desire.

So for weight loss it would be (and this is a short list to illustrate the point, dig much deeper for your market):

Beliefs: it's hard to lose weight, diets don't work, it's genetics

Feelings: this is frustrating, I'm embarrassed I can't lose weight, why me?

Desires: I just want to like what I see in the mirror, I want to feel healthy and lean

And much more.

See how that helps solidify the "which emotions" conundrum? And then you build your sales argument around these three things.

Try it out and see how you go.

The #1 demon within – stops your progress

We all have it. And it hurts all of us. Whether it wins or not is determined by how you defeat it.

So…

What's the #1 inner demon that stops our progress? And keeps you from being your best?

Answer: **SELF DOUBT.**

It shows up whenever you are looking at something new, with thoughts like…

Maybe this won't work…

What if they don't like me?

I'm not sure I'm ready?

Sounds great but I'm just too busy right now.

What if I fail?

What if I can't handle it?

What if I lose money?

What if I end up looking foolish?

Sound familiar?

Hope you were honest enough to say yes.

Coz this little sucker is in all of us.

How do you defeat this demon?

For now, listen to that voice in your head and have your "radar up" and try catch the demon.

Awareness is the first step.

Bump your Yesses

During a consult I gave a client a PROVEN strategy to boost response to his offers.

He was amazed.

But also a little peeved he hadn't thought of it himself.

So thought it useful to also remind you.

The strategy: in your offer, always give the prospect 2 or 3 options.

Reason it works: takes their minds AWAY from "No" and onto which option is best.

So what in effect you are doing is guiding people into YOUR list of choices, not theirs (which includes a "No").

Now here's where you can crank it up…

Test these:

- Choice of options (standard or deluxe)
- Choice of payment (all now or in instalments)
- Choice of benefits (different for each or more for deluxe)

Because suddenly our minds have gone from "no" to another decision altogether.

Remember, all marketing is situational so there is no "right" number of options but…

This "yes or yes" close is a proven and winning strategy to boost response.

Feed the right wolf

Which wolf do you feed?

To explain...

I love the story of the great Indian chief teaching young kids about success in life (which we can apply to business).

The story begins thus, old man in front of young kids:

My children, every day there is a terrible war going on inside me...

It is a war between two wolves.

The Cherokee Indian chief looked at each set of young eyes in turn.

They were awed in his presence... his scarred face and intelligent eyes both intimidated and inspired them.

He went on...

One wolf is full of anger, lies, jealousy, resentment, inferiority, and ego...

The other wolf is joy, love, peace, humility, kindness, truth, and spirit...

He paused again. In the silence one brave young girl put her hand up and said...

Great father, which wolf wins?

The chief paused for effect as he looked each child in the eyes one more time and said...

Depends which wolf you feed.

As you get set for your day today, it's a great business question to ponder, wouldn't you agree?

EVERY minute of EVERY day which wolf do you feed?

Word soup explained

U se this for quick reference…

Every industry has its own "word soup" or acronyms that those "in the know" rattle off rapid fire which can leave someone not as far down the rabbit hole with a head spin. And feeling a little lost.

Fore-warned is fore-armed they say, so here's a list of common acronyms used in the online marketing world with a quick explanation. The list is broken into "macro" terms and then the "micro" that sit underneath these:

MACRO:

TOFU: Top Of Funnel - first touch point with prospects ie ads, email, blogs etc where they get to see you, often for the first time

MOFU: Middle Of Funnel – emails, blogs and more where you build trust, give value

BOFU: Bottom Of Funnel – the sales mechanism… landing page, VSL, webinar… where they buy

MICRO:

ESP: Email Service Provider – the software that does the work for you (there are lots from Mailchimp to Aweber to Keap, Ontraport, and more)

CTA: Call to Action – how you tell them to do something… "Click here now", "Get Access Now" are two examples

OIR: Opt In Rate – the number or percentage of peeps who fill out a form/registration page

OR: Open Rate – the percentage of peeps on your list who read your emails

CTR: Click Through Rate – how many click a link in an email or click and ad

CPM: Cost Per Mille (which is Latin for a thousand… see it's not always obvious!) - refers mostly to ads, how much you pay per 1,000 impressions

CR: Conversion Rate – number of sales

CPA: Cost Per Acquisition – how much you pay to get a customer

EPC: Earnings Per Click – how much you make per click of ad/link

LTV: Life Time Value (of a customer) – how long they stay with you, how much they spend with you in that time

AOC: Average Order Value – how much does each customer spend on average (sometime also called Average Cart Value) per transaction

OTO: One Time Offer – used in upsells/pop ups… once only chance for the prospect to buy more from you while they are in purchaser mode

Hope that helps!

How to get better at writing and make more money

I can't write. I hate writing.

Are two semi-common complaints from business owners.

I get it. Certain skillsets do come easier to certain people.

But if you want true autonomy in business, it DOES pay to master the written word.

So…

Hers's THE secret to getting better at writing…

WRITE MORE.

That's it, yep.

It was golfer Gary Player who said, "The harder you work, the luckier you get".

Same with writing.

Here's another little kicker…

The more words you write FASTER, the more income you generate.

Like everything, writing is a skill and the more you do it, the better you get.

One of today's buzz phrases is, "Content is king".

Well, I've just given you the formula to making more content than your competitor… go forth and make it happen for you!

Huge marketing lesson from a giggling 8-year-old boy

He laughed so hard as he pointed that the giant Cornetto-style ice cream was running down his 8-year-old chin.

Flashback to November 2009. We were at South Beach in Miami, Florida. We'd had a swim, a bite to eat and grabbed an ice cream as we strolled the shopping area with all the cool people.

We stopped in front of one of those novelty t-shirt shops and just gazed. Wall to wall and floor to ceiling novelty t-shirts. A crowded "marketplace" indeed. The rude, the crude, the hilarious and everything in between.

And there was 8-year-old Isaac in the midst of his belly laugh pointing downward to the rack on the left at the back of the store.

What was it that, in all that clutter, what on Earth could have caught his young and innocent eyes and caused the hysterics?

"There! There!" was all he managed to blurt out, his body jiggling with laughter.

And then I saw what he was pointing to.

In amongst all those shirts, his 8-year-old boy eyes had latched onto a plain white t-shirt with just 4 words…

**BOOBIES
MAKE ME
HAPPY**

In all that clutter, one word had caught his attention. I didn't realise it until we got back to the hotel room later that night of the importance of that moment…

Every market has "magic words" which appeal to that specific audience (for 8-year-old-boys it's "Boobies"!!).

What about your market? What are those words that appeal to them, that instantly grab their attention? This is key to writing great headlines and copy… know what those magic words are for your market that instantly catch their eye and stop them in their tracks. It's your job to find your version of **"Boobies Make Me Happy."**

No love any more

I t's been 8 working days in a row now and no love.

Empty.

Absent.

Nada.

And it's sad. I counted them… for 8 working days in a row I went out to the letter box looking for the mail. And I've received none. Seems like no one loves me anymore. Noticed a similar trend at your place?

Does this also give you a little window into a possibly untapped media? Can you smell opportunity? I'm talking about direct mail. Seems hardly anyone is mailing anymore which makes it darned easy to get noticed. While prospects are scrolling through Facebook news feeds at lightning speed noticing very little…

Is this your chance to show up and get attention?

Direct mail is dead you've heard them all scream.

Direct mail is expensive they'll tell you.

Direct mail takes too long to see results.

And on it goes. Be wary. My observations, apart from the 8-day loveless streak in my letterbox…

Discussions with a high-powered marketing guy recently led to his recommendations to stay away from SEO and print ads… but definitely keep up direct mail.

A recent ditty from Dan Kennedy revealed one of his clients increased mailings from 50,000 to 125,000 homes PER MAILING. You wouldn't more than double your spend unless you were getting a nice return, now would you?

To quote Dan…

"People keep right on pronouncing Direct Mail dead. And it keeps rising from the grave… here is what I can tell you as 'insider' stuff: all but one of the clients I work with directly… increased two things this year… one, their incomes. Two their use of direct mail."

Given the emptiness of my letterbox at the moment… just about anything in there will get opened… and if it's a well-crafted sales message, I'll be equally inclined to act on it. Can you leverage this "empty mailbox phenomenon" into an opportunity? If your margins are good, worth a VERY serious test, pronto.

Video killed the copywriting star

Remember the hit song way back at the start of the 80s...

Video Killed the Radio Star.

The Buggles were the artists, and it told the story of how video film clips killed radio... like cars killed the horse and cart... light bulb killed candles etc etc.

Anyways...

Was amused to see another of those online discussions that video had killed copywriting and long copy was dead (if I had a dollar for every time I've heard that one...).

What complete and utter BS. Video is great, no mistake. In most markets it boosts response.

But...

Even a video script has to be WRITTEN... which is, ahem, copy. If you're a bright shiny object chaser, sorry to burst your bubble... copy is STILL king.

Best part is...

Once you learn the principles of copywriting, you can apply them to ANY media... video... social media ... email and on it goes.

A deep and sustained dive into the art of words that sell is one of the BEST investments in self and business you will ever make.

Rant endeth.

P.S. At the time of going to print, AI generated copywriting was emerging with "encouraging" results. By encouraging I mean AI is generating quality content in a fraction of the time it takes a human. One thing a human brain is still required for is the strategy behind the copy. The jury is still out, AI may kill the copywriting star in the future, but my guess is we're a long way from that yet.

Warning signs are here

The world almost stopped…

For some people at least. Shock. Horror. Catastrophe.

Yes, Facebook went down for several hours one day not that long ago.

And the reactions from many were telling… and scary…

You see several successful business people have been warning about social media addiction for ages.

Executive coach Brent Charleton calls Facebook toxic and recommends his clients leave it (although he still uses it as a business advertising media).

Dan Kennedy has said it's like smoking was back in the 1940s and 50s… socially acceptable and promoted as harmless fun… until the REAL dangers of tobacco were outed. He opines it will be the same with social media in years to come.

I don't know if I agree with either sentiment. But the way some people reacted when their "fix" was taken from them aka Facebook when down for a few hours, is alarming…

From some admitting they felt "lost" without it… to others even calling 000…

Have people really given up their sovereignty to such a point a simple media going offline renders them almost paralysed?

This is scary.

And it may have been a wake-up call too if you rely too heavily on Facebook for your marketing…

They say one is the most dangerous number in business…

But I guess the outage for a few hours gave you a taste of what could happen. Heed the warning signs and adjust your operations accordingly. And no, I'm not expecting this to get any "Likes" or "Shares" with such a sentiment.

Just for today, why not unplug for a few hours… get off social media, don't check your emails… nothing bad will happen…

What are you most proud of?

N erd alert…

Yep, I freely admit to being something of a marketing "square"… the geeky kid in the corner his head buried in a marketing book whenever possible.

Like one trip to Brisbane to do a workshop with a client, I (as usual) listened to an interview on CD. This one was with superstar graphic designer (who does all of Dan Kennedy's work), Kia Arian. She shared some cool direct response tips but one of the things that stood out for me was the left of field question and her answer.

The question: What are you most proud of?

Kia's answer (me paraphrasing): *Not giving up. Over 15 years in the industry, including the GFC there were many times I thought just getting a job would be easier. But I persisted. I never gave in to that temptation to quit when it got tough. The fact I'm still here after 15 years and all the ups and downs is what I'm most proud of.*

Interesting perspective… she's obviously worked with some big clients. Helped them and herself create huge successes. But her biggest source of pride was… her resilience.

I think it was Churchill who said, "Success is going from failure to failure without losing enthusiasm".

This can be tough.

But it's not necessarily fatal…

Often times an outsider's perspective, from someone who doesn't have your "negative internal feedback loop" going on where "everything" can seem too hard is what is required.

Fresh eyes, a new approach, quick wins can turn a business and your mindset around very quickly. Do something today to boost your enthusiasm… it will give you a little pick up if you're feeling blah… or it will brighten your mood even more.

Lessons from MAFS

I know...

Watching trashy dating shows like *Married At First Sight* is like staring at a car accident: you know you should look away, but you just can't. Everyone, it seems, is talking about it when it's on.

Social media is abuzz with what a b*tch that girl is (surely it's all scripted... the black dress, playing the devil's advocate all night)... how cut up she was when the previously guarded other "wife" was all over her "husband" even though she couldn't stand her "husband"... on and on it goes. Compelling viewing, right?

Sadly, I could talk about it for ages with you (please don't tell anyone).

What's there to learn from this?

They have been genius at several key marketing tactics which is why the show has been so successful, among them:

- The open loop (where you drop a hint about something without revealing what it is, to keep people reading or watching) - check out the ads for the show and even their coming up after the break teasers... GREAT COPY
- The tapping into our human voyeur tendencies... we are CURIOUS about others' lives, we love STORIES... this show is one big story about how total strangers might go when they hook up
- Novelty... they picked a mix of "normal" peeps with an eclectic mix of "alternative" types... throw a match on kerosene and stand back and watch... there are new and interesting twists every week
- Entertaining... it's fun, even if you feel like you need a shower after each episode... people like to have fun
- They craft story lines we relate to... we can all see parts of ourselves in certain situations... how would we go at dinner... what would we say when we walked in for the dinner party... and on it goes...

So yes, as a MAFS devotee - strictly for learning/work purposes of course! - I can tell you there is much to be learned from this vacuous and trashy TV.

Other media is always a good source of ideas for copy and marketing... watch the next seasons of MAFS and you'll see why.

The penny finally dropped

Reckon you've heard this before because I have too, hundreds of times. And until now, even though I understood it, on some level I never really "got it".

I'm talking about that line of *placing yourself and your business in a category of 1.*

Heard that one before?

Yep, many times.

The penny REALLY dropped for me when I was reading an article by Adam Witty.

If you've never heard of Adam, he built Advantage Books and Forbes Books and a couple of other companies into a $35 million a year enterprise. And he was one-time partner of Dan Kennedy in GKIC (now NO BS Inner Circle).

Anyways, Adam was talking in the article about authority and the need to create it for your business.

This is the little passage that hit me in the face…

Your target prospect is trying to commoditise you. Why? It makes their buying decision easier. Every prospect is trying to justify in their head why you are just like every other person/company that does what you/your company do. If you let that happen, your prospect makes an apples to apples comparison and will then purchase on price… nope not the high price… but the low price. Bad place to be. You MUST not let your prospects do this. You must build authority. You must position yourself and your firm as a category of one…

BANG!

It's what I did with my client in the corporate space for their launch into the lucrative but hyper competitive Aged Care market.

And it can be done at a small business level as well.

Read that quote again…

Because **Category of 1** where price is largely irrelevant?

Now that's a nice place to be.

Guarantee magic words

These are key phrases to use in your guarantee…

In the unlikely event … prompt and courteous refund… no questions asked…

Why?

Consider copy in this 30-day money back guarantee. It might read like…

> **"Try our service out for a full 30 days and if we haven't delivered on everything we've promised simply contact us for a full refund."**

It's ok. But it can be stronger…

> **"Try our service out for a full 30 days and in the unlikely event we haven't delivered on everything we've promised simply contact us for a full refund."**

When you include the phrase "in the unlikely event" it's a powerful mental trigger that implies you deliver for all customers, that a complaint is almost unheard of. It gives confidence in a very subtle way. Thanks Ted Nicholas, for the tip.

Better still…

> **"Try our service out for a full 30 days and in the unlikely event we haven't delivered on everything we've promised simply contact us for a full prompt and courteous refund, no questions asked."**

See how that's even stronger?

When you add a Johnson box and guarantee seal, you complete the job.

Risk reversal is important. Take the time to get it right.

Nasty voice in your customer's head

How to defeat it...

Do you hate that little voice inside your head when you are at work? You know how it goes...

I'll just make that sales call later...

Or...

I'll speak to the staff member after lunch...

Then comes the retort:

Hey, don't you have any self-discipline? This will mean you've not progressed the business today like you said you would!

And:

It's ok, you've got a lot on at the moment, you'll get to it when you can...

And on it goes. Sound familiar? At least a little bit? That voice in your head urging you not to do what you need to do... out of fear... or sloth... or some other negative emotion.

It's the SAME voice in your customer's head which urges them NOT to buy from you. So, if you've ever felt like it's getting harder to sell in today's market, you're not alone.

It's getting HARDER to sell. It's getting HARDER to keep them as long-term customers. And it's getting HARDER to build meaningful long-term relationships.

Never before has a buyer had more power, more choice and more distractions and reasons not to say yes than they do now. No, it's not impossible. But it is harder.

Your copy has to defeat their inner voice which DOESN'T want them to buy. DOESN'T want them to buy again from you. And... DOESN'T want them to remain long term customers.

Today, more than ever you have to work hard to defeat it... never underestimate the difficulty of selling, ever!

Rushed, no time, always busy... see this remedy

I *just wish I had more time...*

Ever heard that or even said it yourself?

In fact, for any business owner, it seems like there are never enough hours in the day...

It's always go go go. And then GO!

Sound familiar? If so, this is hurting your business. Because the success of any business is only ever as good as the thinking behind it.

And if you are go go GO...

All the time, means you're not thinking... you're rushing.

At certain times of the year (June and December in particular) it's especially important to remember this because everyone's tired and jaded.

So here's the solution...

Take time out to think.

Just sit and do nothing for 20 minutes and let your thoughts come and go. I think it was the Dalai Lama who said if you don't have time to meditate every day for 20 minutes, you should meditate for an hour!

Ok, I know... for some the word meditate is too woo woo... but just sitting still and letting thoughts come and go from your mind opens up space to think.

Brendon Burchard in his bestselling *The Motivation Manifesto* devoted his whole last chapter to the need to slow time.

You do this by the deliberate habit of 20 minutes or even 10 every day just being still. Go ahead and try it today... just 20 minutes... set a timer to it... do it every day for a week and watch the difference it makes!

When not to SOS your business

This is about rescuing you…

But not really.

It's about a lifeline for your business…

But also not really.

It's about a moment in time that changes everything…

But it's NOT about saving anything or anyone.

It really isn't.

You see the common understanding of SOS is the international Morse code distress signal "save our souls".

But the SOS I'm talking about is completely different.

SOS = Same Old Shit.

Are you guilty of this?

Where you get in a rut and do the same things (because it's a rut) and wonder why things aren't changing? So do you need to stop the "same old shit" in your business? Food for thought, right?

I wrote a "same old shit" list of the things I need to stop doing in my own business. Ouch. But VERY useful.

What would be on your list of things you need to stop?

Over to you…

When speed is necessary = huge tip for writers

This is one small tip for writers, one gigantic leap in sales (to lean on Neil Armstrong just a little).

What's the tip?

Speed.

Your writing must be easy to read.

They must be able to get the sales message fast.

Reckon this is especially important in emails where you have so little time because of so much clutter.

So yeah…

Conversational tone is important.

Better still…

Make it easy to read fast.

One way = shorter sentences and paragraphs (check out above).

WARNING though…

There must still be flow. Your sentences can't be "bumpy" for the sake of brevity. This will turn off readers just as fast as long winded, hard to read copy.

Speed of the read with flow, my padawan, is key.

Power of emotions

It was a world without war. A world where everyone got along. Order. Precision. Abundance. Peace.

All because human emotions had been eradicated via a daily drug dose and Nazi-style laws and secret police…

So went the story of a Netflix offering I stumbled upon, the 2002 pic, *Equilibrium*.

Interesting premise because the story unfolded that you can't really control or eliminate what makes us human. A song. A painting. A cute puppy. Kids. Your partner. We all have strong reactions to these and many more.

PROOF:

The headline and big idea for the successful real estate promo I wrote a couple of years back…

Four mil or so in sales not too shabby…

Oh yeah, the headline and big idea came to me listening to the real estate sales guy talk.

He was excited. He was animated. He was really "into" the product. And this alone for me was enough to REALLY listen.

More:

When people talk fast with passion and excitement, you know emotion is behind it. So pay attention. Be it a customer. A staff member. A prospect.

Emotion in their voice often means some "gold" is on the way you can use in your marketing. It's worked for me many times. So today, have your "radar tuned" for emotion in what people say and take note… you might just get a great idea for your next promo.

So how did the movie *Equilibrium* end? Don't know… in truth it was pretty crappy, fell asleep about an hour into it after the lesson of human emotions sunk in!

Recommended marketing books

W ant to sharpen your marketing saw further? I read and study the craft. A lot. So I'm happy to make some MORE recommendations.

In no particular order, great marketing books to consider...

Spiritual Power Tools for Successful Selling by Lee Milteer

Direct Marketing Made Easy by Malcom Auld

Meaningful Marketing by Doug Hall

80/20 Sales and Marketing by Perry Marshall

Secrets of Successful Direct Mail by Richard Benson

The Advertising Solution by Craig Simpson and Brian Kurtz

The Official Get Rich Guide to Information Marketing by Robert Scrob

Any of Dan Kennedy's "No BS" series, including

Marketing to the Affluent

Marketing to Boomers & Seniors

Price Strategy (with Jason Marrs)

Direct Response Social Media Marketing (with Kim Walsh-Phillips)

Pitch Anything by Oren Klaff

Magnetic Marketing by Dan Kennedy

Mind Control Marketing by Mark Joyner

Launch by Jeff Walker

Dotcom Secrets by Russell Brunson

Leaders are readers... never stop learning... great marketing books like these are a powerful and cost-effective way to start.

Quick quiz – which headline won…

Which of these two headlines won in a split test?

They were written decades ago by copy legend Maxwell Sackheim for a language training product.

Version 1 = **"Are You Afraid of Making Mistakes in English?"**

Or

Version 2 = **"Do You Make these Mistakes in English?"**

If you're a student of marketing you'll recognise version 2 as the clear winner.

Why?

Simple…

Specificity.

Brought on by the word "these". As in not just any old mistakes…

But "these" ones.

Which?

"These".

Gets your curiosity going, right?

So yes, self-interest (no one wants to make mistakes) and curiosity (these mistakes) are powerful forces to use in any headline. And of course, this principle can be swiped to use in many markets…

Do you make these mistakes in headline writing?

Do you make these mistakes in online marketing?

Do you make these mistakes in Facebook ads?

And on it goes.

What Miley said about business

I t was about 3:55am en route to the airport for a flight to Sydney for one of the mastermind groups I'm a member of.

Instead of my usual mindset or marketing CD… to stay awake I was flicking through the radio looking for something upbeat.

Ads, all ads except for one station… doing an interview with…

Miley Cyrus.

Can't say I'm a huge fan (although her twerking exploits got my attention…)

Where was I?

That's right…

Ads or Miley… so Miley it was.

And I must say it was pretty darn good.

Biggest point she made - and this could easily be applied to your business - is the importance of "beach time".

She was asked what she does when she's not doing her thing.

Response:

"I go to the beach. I need my beach time. It clears my mind and opens up space for new ideas. Many artists are so scared of losing their audience and place in the market that they go and go and go. Not me. I can't work that way, I need my space and clear-thinking time."

Kind of cool, right? And yep, I get it, it's easy to say some version of *"ok for you, coz you're a rock star"* kind of thing. But don't give into that temptation because you miss the important message.

Reckon you need to take a leaf out of Miley's book more often and take some beach time?

Power of numbers

Here's a little tip when you're researching…

It's a well-known truth that scientific data adds to any argument.

For example, I believe better sleep helps you lose weight. Such a statement has personal conviction. But it's easily dismissed, isn't it?

What about…

I believe better sleep helps you lose weight because a 2018 study at Harvard University found that over 3 years, 78.5% of people who reported better sleep also lost 19% more body fat.

Ok, so I just made that up to illustrate the point, but you get the idea.

The second one is much more believable.

Here's one way to find such data…

When you do an internet search, after your keywords, add "scientific study" and see what happens.

You'll be amazed what you'll find.

In this example we might write: "link between sleep and weight loss scientific study"

Boost believability of your copy with data from the world of academia.

Your ability to influence and make more sales will thank you for it!

To greet or not to greet – here is my answer

S chool's in today so pen and paper ready…

Like the "big" question I'm often asked, *where do I get my ideas from,* comes another often asked little gem…

Why no greeting or salutation at the start of your emails?

Hi Steve… Dear Copywriting Student… Hey Friend… are all ways to start a communication.

I can give you tactical answers…

- A number of big name emailers do NOT include a greeting (many still do however)
- If the person makes a typo in their opt-in form, it stays with them forever - and it becomes annoying to be greeted by an error EVERY time (don't laugh, I've done it, it IS annoying - ok, a little chuckle is permitted, it's kind of funny)
- The fewer fields at opt-in, the (usually) better opt-in rate, so first name not needed

So yep, there are good reasons why not to.

But for me the biggie is…

I just love how you can launch into your message, so the reader is "IN" the email right from the outset.

Speed of the read, especially in email, where the space is so cluttered, is vital.

So I like to get into it straight away.

Class dismissed.

How to battle undercutting

P rice cutting is rife.

Commoditisation is everywhere.

Question is, what to do about it?

Is it possible to effectively combat low prices? It's really hard because the one who can afford to go lowest always wins. And this is usually the bigger players.

The answer?

In theory… make the conversation about VALUE, not price.

In reality… one way to do this is to go back to the past and channel the decades-old…

"We fix <insert cheap or undercut service>" strategy.

Examples…

We fix $10 lawn mowing

We fix $59 carpet cleanings

We fix online job board copywriting

And on it goes.

The psychology is clear… cheap = poor quality.

The "We fix" helps position you as the consumers' hero to the cheap (and by extension poor quality) service providers.

Nope, you don't have to be a "price victim".

You can get on the front foot - this "we fix" strategy has, like I said, worked for decades and cuts across just about every industry.

How to express your value part II

Y es, I really did hate it at the start (see #94). I'm talking about the huge importance of you being able to express the 4 pillars of value if you are to sell successfully.

To recap...

When I first started copywriting, I hated asking people for money. This was part past programming, part not understanding my value and how it is to be expressed. I've often said the #1 thing in sales is confidence. But that's tough when you don't "get" the value equation. Your "belief value" is based on clients' results. What numbers do you help them achieve... sales, kilos lost, revenue generated and on it goes.

What of the other 3 pillars?

As internationally acclaimed consultant Simon Bowen says, next you must understand your "contribution value". This is where you see the DIFFERENCE you make to clients' lives. Of course, numbers are involved. But so are personal and business transformations. Like a weight loss ad, what are the before and after "pictures" the client has from working with you? Dig deep here.

Then you must understand your "perceived value". This involves how well you package #1 and #2 and how you communicate it to your prospects. And last but not least is the "sale value" which is, based on 1-3, what you are worth to the market. Most start here... pick a number and guess. Or just base it on industry norms. I believe however, to effectively sell these days, you must dig deeper... only then can you authentically stand in your confidence and sell your product or service.

To recap, the pillars of your value...

Belief value (what you do, results you get)

Contribution value (the difference you make to clients' lives)

Perceived value (how well you package and communicate it)

Sale value (what you are truly worth).

Quick exercise to help your thinking...

Write down each of these values and then write next to them how you provide that value. You'll be surprised the clarity this brings.

Words that sell writing tip

The worst, the hardest, the most traumatic part of your written sales message is... drum roll please...

The editing. Boring. Yep, totally.

It's a bit like using hammer and nail to affix every board on a 10m x 10m deck. Bang. Bang. Bang. Repetitive and well, boring. Don't think you're alone. The great Gary Bencivenga told me it took him 10 years in the craft before he felt really comfortable with his skills.

And to quote Hemingway: "Don't get discouraged because there's a lot of mechanical work to writing ... I rewrote the first part of *A Farewell to Arms* at least fifty times." Good news, right??!!

Here are a couple of tips to help with the grind that is editing...

No cost and basic: the spelling/grammar/FK score built into Word software. Use it religiously (see entry #254 for more about how FK works and why it's vital).

No cost and intermediate: read your copy out loud and whenever you stumble, make a note and come back and massage it to smooth it out.

Low cost and advanced: try one of the many online apps like Hemingway or Grammarly, they are good but do cost (although the latter has a free component).

Key point #1: great sales copy is not easy. Nor is it impossible. It does however require some work... just don't get discouraged. As someone who's written literally 100s of thousands of words... it can piss you off... so hang in there, it's worth it.

Key point #2: you don't have to be a world class copywriter to make a difference. To move the needle in your sales, you just have to be better than your competitors. In most cases, the bar is low, so the opportunity is big.

The skill in writing is the editing for a fast and easy read. Just make sure you don't edit as you write, they are two different skills.

Dangerous new trend?

There is a dangerous trend creeping into the marketing world. I suspect it's in part due to the emergence of "instant gurus". You've probably seen them... people with very little experience and virtually no runs on the board who label themselves a coach or an expert and sell hard.

Quick example...

Facebook ads.

There are many "experts" teaching the ins and outs of this media. Beware.

If they don't teach the fundamentals and the principles of marketing and copy, and why people buy... then you are being set up for a fall.

If the "only" thing taught is the specifics of the media, what happens when there's an algorithm change? Or a law changes?

You're pretty much screwed, right?

So when choosing a mentor, make sure they aren't just teaching for shiny objects. Make sure they teach the fundamentals of sales language.

When you are taught this way, you set yourself up for success because you then have the skills to apply the principles to the different media where your market is.

It's futile trying to be all things to all people, to be omnipresent in all media.

Get the basics right, get good at them. Then find out what works for your market and apply the foundations and principles of great sales language to the media. That is the key.

This mistake again... pls avoid

F rustrating yet so common.

This **subject line** that graced my inbox is an example of a mistake I see time and again...

I'll show you in a sec but keep reading because...

It's important to keep in mind it's rare to find something "totally" bad or "100% correct". We can always improve things.

This one did a number of things right in both the subject line and the first line of copy...

Used "your".

Gave the free product a value.

Used "free".

Used "instant access".

So yeah there was some "good" stuff in there.

But...

Check out this subject line...

"Your 101 page PDF".

Um...

In his book *Thinking, Fast and Slow* Nobel Prize winner Daniel Kahneman talks about "cognitive ease".

Meaning we are more likely to do something if our brain perceives it as easy. Us humans are pleasure-seeking missiles. We want quick fast and easy.

Now I don't know about you but the thought of wading through a 101-page PDF **FEELS** hard.

I don't want to read it. Not 101 pages. 1 page yes... or 10 maybe... but 101 pages...

Delete.

Couple of lessons here...

Sell the result, not the thing.

Sell "cognitive ease". That's what we want.

Sell them at the start with a curiosity invoking subject or headline.

A "101 page" anything just doesn't cut it.

Class dismissed.

Your first thought every day?

H ere's what the masses say to themselves and how you can avoid being like them...

You've probably heard me say it time and again. In fact, I start just about every presentation, whether in person or online, with the mantra:

Words matter

How you use words matters

Words can change your business.

And it's true. And it applies to you and to me and to what we say to ourselves. So take this little test...

What WAS your first thought this morning? For most people it's some version of...

Ugghhhh... is it that time already... if only I could lay here longer... I'm sooo tired... I don't want to go to work today...

Sound familiar? (it's ok, no one will know). It was for me when I was teaching... including wishing it was Friday or Christmas holidays or some other thing than "today I have to face work". Here's the problem with words like that...

The first words you think set up your day. Start negative and you get negative... for all or most of the day. And there's no way you can make money with these words. No way. Money is repelled by negative. It might be woo woo... but it's also true in my humble (but correct) opinion... words as thoughts have energy or vibration or frequency (whatever term you use)... and they create our outer reality. So don't get lazy with your internal words, just like you wouldn't with your external sales message words...

Success coach, author, and business leader Lee Milteer recommends you start each day with a positive (or very least) neutral thought...

Not...

No one is buying my stuff, I'm broke.

But...

How can I more easily make money today?

See the difference? More importantly, FEEL the difference? So yep, don't be like the masses first thing in the morning... watch your first words to yourself... they will create the rest of your day. Wow, imagine a year of "first positive words"... it will change your world.

Sorry, it's over, it all just got too hard...

I'm done with it. Over it. Lost interest. It's a "no". Such were my comments when critiquing some copy recently.

I was focusing on the offer.

It had 5 options. Way too hard. Too confusing. So write this down or seer it into your memory...

Confused people do nothing. And it's a mistake I see often. Sometimes we complicate things so much we stunt sales. This is not just copywriting theory. But actual research...

Dr Sheena Iyengar from Columbia University Business School conducted a study which proved the theory correct. Of all things she chose jam tasting. No idea why. Anyways, she set up 2 different stands in an upscale food shop. One stand offered 6 different flavours of jam to taste. The other offered 24.

Findings...

MORE people stopped at the stand with 24 offerings.

But...

People were six times more likely to buy jam at the stand that offered only 6 choices.

FACT: when the choice got too complicated, people chose not to choose at all.

Conversely, when the choice was easier to deal with, people were more willing to act on their preferences.

Research proves it.

So make the path to the sale smooth and easy. Yes, we want to steer them from "No" with a "Yes of Yes" offer but let's be clear... fewer options almost always win.

I use 2 or 3 at most because it's easier for the buyer.

Remember, confused people do NOTHING.

What I do in the shower

O k, this is not a creepy entry but a truth about idea generation.

Water works.

As in, if you're stuck for ideas, connect with water.

Walk by a river.

Paddle across a lake.

Stroll on the beach.

Take a shower.

For some reason, the "flow" of water helps the flow of ideas.

Don't believe me?

Next time you're stuck. Go take a shower and see what happens.

And...

The other activity that often leads to creative insights is sleeping. If you have a question you'd like answers to, or you're elbows deep in a project and feel stuck, before you close your eyes, either for a 15 or 20 minute power nap or before bed in the evening, ask your subconscious mind for information useful to solving the challenge you will remember when you wake up.

Example:

"Steve, give me the right keywords for the headline in the Smith Company promo."

Give both of these a go, you'll be surprised by the results!

The enemy within

This is NOT about one of the copywriting techniques aka "the enemy in common". This IS about YOUR enemy. The one that stops you from achieving what you want. And no, it's not just "you"… it's in all of us this enemy.

To explain…

I remember way back in my teaching days I was at an administrators' conference at Noosa and the guest speaker was legendary NRL coach Wayne Bennett. The line he gave about leadership has stayed with me to this day…

The two hardest things in this world are diamonds and for a person to really know themselves.

How true, right? I believe this will help… because for every project you take on you face an enemy. This enemy is NOT from the outside world. This enemy is within and it's VERY powerful…

RESISTANCE.

That invisible but destructive force that tries to stop you. It's your ego keeping you "safe". And the resistance shows up in 3 ways…

#1 Anxiety or dread - *what if this won't work*

#2 Insecurity - which shows up after you've started, *is this right, maybe I should reconsider*

#3 Indecision - of both you and your customer, *is this good enough, what if they don't like it*

Here's the thing…

We can feel this EVERY time we try something new. In fact I feel all three every time I put fingers to keyboard (like writing this entry, this book). Key thing is…

Trust yourself. Push on. Do it.

The resistance will ALWAYS be there… so will your determination to succeed… if you allow it. Leave you to ponder next time you try something new and that voice in your head starts up. Remember, it's just the age-old enemy within known as resistance.

Question is, will you let it win…

My market is way too sophisticated for this

As soon as you hear this in your head... STOP!

Be VERY careful here.

Chances are your market is NOT too sophisticated.

To explain...

The average reading age of the Australian population is that of a 12 or 13 year old. About a grade 8 level. Write to that level.

I advocate shorter sentences. Smaller paragraphs. And wherever you can, use a more common form of a word, not its sophisticated version.

Assistance Vs help.

Velocity Vs speed.

Structure Vs plan.

Are just 3 examples. The ones on the right are shorter, more in common usage, and easier to read, fast.

Sure, if you were writing an academic paper, a novel, poetry... ham it up and show your prowess.

Just don't get all complex and flowery if you want to sell stuff, ok?

A wise man once said...

S eek a quick victory.

This comes from Sun Tzu in *The Art of War*.

His reasoning being, a long protracted battle or siege depleted your resources.

Plus, it's no fun, right?

And it's one of the things I look for when working with clients...

What is the simplest path to the victory (sale)?

Is a complex multi-step funnel needed?

Or is a direct mail shock and awe pack followed by two or three step follow up funnel more effective?

Too often, wooed by the latest guru, I see business owners emulate something "cool" and I simply say, "Why?".

The pause that follows is often uncomfortable (for them).

My message to you is this... find the shortest, simplest path to the sale and pursue it with gusto.

Test. Tweak. Test again. And so on.

Only get complex as you need to (which is far less often than most think it is).

Seek a quick victory, always.

Speaking of authenticity...

B eware of too much sizzle, not enough substance... this is why some copy gets the "hypey" tag.

Joe Sugarman, who I was fortunate enough to meet in the US in 2014 is famous for saying, **"If it ain't in the product, it ain't in the copy."**

In other words, to be genuine in copy you have to have an authentic product.

Don't ask your copy to do too much... the product must be proven, the results documented, the evidence strong.

You can probably sell the proverbial "chocolate coated turd"... but when the customers breaks it open, it's still just a turd.

Trust your gut. If you feel uneasy, if YOU aren't convinced, gather more proof.

Remember... *if it ain't in the product, it ain't in the copy!*

The experts are 100% right...

... except when they are wrong... Here's what I mean...

As is often the case the nerdy school kid in me wins over and I study my craft... copy, marketing, business, spiritual development... in whatever media suits... books, webinars, newsletters and more.

I was listening to a podcast by an industry leader who preached...

Get up early, 4:30am, get X done first and then Y.

Now I can't remember what X and Y were but it sounded good, especially when they dropped the clincher...

"All the really successful people I know do this."

Message: if you don't do what I do you can't be successful.

Hmmm... got me thinking... It's not bad advice. But...

What if you don't do your best work early in the morning? What if you are better later in the day? Surely what you do with your time is more important than when?

So be careful... listen to the gurus by all means...

But also remember there are many ways to be right. Find out what works for you (I'm better early than later but know not everyone is). If you're anything like me, you'll probably take ideas from many sources and mould these into your own modus operandi.

Forget what "they" say you should do. Resist FOMO (fear of missing out) that says you must do or be at XYZ. Because, despite what "they" say, you are not being judged like an Olympic diving competition with scores out of 10.

It's just you and the **people** who you sell to...

And the results you see from your efforts. That's the only score that matters. And by the way... you'll never be perfect, you'll have your losses, your battles and struggles... only thing that matters is how you get up from them, every time.

Remember... the gurus are ALWAYS right... except when they're wrong...

Enough to leave you in despair

Hopeless. Careless. Clueless. That's how I describe recent interactions with local businesses. Certainly enough to leave me in despair. And please don't do this in your business.

Take Exhibit #1 - Sandwich board sign

Several times a week Jenny and I walk, usually early in the morning, along the pathway that follows Currimundi Lake. Beautiful. Always there are plenty of walkers, joggers, bike riders who pass us. A block back from the path we take along the esplanade is a small 6-pack shopping complex. Seems a new cafe opened up because one morning a sandwich board was placed next to the pathway advertising the cafe around the corner. Great idea, capture the said passing walkers, jogger, bike riders. Except the sign was name rank and serial number… Name of cafe and the creative tagline of "coffee and cakes". Nothing else. Not even an arrow showing where. Or "Just 20m around the corner". Or something to link the sign to the cafe around the corner which can't be seen from the path.

Remember, confused people do nothing. Do NOT expect them to join the dots, you have to do it for them. Great idea from the cafe owner but an opportunity lost because, if I'd been directed to the cafe and/or enticed with a special offer, we might have walked around the corner and spent some money… if not this time, maybe next.

Exhibit #2 - Interrupting a conversation

We went into a local shop that sells spiritual stuff like crystals, oracle cards, incense and more. Behind the counter was a lady in the midst of a conversation about her grandkids with another lady standing in an inner doorway, which led I think to where they did healing and tarot readings etc. "Hello," was the friendly greeting before she went straight back to the important weekend grandkid catch up chat. We stayed in the shop for maybe 10 minutes. Not once… not ONCE was the conversation paused to see if we wanted to spend some money there. Despair. Because we may have bought a crystal or candle or trinket of some kind… but let's not have commerce get in the way of a social chat. Sigh.

Exhibit #3 - Ignoring altogether

I was scouting for some stationary items for a "shock and awe" marketing pack and went hunting in the local office supplies store. Husband and wife operation by the looks of it because they were in a hushed conversation at the front counter when we entered. As we stepped into the shop, they both looked up. The husband turned his back and made a phone call. The wife went to her computer, eyes down busy. No greeting. Not even a "can I help you". We spent about 5 minutes there, obviously looking for SOMETHING. But any attention from the owners? Nada. Zip. Nil. Despair.

So from just two days, THREE examples of people missing out on my money because they got it wrong.

Here's the good news in all of this: if these experiences are anything to go by, the bar is VERY low. Which means opportunities abound. And don't dismiss any of this as "just corner shop" specific sloth… it happens in big business too. How can you hone your processes and cash in?

It just works

S taff... just about the #1 complaint from business owners...

The "staffing issue" is market and business size agnostic... most leaders and owners mention staffing challenges, and often. How do I know? Easy. When talking to a business owner for the first time, I'll ask them for their top 3 challenges. Almost always staffing comes up. And it can get back to recruiting. Who you attract. How you filter. How you onboard them.

Let's talk about step 1... how you attract the right sort of people. Most companies view recruitment as an admin function. I view it as a marketing function. Thus, it's VITAL you give your recruiting ads a solid dose of your copywriting wand. The ad, online or off, must "sell" the opportunity. In times of almost full employment like now, competition is fierce.

Case in point, from a conversation with a client.

They had always struggled to attract the right kind of people for their IT consultancy. Lots of IT jobs around these days. What they found, when they did what everyone else does - treat it as a simple admin task - was they got a whole lot of ordinary, beige candidates... very few of whom were suitable.

And if they did hire from the beige pool, the person never lasted. Frustrating. And it feeds the "staff!" problem cycle. So when I was working with them, one of the things I did was write a marketing-style recruitment ad.

This was DIFFERENT to a standard ad a HR person would write. Results: they got a lot of the usual applicants, but...

They got **3 high quality candidates** and picked a top shelf new team member.

Boom. All because of the marketing twist I built into the ad. And yes, the quality candidates, in their feedback, said the ad really "spoke" to them more than any other in the industry. Coolest part...

The business owner, who to be fair, was wary of "the outside marketing guy" (me) at various times in our 12-month relationship said...

"Steve's stuff just works".

Yep, good copy is good copy is good copy. In recruitment. In sales. In learning and development. When you speak to and connect with the emotions of your target audience, a yes is relatively easy.

The poor swan just wouldn't fly

As hard as he tried, he just couldn't do it. And the look on his face was one of defeat.

Sitting out the back one day having a cuppa and the family of swans that lives on our water system floated on by.

There was 2 parents and 4 cygnets. The kids could paddle along the water alright and forage for themselves but that's about it.

This one morning there was the mother and 3 cygnets in a group. The mother suddenly starts a take-off. If you've ever seen swans they run along the water, flapping their wings until they have enough momentum to get airborne.

It's noisy and messy and majestic all at once.

So this morning mum breaks from the group…

The elder cygnet follows suit running, flapping… albeit a little unco… The other two watch on ambivalent. We're cheering from the shore hoping the kid can emulate mum…

She gets airborne and flies out of sight.

The cygnet, despite mum's example and its best efforts stays water bound and gives up settling back into the water. And yeah, whilst I'm no swan expert, it had a "Oh crap that didn't work" look on its face.

Which got me thinking about progress in business and life…

No one gets everything right the first time. Or maybe the second. The baby swan, with persistence and example from parents, WILL fly.

And so will you in biz. Despite what "failure" you may be experiencing right now.

And so I just wanted to remind you - maybe you needed to hear it today - that nature has this **stretch-struggle-success** thing which none of us can avoid… not even a cute little swan.

There is always a learning curve which we just have to push through, so go easy on yourself today…

Beautiful family memories

We laughed loud and often. We laughed at ourselves. At each other. At the beautiful memories.

Around 8pm recently one of the kids started opening old files on the laptop and stumbled on old photos.

"Come and look at this," the cry went out to the house.

More laughter. And one by one we were drawn to the laptop. The pics were great. But the videos really brought it to life…

A tantrum on the beach at Hamilton Island…

Chocolate all over the highchair at Easter…

Birthday parties and random videos of kids dancing…

And we laughed to the point of tears, lost in the moment.

My favourite? A video of "the pile on"…

A game we'd play whenever the urge arrived. Someone would be lying on the lounge room floor and the call of "pile on" would go out. Kids would appear out nowhere, often led by Maddie, and jump on the person (usually me)… hilarious watching all these tiny bodies where shorts ran over nappies and down to ankles jumping on and falling off and jumping on again…

Special times now long gone. Funny how fast it's happened… with 4 under the age of 5 at one time it seemed like they'd be in nappies forever, and the hard work would never end…

Wrong. Life goes fast. But it was a special moment of connection that night. What seemed like 5 minutes in front of the computer together, because we were so lost in the moment, was actually over an hour of fun.

So as you get ready to head into your workday, might be a good time to relive some of those special memories, the most important times with the most important people in our lives, again.

Helps too I think to keep perspective, that not EVERYTHING is about business… about leads, conversions, profit. These are important, sure, but only one part of your life picture. Keep perspective. Have fun. Enjoy the small moments.

Why should I care?

This question is pretty close to #1 when critiquing headlines. And it's what I hit a client with when I saw their "**Results we swear by**" headline.

"John, why should I care about that?"

"Well…"

And then silence. He couldn't answer that question. Note: "John" is not his real name… got to protect the guilty…

But no.

Stuff like that never works. You have to put in more sweat than that to get people's attention these days. Write 20, 30, 50 or more headlines (the late great Ted Nicholas recommended at least 100).

Try different angles and ideas. And pick the top 10 or so you like and put them to the test…

WHY SHOULD I CARE?

If you can't give a CLEAR answer to this question when you read your headline, more is required if you want success. Quick example:

"6 Simple Tips for Shopping That Will Save You Up to a Third of Your Grocery Bill Every Week"

Why should I care? Simple: I'm going to save money on food every week. Makes you want to read on, right? At least more than "John" and his "Results we swear by" style no one will stop and read.

Remember…

Why should I care… why should I care… why should I care…

And apply it to every headline you write.

Boozy Russian leader's marketing lesson

C an a bloke known to be heavy on the old sauce bottle really offer you a marketing lesson? Yes. If his name is Boris Yeltsin.

Here's a quick story from history for context:

Yeltsin was president of the Russian Federation, the first post-Soviet iteration of modern Russia. He had his challenges for sure. And depending on who you listen to he has been portrayed as anything from a hero to a drunkard. Google "Boris Yeltsin dancing" and there's a rich tapestry of material to support such claims.

Anyways, the story goes one day in the 90s old Boris faced a moment of crisis…

The country was on the brink of a military coup as old guard hardliners rebelled against the horrors of democracy style reforms the people and Yeltsin wanted. The military, complete with tanks and battle gear, arrived to arrest Boris.

What did he do? Apparently he strode out to the lead tank, climbed aboard and knocked on the hatch. When the tank commander opened it, he was met with a warm handshake with the words (my paraphrase), *Thankyou you so much for coming, the people really need you in this hour.*

Crisis and coup over.

When asked later why the sudden change of heart, the tank commander replied with one word: CONFIDENCE. Boozy Boris showed up so calm and confident in that moment of crisis the tank commander was "sold" and would go on to say (again my paraphrase) it was Yeltsin's confidence that won him over to the point it felt like he was on the side of "right".

And the rest, as they say (including those boozy YouTube clips!!!), is history. THE biz lesson from Boris… How you show up at the point of sale is VITAL to your results.

I'm not talking here about bravado or tired used car salesman tactics… I'm talking about real confidence in the RESULT you get for clients. If it's missing or false or weak… prospects will sniff it out in a heartbeat and its game over.

So yeah learn from Boris… confidence, real confidence in you and what you do matters to your sales results.

And confidence comes from runs on the board.

Criticism and what to do

I s there anything in life worse than being exposed, publicly? The criticism. The ridicule. "Them" laughing at you. Of course, today on social media it's all too raw and visible. And people are merciless.

I can remember as a kid, one of the mantras of a civil society was, "Keep your opinions to yourself".

Now? Well, unless you're out there, outing people, screaming for change, seems like you're some kind of wuss.

As a writer, I'm vulnerable every day. First, to the client… will they "like" my work. And then more importantly to results… will the market "like" my work and buy.

When you fail, and fail you will, it hurts. And don't believe the snapshots of success social media gives you. So few share their failures. Like I said, being a writer and being in business leaves you VERY exposed. You're open to criticism with nowhere to hide. All of which can ruin your day if you let it.

So this message is for you if ever you've failed at something and then had the courage to get back up and keep going. One of my all-time favourite quotes is Einstein's:

"A person who has never made a mistake never tried anything new."

What about you? Fingers crossed you've made plenty of mistakes because it means you're trying new things and moving forward.

Everyone Needs a Cuddle...

S o give them one.

This copywriting "click" works in most sales situations. Whatever the problem your product or service solves, it's not the fault of the customer.

Let them off the hook by telling them 2 things...

"It's not your fault"

And

"You deserve" to have the problem solved.

This bonds you to them, lets them know you are on their side and paves the way for a smooth purchase.

Different markets dictate how you do this. In mass consumer markets like weight loss the tone of this is very different to B2B or C suite marketing.

That said, the principle remains the same... where appropriate, give them a copy cuddle.

One heck of a headline

C heck this out…

From the *Betoota Advocate* (far western Qld online newspaper - where else?) came this gem of a headline…

"FIFO Worker Accidentally Roots His Own Wife During Week Off"

C'mon, there's NO WAY you aren't going to read that story!!!

The article explains how a FIFO worker books an online escort only to find it's his wife, who, unbeknown to him is working as a "professional".

And they well, let's say, "hook up".

Anyways, that's their business.

But the headline… wow!!

Whilst media outlets like the *Betoota Advocate* are more fun than serious marketing, a good headline is still a good headline… and why it works can be transferred to other media and markets (maybe not the exact words… but the reason why something works).

Note: this one also falls within the 8-12 word sweet spot for headline length.

The anti-hustle

In these pages I've riffed on about my loathing of the buzzword "hustle".

All the social media gurus telling you to get out there and hustle. Push. Rush. Crush it. Kind of rubs me up the wrong way, just a little. Don't get me wrong…

Not suggesting laziness or ill-discipline or "whatever" are good plans. To me it's more about knowing yourself and your productive times and how you work best.

And…

That sometimes it's ok NOT to hustle. Sorry gurus.

Anyways, came across this nice little anti-hustle memo to self and just wanted to share. It's from Lori Deschene, creator of tinybuddha.com and it goes thus…

You don't always need

to be getting things done.

Sometimes it's perfectly

okay, and absolutely

necessary, to shut down,

kick back, and do nothing.

Amen to that! Especially in our "always on" world. Yep, it IS okay.

On a workday however? I WILL be focused and productive. But I will switch off at some stage and do nothing.

And just be… me… a husband and a dad…

What do you think?

Missing piece

Persuasion is a multi-faceted, multi-dimensional beast. Like an aeroplane, one thing doesn't make it fly. Would love it to be not so but that's not reality.

So listen up because one piece of the sales conversation I see missing often is this…

And look, it's NOT new, but it IS missed with regularity.

Also, it doesn't matter which formula you use… AIDA, PASPA etc…

Just make sure you make the reader/listener aware of…

Drum roll please…

The cost or pain of inaction.

It's big and like I said, often missed.

If you want to continue to lose sales, by all means gloss over this reminder…

Is an example (go back and read it).

Sure, we agitate the problem. Tell them how they get relief. Call them to action.

But what happens if they don't act?

Which is why you need to bring to their attention the cost or pain of inaction… nope, that problem won't go away by itself.

They need to feel it (*If you want to go on missing sales, by all means gloss over this reminder*).

So yeah, make sure they feel the pain of not acting on the solution you provide, it's a game changer.

Everybody has a plan until...

I t's one of my favourite quotes.

And it comes from Mike Tyson of all people, the erstwhile undisputed heavyweight boxing champion of the world who terrorised the sport in the 80s and 90s.

And it's so true in business, he's quoted thus...

"Everybody has a plan until they get punched in the face."

A business punch in the face is anything that throws you out of whack and challenges you.

A new cashed-up competitor.

A change in government regulation.

A sudden dip in the economy.

And on it goes.

There are punches aplenty out there in the business world.

Which makes having a consistent, reliable, predictable marketing system vital to your success and longevity.

You don't want to wait till you're thirsty before you start to dig the well.

Me bets you don't do this enough

Y ou have habits… Some good. Some not so good. Me too. But I'm betting you don't do enough of this critical business success habit. Quick backstory:

Was chatting to a client and he mentioned how busy he was, how rushed, how he never seemed to have time for anything. My advice: You need to make "thinking time" a habit. As expected, I got the usual, self-defeating "you don't understand my business is different" BS. And it is BS with a capital B. Am sure you've never engaged in this (me neither)… um… ok let's move on, nothing uncomfortable to see here folks…

So… When was the last time you took time out to think as part of your WORK? I'm talking about… blank sheet of paper… coffee and pen in hand… and just sat and let ideas comes to you. Or… Cold beer/glass of wine and pen and just chilled. Or… Went for a walk with no intention other than just clearing your head. Bet it's been a while?

Unsolicited advice: take time out to think. I constantly remind myself to do same. You see I'm an avid reader of biographies. One of my favourites is *About Face* the story of the late US soldier David Hackworth's extraordinary life… long story short, one of his mentors was a guy named Colonel Glover Johns who developed a certain leadership style he boiled down to 15 principles, you'll find below… #2 giving me and you the time to think advice. Here they are:

1. Strive to do small things well
2. Be a doer and a self-starter – aggressiveness and initiative are the two most admired qualities in a leader – but you also must put your feet up and THINK
3. Strive for self-improvement through constant self-evaluation
4. Never be satisfied. Ask of any project, *How can it be done better?*
5. Don't over-inspect or over-supervise. Allow your leaders to make mistakes in training so they can profit from errors and not make them in combat
6. Keep the troops informed; telling them "what, how and why" builds their confidence
7. The harder the training the more troops will brag
8. Enthusiasm, fairness and moral and physical courage – four of the most important aspects of leadership
9. Showmanship – a vital technique of leadership
10. The ability to speak and write well – two essential tools of leadership
11. There is a salient difference between profanity and obscenity; while a leader employs profanity (tempered with discretion) he never uses obscenities
12. Have consideration for others
13. Yelling detracts from your dignity; take men aside to counsel them
14. Understand and use judgement; know when to stop fighting for something you believe is right. Discuss and argue your point of view until a decision is made and then support the decision whole-heartedly
15. Stay ahead of your boss

Could do worse than adapt a few of these, right? Go ahead… take time out to THINK…

Leverage off your competitors

It's always a good idea to keep an eye on your competitors.

See what they are doing.

Because you never know when it will spark a marketing opportunity.

Exhibit A below illustrates my point, and hopefully get you thinking about "how" you can apply it to your business.

Exhibit A:

When Pizza Hut was a thing, they did this promo to give away 10 FREE margherita pizzas to the first 10 customers in each store across the country.

About 10,000 pizzas in total.

Why?

It was in response to rival Dominoes ditching the pizza from its menu.

You don't have it anymore, we do... come and get it for FREE from us.

A large percentage would also have bought something else when in store.

Nice one Pizza Hut, stick that one up your jumper, Dominoes.

How can you leverage what your competitor is doing and flip it into a marketing opportunity for your business?

Have your radar up to what they're doing. Helps if you take time out to put your feet up and THINK.

Drink beer for health

I t's true, drinking beer can make you healthy.

I have data to back this up so it must be true.

Behold...

- a study in the Netherlands found people who drink up to 10 beers a week have a reduced risk of type 2 diabetes
- according to US research you're 41% less likely to develop kidney stones if you sip beer and not sugary soft drinks
- regular intake of dark beers reduces the risk of cataracts by as much as 50% says the American Chemical Society

Buuurp... and cheers...

KEY POINT: no matter what you're selling, you can find data to support your sales argument, if you...

#1 - have your radar up (like I've been banging on about for years and in these pages – this beer info came from the Sunday papers)

#2 - you take the time to dig a little

So make sure you research the heck out of your product, the market it's in, and the people buying it. Numbers don't lie. People believe "research studies". And when you combine proven facts to the right emotions your results skyrocket.

Avoid this danger

O n a bright sunny day, a door-to-door salesman walked up to the front of the house. A young boy was sitting on the front steps. A dog was near his feet on the grass.

"Is it ok if I pat the dog?" the salesman asks to break the ice.

"Sure," says the boy.

As he reaches down to pat the dog, it lashes out and bites him.

"Hey, I thought you said I could pat your dog!" the salesman rages.

"Not my dog," the boy replies.

And so it is in business… assumptions are VERY dangerous things. They can cost you time, money, and a whole lot of mental hurt. Case in point…

I hadn't heard back from a prospect for a couple of weeks.

Well, that deal's over… I thought. Reasonable assumption given that the longer a deal takes to get across the line, the greater the chance of it falling over. We "know" this instinctively. Reasonable… but also wrong…

Notice that sentence contained the word "assumption". Turns out the client had a death in the family which naturally threw everything into a spin.

In delay situations like this, it's easy to get a little indignant (*"I haven't heard from you, I have other clients waiting"*) or pushy (*"this is your last chance to move forward"*). But such responses are based on WRONG ASSUMPTIONS and would have killed the deal there and then.

Be alert in every business situation… are you basing your thoughts and next steps on known facts… or on assumptions which may or may not be true? You may need to dig a little before you take that next step… could save you a whole lot of time, money, and angst.

This little sales device...

Do you miss this important little sales technique? If so, it could be costing you conversions and income. What is it? The humble PS or "post scriptum"... the bit of copy that goes on the end of a sales letter.

I use it just about all the time (see the end for circumstances when I don't). Now there is a feeling out there in some quarters that this is old fashioned or too "salesy". No. When you understand HOW people read you see its importance...

You, me and everyone else does this: we look at the headline, if it interests us, we then generally scroll/flick to the end before we decide if we will devote any more of our precious time to it. Follows then that the headline and the SECOND thing they see should be where a lot of energy and thought must go. Don't fall into the trap of just chucking any old thing in the PS because you're tired of writing at the end of the sales message.

Always come from the mindset of... if they just read the headline and the PS will they buy? Yes, it's that important.

Here are some PS tips, it can...

- Be a summary/reminder of the offer
- Emphasise the most important benefit
- Re-state the guarantee or special bonus

ALSO... most of the time multiple PS's outperform a single PS. Length is dependent on factors like media. I've seen PS's of a sentence and even up to 2 and a half pages long!

ALSO ALSO... to make the PS stand out, you can vary the font in both style and size, use all capitals (if it's short), use a different colour or even put the PS's in a Johnson Box with a lightly shaded background. Often, I just use same font and size as rest of the copy.

One PS formula (try this but remember it's not "the only" formula)...

PS #1 = reiterate the headline

PS #2 = reminder of the deal they get

PS #3 = re-state the risk reversal process so it's "safe" for them

When don't I use a PS... Hardly ever but may consider it if it's a single page letter and there's absolutely no room – although I almost always include: "PS See over for what recent clients say" (and on the back of the letter insert testimonials); also sometimes in a short "connector" or "teaser" type email and there's no action I want you to take I'd leave it out... otherwise it's a PS!

There you go... next sales message you craft, include at least one PS... and watch for the bump in your response.

Ignore them at your peril

It's one of the most ignored income generating strategies I remind clients about... reactivation of "lost" customers.

Here's an interesting little tidbit and reminder...

Sitting in my inbox one day was a message from a long past client asking me about my availability for a project.

Part of his message read...

It would be great to have you work again with me on this...I think you have worked on every business I have owned in the last 10 years!

Pretty cool, right? And nice feather in my cap. But it also got me thinking...

Do I contact (or reactivate) past customers enough?

Sure, they get my emails... but do the loyal and long termers who write such nice things get enough "love" in return?

Plus...

Do I value enough the lifetime value of clients?

Hmmmm...

Of course I ask myself these questions out loud in the hope you too will ask yourself similar...

Will leave it there and let you ponder today some more...

About how you can mine deeper into your list to help more people and profit more.

Beef jerky

Zero was my intention to buy a packet of beef jerky when I went shopping this one time. But I forked out $9:00 for a gourmet packet at my local butcher. I'm a fan of beef jerky. So are my boys. It never lasts long. But $9?

And I admit, I've never paid $9 for beef jerky, ever.

What lowered my resistance? What overcame no desire to buy?

One thing…

Product in action.

They had free samples on the counter at eye level with a big sign.

So I sampled.

I liked.

And I bought.

No, this is NOT new.

But it may be a timely reminder… how can you give a free sample and/or show your product in action so prospects, even completely disinterested ones like I was about beef jerky, part with way more than they ever have in the past?

My 9 recent favourite subject lines

T his is good for generating ideas and an example of a swipe file… where you leverage off others' ideas to create your own. Not copy. But use as inspiration. Example:

Mel Martin's famous…

"What never ever to eat on an airplane" could be used as inspiration in the finances niche…

"What never, ever to invest in if you have a mortgage"

Or Health and beauty…

"What never ever to put on your lips"

You get the idea.

I'm on lots of people's email lists and I keep a swipe file of subject lines which compelled me to open them. Here are 9 of my favs from recent times…

1. **When you feel a tingle in your balls, you're about to get kicked in the nuts** (by Ben Settle… no explanation needed – and yes, Ben is "out there"!!!)
2. **How To 5X Your Referrals In 7 Days (Guaranteed)** (by past student Drew Slater – love the specificity of the numbers because they create curiosity)
3. **Didi Mau!** (by Perry Marshall – side note: my first job was mowing lawns at an old people's home which was run by a Vietnam veteran who told me the first thing he learnt in-country was "didi mau" which he translated to "p*ss off"… as in "You got one dollar mista?". "No! Didi mau!". Apparently, it also translates to "go quickly"… either way this got my attention due to the story, but it was Perry's different way of saying hurry!).
4. **Gary Bencivenga's "lost" copywriting formula** (by Bob Bly… any line with GB name in it gets a copywriting nerd all flushed and bothered)
5. **General Eisenhower's Final Warning** (by Early to Rise… I'm a history buff so there was lots of curiosity here)
6. **The moose on the table…** (by Brian Kurtz… curiosity there big time)
7. **The numbers Australia won't want to see** (by Fox sports news… this leverages off the "secrets" click and came after Aussie batsmen folded like a road map in the 2nd innings against Sri Lanka's spinners)
8. *Nudity, Chains & Beating Procrastination…* (by Pete Williams… maybe it's a guy thing but anything with "nudity" is worth even a quick peek, right?)
9. **This one sentence melted our inbox** (by Dale Beaumont – again high curiosity factor)

Note to self #1 – keep a swipe file

Note to self #2 – understand the high curiosity thread above

Note to self #3 – how can you use these for inspiration?

Coolest guy in the world's business secret

I once wrote that I don't watch much TV. And it's true. Outside of sport (ok and the odd trashy dating "reality" show and Seinfeld reruns), I'm a bandit for documentaries on the History Channel.

Love the ones about famous people because they offer a roadmap for success. At the very least, there's always something you can pick up.

A recent favourite was on the greatest showman of all time...

Evel Knievel.

Remember him... the flashy motorbike rider who used to jump cars, buses and even the Grand Canyon?

So successful was he, he earned huge sums of money and was said to be more recognizable than the US president. A true showman, he promoted himself tirelessly and was a regular guest on the likes of The Johnny Carson Show. He knew what he wanted and pursued it until he made it happen.

Key point: for all his success he was a serial "failure".

Many of his jumps ended in serious crashes. His list of broken bones is long, and he spent his later years limping around on a cane.

But he kept going.

As an aside, the documentary claimed he wasn't a great role model (was a serial cheater who boasted he could have any woman he wanted and was renowned for treating people such as journo's who gave him bad press, mercilessly).

His biggest moment? His brash proclamation he was going to jump the Grand Canyon... even when he had NO IDEA of how it would happen.

A couple of years later in a rocket propelled "bike" and an audience in the millions he took off only to make it halfway across before a mechanical failure saw him and his parachute splash into the Colorado River.

Yep he knew what he wanted and made it happen and was NEVER deterred by his failures...

You'll have failures in marketing and business, key thing is, as the great Evel showed... don't be deterred, push on.

Boost readability of your copy

Your word processing software has readability data levels built in, it just has to be turned on.

As a general rule we want our copy aimed at the level a Yr 8 student can read (note there are some successful copywriters who disagree with this, arguing they deliberately write at a higher level to attract a more sophisticated buyer, and repel a "less" quality buyer).

Me? I aim for the Yr 8 level or less because it more closely aligns with the general reading age of the Australian population. To do this I rely on the FK score and readability statistics. These act as a "check" for my writing.

Microsoft Word has "readability" included. Now it depends on which version of Word you have but to make sure it is turned on all you do is open a new doc and…

Select Options from the toolbar.

Click the "Proofing" tab.

In the "Correcting spelling and grammar section" click "Show Readability Statistics".

Once this function is turned on, Word will do a "readability check" whenever you do a Review (Check Document).

FK stands for "Flesch-Kincaid Reading Level." Using the size of the words, length of sentences and "chunkiness" of the paragraphs (a technical term, lol) it calculates "reading grade level" of your document.

For example: 5.3 = low 5th grade level, 6.8 = high 6th grade level.

Like I said, I recommend you keep your FK score at 8.5 or lower.

The other number that's important is "Flesch Reading Ease" which refers, as the name suggests, to how easy the document is to read.

You want this number to be 60 or higher.

This helps to take the guess work out of the copy for you.

Just remember… no number should ever trump emotion and connection in your copy.

I use this as a guide only and it's one of the last tools I use in the critiquing process.

No one is that good

S o, you're on a few email lists, hey? Me too. And…

You have been bombarded of late by the next shiny object program, training or system that promises fast clients and cash, hey? Me too. And…

You've probably not watched every pitch, maybe even deleted some or unsubscribed from a few, hey?

Me too. And…

If you're anything like me, there are times when it's hard to swallow all the big promises. Wouldn't you agree? Which is why this one was refreshing…

I listened to one particular pitch online and the presenter told of the success they'd helped certain people create. Nothing new there, and a necessary part of the sales script. But here's where it was a little different. Amongst all the promises there was this nice little line, tempering the big claims.

"We've helped lots of people create extraordinary results, but it has taken work AND you can expect your fair share of misses and disappointments. You won't make $18,938.00 with every campaign, like Paul. No one is that good."

From the whole pitch I wrote that one line down for my swipe file and will deploy it strategically in the future.

No one is that good.

Nice.

And it's also instructive to your business and sales this week. You will have your winners. You'll have your losses. No one is that good to win every time. No, this is not a license to be sloppy or lazy or expect it all to just happen. You have to be excellent at what you do. But also gentle on yourself if you don't quite smash it out of the park every time.

No one is that good.

Remember this as you create a productive and successful day.

Push or ease off?

"It's like landing a jumbo jet... gently, gently, gently... ease her in... no dramas".

So said one of my school principals way back in my previous life as a teacher, as the end of year loomed.

Solid advice in steamy December when dealing with tired kids and exhausted staff at the end of a long year.

But does the land her softly, cruise to the line with few waves and disruptions work in business?

In my humble opinion, no.

What you do in November and December can help you start the next year the RIGHT way, on the front foot, ready to create new success.

From scratch in early January is hard.

Picking things up from November/December efforts where meetings were booked for January, new clients were landed ready to be on boarded is a MUCH better way to end your year.

Many have this soft landing philosophy. For consulting/coaching I've found November/ early December a productive time to win new business.

I say go hard. The New Year will thank you for it.

B2B Vs B2C, what's the difference?

Here's the DEFINITIVE answer to the age-old question... Is writing for the Business to Business market different to writing for the Business to Consumer market?

Answer in a sec... quick back story...

I get asked this semi-often. You may be aware I consulted to an ASX listed top 200 company for more than 18 months and have written winning promotions for just about every B2C business large and small, start-up to mature over the past decade. So yeah, I'm well placed to answer this one.

And here is THE answer... Is writing for the B2B market different to writing for the B2C market?

Yes and no. What the?

Settle down my padawan, to explain...

There are nuances to both markets which you have to be fully aware of. If not, it's curtains. That's where the "no" part of the answer comes in. They are not the same, you have to know both intimately.

Where they are similar - the "yes" part of the answer - is that you can't get away from the fact that a human set of eyeballs, complete with human emotions, sees the message and STILL makes the buying decision.

And this is where many fall down in B2B marketing. They focus almost solely on slogan, product and price and miss the fact that even CEOs make decisions on emotions. Sure, the emotions at play are (mostly) different to consumer emotions. And the language you use to poke the emotions is different to the consumer market... and B2B decisions are often made by a board or committee... but any decision is an emotional one... you have to find what that is for B2B.

That is the challenge and where many direct response marketers come up short, they come across as too "hypey".

KEY POINT: know your market and talk to them in THEIR language, understanding HOW they buy.

Best movie line

Cast your mind back to the 80s... Taffeta, high hair, Rick Astley... And some great movies. One of my favourites was *Rocky III*. I just loved this line from Clubber Lang (aka Mr T) at the press conference before his fight with world champion Rocky Balboa...

Reporter: "Clubber, what's your prediction for the fight?"

Slight pause and mean as hell stare down the camera...

Clubber: "Painnnnn"

And the rest of course is movie history. Clubber destroys hero Rocky in 2 rounds. Trainer Micky dies (which was almost as heart-wrenching as Goose dying in *Top Gun* I reckon). And so sets up the redemption story.

What's this got to do with you and your business? Glad you asked. And I'll answer it with a question...

Why did Rocky, with 10 title defences under his belt and on top of the world, get smashed by Clubber Lang?

Simple answer...

He flatlined. He lost the edge. He put the work in, sure, but his heart wasn't really in it. And the result showed in the ring. Ever had that feeling in your business? A bit flat. A bit dull. A bit numb...

Happens to all of us at some stage. Has me even asking you that question, right now, caused a little unsettling in your tummy?

Hmmm... If yes, perhaps it's time to branch out and do something new and different to get the juices flowing again, before you meet your own version of "Clubber Lang" and feel the *paaiiinnn*...

What can you do to get the passion flowing again?

Make it crystal clear... here's one way

I f your offer is complex, NEVER assume the reader will "get" it.

If you do assume they understand all they get for the money they invest, you run the risk of confusing them. And as we've seen a confused buyer does nothing.

Here's the solution...

Say your offer contains the main product XYZ. But it also has other components, ABC and DEF.

Then to make the offer irresistible you add Bonuses 1, 2 and 3.

This is a lot to take in and do that little calculation in our heads we all do... If I pay $X, I'll get Y and its good value, yes.

So you need to make it as simple as possible or doubt may creep in.

To remove the confusion, one of the best ways to do it is to summarise your offer in a table. It's also a great tool for the skim readers... their eyes will focus on the table, so they get the sales message fast.

A summary table usually has 3 columns:

Product Component – The Individual Value – What You Pay (for it in this offer).

Then you total the value. Show what they pay (which is less than the total value because it's a strong offer).

This makes it quick and easy for the reader.

Take the attitude, if this is all they see, there needs to be enough information in the table for them to make a buying decision.

How to prime your sales pump

Ever had one of those moments where you just couldn't be bothered? Where you felt *aaargh… marketing is "hard" or takes too much time?*

No arguments there. We all get like that at times.

An 800 to 1,000 word blog takes a chunk of your day to write. An email to your list requires thought and effort. An ad campaign even more work. A social media post that's different causes you to think. And on it goes. But…

If you think marketing is hard, try running a business without customers.

Here's a little short cut, or as they say these days, a "hack"…

Every day **DO AT LEAST ONE THING** to generate sales. Make that at least every working day. Just do one thing. It's how you create deal flow. What do I mean by this?

Here's a typical example from my week…

Monday: send email to my list with a special offer

Tuesday: contact a prospect to arrange a meeting (for the next day at 10am); send offer reminder email.

Wednesday: client meeting to extend the deal for another 4 months; email my list.

Thursday: email my list; do podcast interview and post on socials.

Friday: email my list; followed up with two prospects and responded to a referral.

Every day… do at least ONE thing that has a DELIBERATE sales focus to create that deal flow. Even if it's only one thing, it's way better than nothing. And it's amazing what happens when momentum builds… pebbles turn to rocks which turn to boulders which build mountains.

What's your one ACTION today to prime the sales pump?

It's hard, for everybody...

The #1 fear for just about EVERYONE is... Drum roll please... You ready for it? My biggest fear... your biggest fear... their biggest fear is...

Failure which makes us look bad. I mentioned it already in these pages that no one wants the "embarrassment" or "shame" of public ridicule. I well remember the first time I stood in front of a class... stepped foot on stage... sent my first email...

"That" feeling in the gut.

What stops talented people from breaking free of a job they no longer love and doing something different? Probably the fear of it not working out... of failure... of looking silly.

Evidence:

- Spoke recently to a top coach who's worked with elite tennis players (ie world top 10, names you'd know)... their biggest issues were self-worth and fear of losing... yes, elite people
- Apparently John Lennon, after he left the Beatles, the first live gig he ever did was preceded by him throwing up before going on stage
- And the great Johnny Carson was said to be a nervous wreck backstage before the music started, every show

We all have insecurities around failure. What's the difference then between successful people... like Carson, Lennon, the tennis players...

And those who settle for safety? Answer: the successful ones, despite "that" feeling do it anyways. Yes, life and business it seems, is hard for everyone. But if you want success...

Suggest you grit your teeth and do it any way. You might be surprised how well you go!

The MW + PW Headline formula

H ere's a powerful headline formula.

It's my go to, at least as a starting point.

Ready? Ok, here it is…

MW + PW

MW = Magic Words (those special words only your market responds to, think "boobies")

PW = Power Words (the list of proven successful words eg new, amazing, secret and more)

When you combine these into a headline, you give yourself every chance of success.

Example from one of the online trainings I ran:

Unlock the Genius of Great Sales Language in Your Business

7 Little known ways to present price so you close more deals and boost profits

Magic words here (only appeal to the market ie business owners): price, sales, close, business, profits

Power words here (proven to work): Unlock, little known, boost, you

Next time you're stuck, have a crack at MW + PW… you'll surprise yourself what you come up with!

Personal touch

How often have you sent a handwritten personal thank you note to a customer or even a staff member? Reason I ask is to remind you of the power of the personal touch. Case in point...

We do a bit of online shopping (by "we" I really mean "Jenny" because apart from books/training resources, I don't). For "us" there is a fairly steady flow of goods via delivery. Some good. Some returned to sender.

This one caught my eye because with the package was a small postcard.

Side A = Thanks

Side B = "eBay Your order made my day. I hope this package makes yours!" Standard card they shove in with the order. Nothing new.

Plus... and here's where it differs...

There was a handwritten note that said...

Thank You!

Your business is greatly appreciated!

signed with name of the biz.

Small. Simple. Easy to do. But it made an impact. Someone had taken the time to do this, in real pen.

Result?

Happy buyer because the personal touch is "felt".

Do you send enough handwritten, personal touch notes?

Little nudge for me and you, it's something we could all do better I believe.

It worked!

S o came the excited email from client, Mary. We've been working together to grow her writing business. She'd tested a couple of strategies we'd devised and had success.

Cool, right?

And this from Darren, a recent client in the IT consulting space...

"I just wanted to say thanks. I'm not a marketing/salesperson at all... we now better understand and position ourselves for current and future clients... the overwhelming feeling after working with you is one of satisfaction."

Cool again. The point? Not swagger... but an important illustration of the psychology of your market which so many in business miss...

The herd mentality.

For example, the first line on the first page in Mark Joyner's 2008 classic, *Mind Control Marketing* reads thus:

"Humans, like cattle, tend to move in herds. In action and opinions, Homo sapiens are natural followers. We like to act and think in groups."

Which makes social proof VITAL for ALL marketing you do.

Mr Joyner on page 3 takes it further...

"Aggressively compile information about your herd and display this information for all to see."

Testimonials, case studies, success stories, awards won are all examples of playing to the fears (*Will I be the only one to use these people?*) of the herd.

If you understand this psychology and ease their pain of being alone and exposed, you're one step closer to the sale.

Copywriting Click – Future pacing

This is where you cast them into the future to show the RESULT they will get. What you do is paint a word picture about what life will be like with your product or service.

This is powerful because it helps you sell why they should buy your product or service. And this is what your market wants… the RESULT… not the thing.

When you get to #366 of this book you will be armed with all the tools for deploying great sales language in any situation. This means more confidence, more clarity, more sales, and greater influence. Who doesn't want that!

Is an example of future pacing.

Wrong answer to the right question

S hocking but true…

I still get the "everyone really" answer to one of the first questions I ask a prospective client…

Who's your market?

"Everyone really" is NOT the right answer.

Here is one quick example why… what A list copywriter Dan Ferrari calls "generational energy".

You see your target audience demographics are vital to understand.

Baby Boomers for example are not so much looking for a transformational experience, more comfort/enjoy what they've worked for.

Not much point selling them something that requires work.

Gen Y on the other hand?

They are in the phase of life where they are searching for identity and are prepared to get their hands dirty to achieve it.

So know who you are selling to and leverage off the energy specific to that group.

Can save you lots of failed tests and angst.

Food for thought for today.

Take away the sale

As I've already said, copy is not written like a story... start at the beginning with the headline and write all the way down to the PS. You don't "write" copy... you "assemble" it, from parts written over time.

Working this way is much faster.

Plus, you also get to insert the persuasive devices or "clicks on the copywriting dial" strategically.

Every good writer has 20+ of these they weave into their sales message. When planning your writing, you factor these in (ie you "assemble" your sales argument).

Here is the "take away selling" click.

Good copy forces people to make a decision about themselves.

The technique of takeaway selling works because it positions your product or service by telling the prospect who it's NOT for. The power of this is twofold: we all want what we can't have... plus, it is an interesting psychological device.

You say who the solution is for.

You generally start with the positive types of people your market wants to be.

Then you take away the solution by telling who it's not for. It's not for this type of person, that type of person. Take fitness for example... you'd use words like this program is not for the unmotivated, the time poor, the excuse maker and so on.

Get the idea?

What happens is... and this is cool... no one wants to be the "loser" of their market, the type of person you just listed who it's not for.

So they silently place themselves on the "yes" list which psychologically moves them closer to the sale.

This is a VERY powerful persuasion tool because, like I said, it forces people to make a decision about themselves.

A love letter to your genius

*H*ello there dear genius,

How are you today? I've been neglecting you for some time, so thought I'd swing on by and say hi and that I appreciate you. Thanks for being there, always.

Have a great day.

No, I haven't lost my marbles. What I can say however, because I'm human, is that it's easy to lose perspective.

Here's what I mean…

Recently an email I'd sent to a client came back to me within about 6 minutes of hitting send. It read…

"You're a genius! Thanks, that looks great."

What was so mind-blowing? A short bio for a website. I'd waved my magic wand over some copy for a client's "About us" page featuring their staff, sent it to the staff member to check for accuracy, and so came back the "you're a genius" response. Nice and all. But it did get me thinking…

The short piece of copy took very little effort from me. It was easy.

For the client? Being in the IT niche, the weaving of words is not their sweet spot. So yeah, it was some kind of "genius" from their perspective.

And here's the thing…

It was a good reminder, because if something is "easy" for you, it doesn't mean it's easy for everyone… AND… it also doesn't mean it's not highly valuable in the marketplace.

Plus, "ease" can be quickly dismissed and that's a mistake.

So keep perspective. Nurture your talents. Work on your genius.

No one else does it the way you do.

It's the offer, stupid!

B ack in 1992 the first George Bush was considered unbeatable in the upcoming US presidential election against then-Arkansas Governor, Bill Clinton.

You see Bush had successfully prosecuted the first Gulf War and was miles ahead in the polls. Clinton's campaign strategist, James Carville, a smooth operator, saw a weak link in the Bush armour. Carville knew he couldn't beat Bush on foreign policy (Bush had a 90% approval rating at the end of the war in 1991) so he found a soft spot... the economy.

He coined the phrase, "It's the economy, stupid". Sharp, simple, to the point. And it really hit home by implying that Bush hadn't adequately addressed the economy (which was in recession) and the rest, as the saying goes, is history. Clinton ran on economics and went on to win.

The phrase has been used ever since whenever someone wanted to instantly cut through the clutter and focus on an important issue.

It's the deficit, stupid... It's the corporation, stupid... It's the voters, stupid... are examples.

And what about marketing?

It's the offer, stupid!

Legendary Gary Halbert said it was by far the most important part of a sales message. That's right, success or failure of any promotion can get down to the offer.

Here's a checklist for every offer you write...

⇨ Does the offer appeal to the market's pain and offer "easy" relief?

⇨ Is the offer easy to understand?

⇨ Is the price right for the market?

⇨ Is there a "yes or yes" option?

⇨ Is there a money back guarantee?

⇨ Is the call to action clear – they know what they have to do?

⇨ Are multiple means of contact used and are they easy to find?

Use this checklist for your next offer.

They got this wrong

H ere is THE formula for an effective marketing campaign…

Relevant + Entertaining = Effective

So said a report I read recently by a B2B agency.

Ummm… kind of.

You see I get concerned when I see words like "entertaining" or "creative". The big ad agencies love to be creative and win awards. In some instances, these can be very effective.

Other times?

Well, saw this one recently in the tech space with a headline that went something along the lines of "pigs might fly" with an entertaining pic of a flying pig… the message being, great service in the market is non-existent (pigs might fly) unless you come to us.

So it was entertaining and relevant. But, if my insider info is correct, it flopped.

What's a better formula then?

For mine…

Success = strategy x execution.

You can have the best most relevant and entertaining content but if the strategy behind it is wrong? It bombs. Same with execution… if it's not executed with precision… it bombs.

Just remember, planning and thought before action (using the second formula I told you about today) tips the scales in your favour.

The REAL reason why you must do more of this

Beware of tired old sayings and beliefs you just take for granted. Remember I told you collecting testimonials is good to provide proof in sales, but also important for YOU for those times when you're feeling a little down?

How you FEEL about you what you do is important to monitor because as I've said, business gets tough at times and this can affect, at least subconsciously, how you "show up" when it comes time to sell.

To quote on of my favourite deep thinkers about business and life in general (and the writer of the Foreword of this book), Simon Bowen:

"Customers can't buy at a level of confidence higher than your own".

Read that again. At least twice more. Testimonials, how you've changed other's lives, are important for you and your confidence.

Case in point, from Martin, one of my clients in the corporate space who sent this to me:

"Steve becomes your ally, a neutral sounding board, primary strategist, crap filter and ideas amplifier. Your staff and teams that work with Steve will become empowered, motivated and energised with new tools, approaches and psychologies to take on new markets, optimise existing customer bases, launch new products and services, solve the insoluble and resolve that intractable blockage that you have been losing sleep over for way too long. With Steve on-board you will create, plan and move mountains in ways and by means previously unimagined."

Next time I go to sell into the corporate space, I'll take this out and read it. Several times. And thanks Martin, was a pleasure working with you and the team.

So yeah, testimonials are important social proof elements… plus they have REAL value in the confidence they give you. Time to collect more for your business?

Why this dud headline works

There's a phrase in this headline I think is a complete mismatch for the market. But it's a great example of two things…

#1 - never let your own opinions cloud your judgement

#2 - radar up for things that are working

So here is the headline…

"Pensioners go crazy for free hearing aid."

The call to action was phone a 1800 number or go to their website. The ad appeared in News Limited papers for several months, usually at the bottom of page 3.

Anyways to the ad…

Number #2 first. Radar up. This is about the fourth version of this ad I'd seen over a 12 month period but, this "go crazy" angle has run the longest. So it works. Which leads me to #1…

I really don't like the "go crazy" language, I think it's a mismatch for the pensioner market, not sure it's language they would use.

But…

According to the longevity of the ad, it works. And why it works is the social proof element of the headline… if "everyone" is doing it, it must be good, right? Which is why this is a winner. Oh and it was "free".

Social proof in copy is HUGE. Use it wherever you can. What?

I SAID, USE SOCIAL PROOF WHEREVER YOU CAN. Oh c'mon, it's a hearing aid ad, that's funny.

Humour aside, ignore ye today's two big lessons at your peril.

The curve is real

I f you've ever been frustrated by not smashing it out of the park every time... If you're cheesed off that 3 of the last 5 things you tried were a complete flop... Or if you just hope this next thing you've got planned works...

Then here's the TRUTH:

You are normal. Two key things to always keep in mind...

"No one is that good" to get it right all the time (or even the majority of the time - NO ONE... ignore the guru boasts on social media, they rarely tell you about their mistakes and failures).

And...

The curve is real, meaning...

Think of a long J curve on a graph. It starts close to the bottom left corner where X and Y axes meet and only rises slowly at first. Then at a certain point things "take off" in the upswing of the long J.

Thing is...

To get to the upswing, you have to go through those annoying times when things often suck. This is when you learn. And it's a "REAL" phase is any endeavour. No one starts at the top. Yes, there are shorts cuts (like learning how to write copy or engaging a gun marketing strategist such as me), but you still have to go through those early phases - it is REAL.

What's the solution? Step up to the plate and keep swinging... the curve is real and if you persist you have a chance of enjoying the upswing. Give up, and well, you start at the start again. As frustrating as this is, there isn't any other way...

Keep working towards your success, the curve is real.

Avoid fugacious success

Remember the hit "Come on Eileen" by Dexie's Midnight Runners in the 80s? What about the "Macarena" by Los Del Rio in the 90s? And "The Middle" by Jimmy Eat World from the 00s?

Remember those gems?

They all had one thing in common... one hit wonders. Great while they were here but like hail on the ground after a summer storm, they quickly melt away.

They were, as a very smart lady told me, fugacious.

What?

Fugacious... success that doesn't last.

And so it is with many businesses' marketing efforts. You can jag success occasionally, but because there's no real system, that success is fleeting and can't be repeated. It happens a lot.

What to do to avoid this big word in your business?

Easy.

Create a marketing system. And it doesn't have to be some 52-arm monster. It really only needs 3 simple parts...

1. Lead generation - the continual attraction of new prospects
2. Conversion - moving those leads to paying clients
3. Retention - keeping the growing number of existing customers

Anything else is, well, fugacious.

If you don't have systems to attract, convert and retain clients, chances are your business is a "Come on Eileen" in the making. And that's only fun for a little while.

Random response boosters

H ere are three easy and proven ways to boost response...

Create curiosity. For direct mail, to the outside of an envelope add some teaser copy eg "Do not bend" or "Photos enclosed"... this almost always boosts open rates.. often works in email subject lines too!

Create exclusivity. Everyone wants to feel special and appreciated. Certain phrases have been proven to trigger a special feeling... "exclusive offer," "invitation only", "limited edition" and "To our top customers only".

Free still works. Free trial. Free special X this month. Free Y with your next purchase and more.

You don't have to be super creative all the time... things work because they work, especially if you implement them!

Email Open Rates and Other Important Stuff

Whatʼs a good open rate for your emails?

Again this is a how longʼs a piece of string type question. And you want to be careful this doesnʼt become a vanity type metric like "likes" on social media often are because a "Like" does not = sale.

Quick example… say youʼre selling a high-priced product or service and you send an email to your list and only a small number open it. Youʼd have a low open rate of, say, 6%. Bad. But say from that small number, 5 customers bought. Happy days.

Low open rate = success, you made 5 big sales. Great.

On the other hand… if you have a huge open rate eg 55% but make zero sales… really bad. Which would you prefer?

So be careful chasing a vanity type metric. That said, in most cases Iʼm looking for an open rate for campaigns of at least 15% and really into the 20ʼs is desirable as a rough guide.

A few more commonly asked questions:

Best times to send? Depends on your market… general rule of thumb… when they arenʼt sleeping or busy… in the mornings works well for B2B… Iʼve found Saturdays to be the worst day in every market Iʼve tried… and on the contrary, for some reason, Sunday afternoon works well.

How often do I send? This one always makes people cringe but in most markets "the more the better" is a general rule of thumb… daily works well… several times a week is great… the thing is, you canʼt sell via email if you donʼt have a relationship with your list (because you donʼt send emails).

What do I put in my emails? As Iʼve said all marketing is situational, but as a guide… stories work well… so do industry updates… testimonials are useful… and of course, when you have a relationship with your list you make offers.

Contrary to some popular opinions email these days is NOT dead and it should be an important part of your "influence arsenal".

Edison's Secret

Frankly, failure sucks. The truth is, in marketing, nothing works all the time. So if failure gets to you occasionally, this may help. Ask yourself...

SO WHAT?

An ad didn't work... well, ok but so what? What's the worse that happened? Not much "bad". Learn the lesson and try again.

Consider the legend of Thomas Edison and his 10,000 attempts before he got the light bulb right. He apparently was quite ambivalent about his 10,000 failures, saying all it told him was 10,000 things that didn't work. As in SO WHAT... thanks for the lessons, I'll move on to find one that does.

So give yourself a break when things don't go the way you wanted them to.

What's the worst that can happen? Nothing truly "bad", right? SO WHAT? And move on. Be gentle with yourself, get back up and get going again.

Last thing: this isn't permission for laziness or half-arsed effort. The buck stops with you and yes, your outcomes are the results of your last 1,000 or so thoughts... so take responsibility.

Just do so in a gentle way.

Not the outcome you wanted?

SO WHAT... let's move on...

Another gentle reminder next time things go arse-up.

Do you make this headline mistake?

E xactly how do you get people's attention in a headline?

It really is the #1 question you must answer.

Like I've said, if you don't grab them at the start, it's over. They've turned the page, swiped or clicked away. And it's bye bye money.

But how do you do that?

Dan Kennedy has a saying, and I love this because it lasers in on it…

"It starts at the start. You have to leave your reader with NO CHOICE but to read on".

Cool right?

Leave them with no choice.

Are your headlines so powerful you remove a reader's choice such that they just "HAVE" to open the email or read on?

Spend time on those headlines!

Radar up 2.0

If you're looking for inspiration for any copy project, check out other media.

Three examples…

First, the **nightly news and/or current affairs shows.** They are VERY good at curiosity…

"Coming up after the break…"

And then they tease you with a tidbit of information that leaves you hanging around through the ads to see what the answer is.

Newspaper headlines. Again, note how they make it "newsworthy" to get your attention and draw you in. It takes a high level of skill to do this consistently. Note the words used. The language patterns.

Magazine covers. Those teasing 4 to 8 words that summarises in a very powerful and enticing way the articles inside.

Again… word choice… high curiosity… newsworthiness…

If ever you're stuck for inspiration, head to the newsagent or supermarket, turn on the news occasionally with your marketing radar up and you won't be disappointed.

The 1-2-3 Punch Headline Formula

W ant another headline formula to test?

Try the old 1-2-3 punch.

This is where you use a prehead, a main headline, and then a subhead. You...

1. Call out who it's for (prehead)
2. Create the problem (main headline)
3. Solve the problem (subhead)

Here are two examples for a lead gen funnel:

Attention Property Investors...

"Are You Worried Your Rental Property is Costing You Too Much Money?"

Free Report Reveals for the First Time the 9 Secret Ways Landlords Can Save Money Which Most Property Managers NEVER Reveal!

Retirees feeling the financial squeeze...

"Here's the Fastest, Easiest, Most Cost-Effective Way to Travel on a Budget and Still Live like a King"

Free Report Reveals for the First Time the 7 Ways Over 65s Can Save BIG $$$ While Enjoying a Minimum of 4 months Travel EVERY Year!

Remember, the easiest way to get someone's attention is to call their name. Next best is to call the "group" they identify with, which is what you do in the prehead... and then you use a version of problem/solution in the headline and subhead.

Give it a go.

Addictive profit killer

G o on, just check Facebook one more time… or quick scan of the emails… or an extra half hour on the PlayStation… Can't hurt, right? Not so fast. Check out these nuggets about addiction…

In their bestselling book *Stealing Fire*, authors Steve Kotler and Jamie Wheal explain how video game companies employ top notch neuroscientists and psychologists to make video games as addictive as possible. They quote one of America's top addiction specialists thus: "The developers strap beta-testing teens with galvanic skin responses, EKG and blood pressure gauges. If the game doesn't spike their blood pressure to 180 over 140, they go back and tweak the game to make it have more of an adrenaline rush…"

Scary stuff.

They go on…

"Video games raise dopamine to the same degree that sex does, and almost as much as cocaine does. So this combo of adrenaline and dopamine are a potent one-two punch with regards to addiction." Ouch. And a huge wake-up call if you have teens who love their Xbox or PS5 (or whatever the latest is). And this, if you're a Facebook tragic (read addict) stop reading now…

From a Dan Kennedy newsletter, under the heading "Facebook Psychosis" comes data from a report in the *American Journal of Epidemiology*…

"The more hours Facebook users logged on over time, the more their sense of wellbeing and happiness declined" and those who gave the biggest chunks of time to Facebook showed "meaningful decreases in mental and physical health". Ouch again. Might pay to monitor your screen habits. Less, I'm banking, is more…

Less screen time = more happiness = a better, more profitable business. Definitely food for thought.

Think this is alarmist crap? Well, as mentioned already, so did people say of the early health warnings about smoking.

Can clearly remember as a kid the Benson & Hedges Test series (cricket) and Winfield Cup (rugby league). Only took us a few decades to realise the truth. Check your screen time… maybe a walk is better instead?

Don't do what these teams do

S even of them NEVER make it each week... 7 players...

That's right, each and every week they are "surplus to requirements" and considered "non-essential".

It was one of the most surprising things from my tour of the stadium in Cleveland, Ohio, where the NFL franchise the Browns play, when I was there a few years back.

Every NFL team has a roster of 53 players and only 46 of them make the game day squad.

I love the NFL but having 7 players "at work" who don't do anything every week is a little weird... but I also believe it mirrors many businesses.

You see there are things you do every week that take up time which are "important".

But are they essential?

If you think about this, reckon you can come up with a list of 3 to 5 things you could stop doing today without near-death experience of your business. It's one of the BIG but hidden benefits business owners get when they work with me...

I help them focus not on the important things...

But on the ESSENTIAL things... so they get more leads, convert more of them and grow their business.

Often it takes a fresh set of eyes, an independent "critical friend" to help you separate the important from the essential. And focus only on those things.

When you do, it's surprising how much your confidence grows.

There's much to love (from my point of view at least) about the NFL... but I suggest, carrying extra "non-essential" players is NOT one of them.

What non-essentials can you get rid of this week? Worth thinking about...

Crazy headline ideas

Believe it or not but vintage Cosmo magazine covers are a VERY good source of fodder for your headlines.

They are BIG on curiosity.

I'm a strong advocate for paying attention to what other media do because you can use similar ideas in sales copy.

Sometimes just a string of words or key phrases or a headline structure can spark an idea. And if nothing else, these are good for a giggle to brighten your day. Win-win. But especially if you get ideas from them. Example:

Crotch Crisis: 4 Scary Things Gynos Tell You and Why You Shouldn't Wig Out

Wow… You could use this formula for a headline in a new campaign. Say you're in business consultancy services it could be……

Tax Crisis: 4 Scary things Accountants Tell You and Why You Shouldn't Wimp Out

Ok it needs a massage, but you get the idea.

Note, fun as it is, I'm struggling with how you'd massage this one, however…

"She Caught Rapist with a Straw"!!!

Those vintage mag cover teaser headlines are interesting and good to get the brain ticking over.

The dangers of waiting

S cientific research provides proof that the old saying, "delay is death" is fair dinkum. In fact, for a business owner, procrastinating or delaying the launch of something can stall your profit and success, big time.

And you've heard me say stuff like, "money loves speed". Well, here's the proof:

Lawrence Blair's 1975 book *Rhythms with Vision* cited a study of acaque monkeys on the Japanese island of Koshima in 1952. It's become known as the 100th Monkey Theory.

These scientists observed that some of these monkeys learned to wash sweet potatoes. Gradually this new behaviour spread through the younger generation of monkeys. Nothing unusual, right?

But then, and this is rather spooky…

The researchers observed that once a critical number of monkeys was reached (ie the 100th monkey) this previously learned behaviour instantly spread across the water to monkeys on nearby islands. No, the monkeys didn't swim across and teach the spud washing technique. Somehow though the idea spread to other monkeys…

And I believe it's similar in business. In short, the 100th Monkey Theory says that once you get an idea for your business, somehow, somewhere, another person or persons gets the same or similar idea. When you get the idea, really only 2 things can happen…

You pursue the idea and profit from it. Or… You think about it and ponder how it might work. And get busy and come back and think about it later and so on.

Here's the thing…

Who profits most from the idea is whoever gets to market first. Now to get to market first, effectively, you have to know what you're doing in a marketing sense. It's an area where many business owners, who are great doers of their thing, fall down because they're not great marketers of their thing.

You have to have the skills and confidence to craft your message the right way, so prospects see it in the right media. It helps to have the templates, examples, and shortcuts to beat the opposition to it.

Because in business, speed is vital to success.

I cried yesterday

What do you do when you lose your hero?

Vince Plummer, my dad and my hero, passed away yesterday morning.

We got to the nursing home about 15 minutes too late.

My siblings then arrived one at a time.

And we said goodbye. It was a long and emotional day.

He would have been 92 next month, a good innings indeed.

Well played, Dad.

You were my role model and my rock.

Miss you already.

It will be a week of sadness and celebration at my end.

But because I'm a writer, I just had to put fingers to keyboard and write… something.

So have a great week, will be in touch again sometime soon.

NOTE: this is the script of the email I sent to my subscribers the day after my dad, to whom this book is dedicated, passed away. I include it here for a couple of reasons: first as a tribute to my hero, and second, as a teaching tool… it's ok to let people into your world, to show you're human… I was flooded with messages of support over the following days… plus, the second last sentence is key… when you are a writer, yep, you just have to write… Vincent Grayson Plummer 23/11/25 – 1/10/17 – RIP dad…

Body marks in the sand

Honestly, it looked like someone had dragged a body through the sand. There were two furrows made by knees or ankles. They went from the end of the concrete path at the top of the dunes down about 50 metres onto the beach. Such was the scene that greeted me one early morning walk as the sun rose.

I couldn't work out what it was and there was no blood or any other clue around. So, with a slight shiver, I kept walking. This happened several times over the next few weeks until one morning, finally, I saw what made the tracks.

And bloody hell, it shocked me.

There was this man, looked about mid-30s, his body twisted and deformed from MS or some other condition… down on hands and knees in the sand.

Left hand in front. Plonk. Right knee dragged. Plonk. Right hand forward. Plonk. Left knee dragged. Plonk.

Each movement a slow and seemingly painful inch back towards his wheelchair. Thinking he'd fallen out and needed a hand I asked him if he was ok.

"Yeah mate, beautiful morning isn't it?" was his garbled reply.

Courage. Determination. Will power. And I've since worked out the guy does this electric wheelchair to path's end, crawl and bulldoze through the sand for 50m onto the beach and back to his chair. Most mornings. And I decided then and there, next time something in business pissed me off… customer, copy that didn't work, technology… whatever it was that got under my skin… I'd remember this guy and the example he set.

I saw him again recently…

Do I still get pissed off? Yes. But not for long because I think back to what that amazing guy goes through just to enjoy what I take for granted… and my issues melt away pretty fast. When you get annoyed in your business… remember… TRACKS IN THE SAND… it changes your attitude pretty fast.

Make it about them, even when it's about you

One mistake even experienced writers make is to not include the prospect in their copy, even when telling a story about themselves or their product.

The common push back here is some form of... How can I make it about the reader when the story is about me...

Easy. Here's how...

Change the me/I to you.

Example:

The reason I created XYZ was because I hated ABC problem. This is all about the business owner. Fair enough. But you can go a step further by including them.

The reason I created XYZ was because I hated ABC problem, maybe you felt this too? Many people in our industry have.

Or...

My legs cramped so badly after a long ride I was in agony. It's why I just had to develop the new X muscle spray.

Can be tweaked to...

My legs cramped so badly after a long ride I was in agony. Can you relate? It's a common problem for us riders over 40.

See the difference?

Include your reader at strategic points. It helps connect to and bond with them which is important because people buy from people they know, like, and trust.

Willpower alone = epic fail

E ver pondered the difference between success and staying stuck? You see I was at 2 VERY high-end masterminds in Sydney this one time, one as a presenter, the other as a participant. And it got me thinking…

Why do we need such groups (or books like this for that matter)? Because here's the truth: the people in both these groups were well educated in their fields, very motivated and super talented. So why can't they just do it?

My honest conclusion…

Willpower alone is NOT enough. If it was, EVERYONE would get to and be at a level they want. And you and I know this is NOT the case. So yep, willpower alone = failure (or at least staying stuck).

What's the answer then to getting ahead? It's my belief that you need an external "mechanism" to move beyond where you are now and get to where you want to be.

Proof:

#1 – I remember seeing a low number on the scales one day for the first time in 20+ years… yep I was the fittest and healthiest I'd been since I stopped playing competitive sport… in the past it didn't matter how hard I exercised, how disciplined with diet I was, still couldn't crack the 82kg barrier until… I recently found a mechanism to lose fat – therapeutic ketones

#2 – Life and business coaching this past year, according to industry figures, is estimated to be a $2 billion global phenomenon

#3 – My kids did well at Senior English in school… they used former English teacher me as their mechanism to leverage what they are taught in class (it's ok, I helped them, I didn't write it for them!!)

So yeah, think about where you are now. Where you want to get to. And then work out what the best "external mechanism" is to help get you there. Because your willpower alone just won't do it.

How do I know this?

You are human. So am I. We need that external fresh set of eyes, ideas, and impetus. What's the mechanism for your next success?

How to write crackin' headlines

How do you write a crackin' headline?

It's a question I'm often asked. Let's face it, you get this wrong and well, nothing else matters, right?

So what's the answer?

Well, like lots of things in marketing, there are many ways to be right.

Here are 9 questions which give you focus when writing your headlines…

- Have I told my prospect what he or she will be reading in my ad?
- Is it believable?
- Does it make him or her want to read it NOW?
- Have I focused on the prospect and WIIFM - instead of focusing on business/product?
- Is it laser-focused on a specific target market, written in their language?
- Is it interesting or curiosity provoking?
- Is it clear, to the point, easy to understand?
- Am I talking in the 1st person and in the present tense?
- Does it show uniqueness?

Hope that helps next time you sit down to write a headline.

When the f-bomb works

For a recent wedding anniversary, I decided to f-bomb Jenny. Hang on, it's not quite what you think, and there IS a strong marketing message here, so keep reading.

You see this f-bomb brought me brownie points, not a VERY cold shoulder.

Why? Well, the "f" stands for flowers. There is a company in my local area that "flower bombs" people.

You go online. Pay the moolah. And at the designated time… ta-da! A flower bomb arrives for the lucky person. It's a posie of about 6 small flowers in a small paper wrapped jar. Nice. Quaint . Different. BTW… how long since you heard the word "posie" (since ring a-ring a rosie???).

Back to it:

Nice story Steve, so where's the marketing lesson? C'mon, let me bask in my obvious "perfect husband" glow for just a second…

So how is this "f-bomb" a marketing lesson? Simple…

Just about everything's already been invented. Like the flower bomb people… they just deliver flowers.

But… And here's the BIG but (and marketing lesson)…

They show up differently in the marketplace. They have a new twist on an age-old product/service. And it works.

Very well.

So let your mind wander… how can you show up differently in your market? You don't necessarily need a new mouse trap… just a new twist on what you do.

How to use indirect proof

It's a phenomenon every business needs to leverage. It taps into a deep-seated human psychological trait. And I'm guessing you don't use it nearly enough. It's called…

"The Rodney Lush Effect"

Well, it is now, because I named it thus. What the heck is "The Rodney Lush Effect"? Glad you asked…

One of my clients sells big farm sheds to landholders all over South Australia. Hay sheds. Machinery sheds. Grain sheds. Fertilizer sheds. And more. All custom built and manufactured in their factory in Monash (a small town to the northeast of Adelaide).

In one of our regular marketing calls, the client mentioned several times a particular customer of theirs (he has several of their sheds), a highly respected farmer named Rodney Lush. My marketing radar being "up" as it usually is, homed in on this. Because Mr Lush is widely respected among his peers, whatever he does gets "noticed" and even "followed" by others.

It's safe to say, he's a celebrity no one outside that niche has ever heard of. But farmers have. So what we did (with permission) in marketing the business is leverage off Mr Lush's status as a "respected farmer".

If it's good enough for Rodney Lush, it's good enough for me… Is the seed we are planting. Understand the psychology at play…

Humans are herd creatures. We gravitate to others. And we especially gravitate to respected or famous or celebrity peeps. If they are doing it, it's "safe" for me to do it.

In every market. In every business. In just about every situation… there is a "Rodney Lush". And that means you too can leverage **"The Rodney Lush Effect"** to boost sales.

The thing is, when you "name drop" like this "in passing" it's a more subtle or indirect persuasive device, not a worn out "hypey" hard sell technique everyone is sick of.

Your task is to think up who might be the "Rodney Lush" of your market… AND… work out how you can leverage their "star" power. Known people. Respected people. Successful people… are everywhere… who are yours?

By the way… I have a patent pending on "The Rodney Lush Effect"!!!

Wordsmith tip

We want our sales messages to read fast. To be smooth. To flow. If it's hard to read, if they stop to re-read your words, they'll get sick of it pretty fast and it's sale over. Copy success is about creating the "greased slide" everyone talks about. Here's one way to do this…

Eliminate trip points in your copy. What?

Trip points… those parts of the sales message that either don't make sense or cause the reader to stop and go back and read it again to be sure they got it right. Key word here is "stop". We don't want them to. We want them to read from start to finish, fast. Consider these two headline examples:

"Finally, a One-Stop Service for Everyday Australians which Co-ordinates ALL Your Financial Services…"

Or

"Finally, a One-Stop Provider for Everyday Australians which Co-ordinates ALL Your Financial Services…"

When you read them which one "felt" better? If you didn't get a feeling, go back and re-read them a couple of times. One will "feel" better/easier than the other.

Most people pick the second. Want to know why? The word **service** is not repeated. You see, **same word, same sentence** is one of those trip points. When the same word appears a couple of times close together, what the human brain does is say, *"Hang on, I've just seen that word a second ago"* and your eyes scan back to look for it to confirm the thought and/or check to see if it is an error.

The problem with this is…

YOU HAVE STOPPED READING.

The sales message has been interrupted. Once is bad enough. If the reader has to do it three, four or more times, chances are it will become too hard for them and without realising why, they will have clicked off the page.

To smooth your copy out, eliminate same word same sentence… now you know why the second headline "felt" better!

To sell hard... yes or no?

It's an interesting question... Is selling hard, upselling, and doing everything you can to get your product in your prospect's hands manipulative?

To a point, I'd say YES. But that's not necessarily a bad thing, depending on the circumstances.

Take me for instance... am I glad the likes of Ted Nicholas, Mal Emery, and Dan Kennedy sold me stuff, and upsold me and worked hard to do so? Answer: hell yes! If they didn't, big chance I'd be stuck still working in schools not really liking my life. And you wouldn't be reading this.

But this isn't the case for everyone. And certainly, if the business sells crap, then it's a huge NO.

More: One of my past students, the Dan Kennedy certified copywriter Mark Mehling who runs Take Control Marketing out of Florida says, "If a product or service is offered with honesty and integrity, based on a true need designed to help the consumer, then every effort should be made to help them choose the best option for their individual needs".

And he's pretty much right.

BIG POINT: the key elements are **integrity, honesty, need,** and **help**. No upsell is manipulative unless it violates one of these pillars.

High pressure tactics for ordinary products or services violates these 4 pillars.

LAST THING: selling good products and services makes the world go around... dodgy products, scams and high pressure upsells just annoy.

"You want fries with that?" (because burgers taste way better with a side of fries) helped build a business monolith and done right, with the right intentions, the right upsells can build your business too... all the while helping people even more.

Recommend considering these 4 pillars with every product and upsell.

Ever felt chaotic... this one little strategy may help

L et's talk again about your productivity... and this goes back to the truth I've already mentioned...

"Environment wins EVERY time". Remember, put a person in the desert without water and they're dead in 3 days.

So are your work surroundings geared for max productivity or are you all over the shop? If you feel like you could benefit from better focus, try this...

Visual cues.

What visual cues do you have in your work environment that help you get the job done?

Couple of examples...

Dan Kennedy has a sign on his desk that reads: "Do Epic Shit".

Mal Emery, if ever you did a Zoom or Skype call with him back in the day, had on the wall behind him in plain (and choreographed) view framed client testimonials.

Client and friend Ali Halupka has a little sign at eye level above her computer that reads, "Just fu*#ing do it, Ali" (because in the past she has been known to procrastinate – now they turn over more in one month than they did in a whole year).

Me?

I have my business Genius Model, my 7 Golden Rules of Marketing and my favourite saying: "Greatness ALWAYS comes with ease, it is never forced" in plain sight so every time I take my eyes of the screen, I see them.

You? What visual cues do you have in your environment that help you win?

Who can you depend on?

This is the story of Argentine boxer Sergio Martinez. From 2010, he was world middleweight champion for 50 months. It's one of the longest title reigns in the history of the division.

Known as a "good guy" of the sport, in his 2012 title defence against big name Julio Cesar Chavez Jr, he survived an 11th round knockdown to score one of the best victories of his career. He was a star.

That said, Martinez suffered several knee injuries which required surgery. And like many who go under the knife, he was never quite "the same".

Two years and one title defence after defeating Chavez Jr he took on big hitting Columbian Miguel Cotto. Martinez was knocked down several times but fought on into the ninth round. His legs (or rather knees) were shot.

As he was sitting in his corner after the gruelling ninth, his trainer Pablo Sarmiento, wouldn't let him stand for the tenth round. As the crowd started to yell in anticipation of the next phase of action, Sarmiento said to Martínez, *"Champion, your knees are not responding. Sergio, look at me … I'm gonna stop this one. Sergio, you are the best for me. You'll always be the best champion, Sergio. It's over"*

And so ended a career.

Several months later, as he was reflecting on his achievements as one of the world's best middleweights, Martinez had this to say…

"I finished the big fight with Chavez Jnr and had 1,060 missed calls. And when I lost my last fight against Miguel Cotto, I had 4 missed calls. One was from an unknown number, the other 3 were from my mother. That put everything in its place."

And so I ask you… Who is there for you when you close the doors of your business every day? We may not have the bright lights and adulation of prize fighting but, like Martinez, we are in an arena, in business…

Who is there for you when things get tough? Because, again like Martinez, you'll find there are a few more people that hang around when things are going well, compared to when they are not.

Food for thought about who and what matters most to you in business and in life.

Finally, it's fixed

Be wary of this thought.

I saw recently one of the big online players show their website from 2015.

He said what he put online back then now makes him cringe.

What really struck me though was this line, paraphrased here:

We fixed it. And we fixed the fixes. And fixed them some more.

And that pretty much sums up marketing and business…

One and done doesn't work, at least for long.

You have to go and fix things. And tweak and adjust. And fix some more.

Just wanted to remind you of the changing nature of business… there is always things to fix. And re-fix.

And fix some more.

All for now, have a great day, go ahead and fix something.

Bullet formula

When writing a list of bullets, does it matter what order they go in?

Yes. Understand how we read, especially skim readers…

When confronted by a long list we generally start at the top and read the first couple and then our eyes slip to the end. Only then do we decide if we're going to go back and read everything else.

Which is why, when using bullets, this is the formula I follow…

✓ Biggest/most important benefit bullet MUST go FIRST
✓ Second biggest/most important benefit bullet MUST go LAST
✓ Third biggest/most important benefit bullet MUST go SECOND

After that, the order is not so important.

Cracker of a headline or fake news?

Y ep, words are powerful as this cyclone horror story shows…

One summer recently we were lashed by the remnants of Tropical Cyclone Oma. By the time it hit us it had been downgraded to a Tropical Low. Effects were "solid"… strong winds… very high tides (which coincided with a "super moon") and the odd scudding shower.

We live on a canal and have done for over 20 years. Water overlapped the bottom wall which resulted in dead grass. Such is life. These events are not uncommon. Water over the bottom wall happens about 5 times a year. We get serious weather, like everywhere, at certain times. So it was with some amusement I read this headline on an online news service. Now before I tell you about it, I'm not advocating ignoring weather warnings or doing foolish things in defiance of Mother Nature. But the headline for the story…

BREAKING NEWS: Mega storm from HELL about to strike Australia - what you need to know

Damn good copy, right? Look at the emotive and trigger words in it. Good attention getting stuff. But true? Hardly. And this also got my attention… The first pic in the story was of a 4wd that got stuck at Mudlo Rocks near Rainbow Beach earlier in the week. The inference being "the storm from hell did this".

No.

If you've ever been to the Rainbow Beach pub or one of the service stations there, you'll see pix dating back decades of vehicles that got caught racing the waves around the rocks. It was an interesting example of how you can use "facts" to "sell" your story.

Storm from hell? Nope. Vehicle swallowed as a result? No more than any other intrepid 4wder who got their judgement wrong.

Ethical reporting? Will let you be the judge of that. But it was good attention getting copy.

Couple of lessons here… you can find facts, figures and illustrations to support just about any argument. Plus… you can leverage off what people are already thinking about or what's in the news to get greater traction…

Boring

Here's a simple truth: success can be BORING.

Think of a pro golfer. Hours and hours of repetition hitting a ball. Boring. A Pro basketballer. Hundreds of shots from the free throw line. Boring. The pro boxer. Thousands of punches hitting that bag. Boring.

You get the idea. Now if these pros have their basic techniques right and...

They know how to do things in a sequence for the right reasons...

And they practice it again and again and again...

With slight tweaks and adjustments as they go...

They get success! And all the accolades that go with it.

But...

And here's the big but...

They would NOT reach their success without the RIGHT fundamentals and "secrets" in place. And in my humble (and correct) opinion, it's similar in business...

As the pro biz owner, you've got to get the fundamentals right. And practice. And implement. And repeat your successes with tweaks along the way.

The repetition part can be boring. And this is when we go chasing shiny objects, often ignoring the success principles in the process.

Be aware of this and understand the tedium that builds success, it will hold you in good stead when the shiny objects tempt you...

Key to EVERY successful promotion

I s THE BIG IDEA. The **Big Idea** is the concept that drives the promotion and sets it apart from all the clutter. It's a fresh way to say what everyone else is saying or has said many times before.

A promotion that contains a Big Idea will make your reader stop, take notice, and want to find out more. Exactly what is "the big idea"? It's also called…

- ✔ Theme
- ✔ Hook
- ✔ Angle
- ✔ Controlling thought
- ✔ Selling concept

Key, it must be NEW and DIFFERENT and be weaved throughout the copy

According to A-List copywriter Paul Hollingshead "The Big Idea" has 5 key components. It is:

NEW

TIMELY

UNIQUE

BOLD

IMPACTFUL

How do you find it or create it? RESEARCH, RESEARCH, RESEARCH.

Some examples of "big ideas" I've used in promotions…

"Perth Real Estate Revolution"

"Respected Farmer"

"Crack the Copywriting Mastercodes"

These "themes' ran through the copy and tied each promo together. To nail a winning "Big Idea" takes time… and deep thought.

Enter the manzone at your peril

O ne day recently I took the plunge…Went out on a limb…And decided to risk it…

Yes, I entered the "Manzone" for the first time. And boy was it fun. And a powerful little marketing lesson too, so keep reading…

Ok, so me and my boys, Isaac and Nate, fronted up on a Tuesday afternoon to Manzone.

It really is a place for secret men's business. Beer in the glass front fridge – take one if you want. PlayStation waiting for you – play if you feel like it. Men's mags on the coffee table – have a read and relax.

No, not "that" type of magazine… Truckin'. Boating. Fishing etc. Bloke's stuff. What were you thinking?

Plus…

You can crack a joke without fear of offence. And just generally be a bloke for a while, guilt-free. Yep, a real man's haven. What were we there for?

A haircut.

Yes, "Manzone" is a barber. But…

One with a difference BECAUSE they've got their target market nailed. Men. And men only. They give you stuff blokes want… beer, PlayStation, mags, all included… while they cut hair. Price is comparable to competitors. The "experience" is NOT.

How is this relevant to you?

How well do you know your market… And… How well do you really cater for them to the exclusion of others who will never buy from you anyway?

Can your business do with a dose of "manzone"?

Worth thinking about isn't it?

Embarrassing word obsession

Confession time... I'm kind of obsessed with words. It's ok if you find it weird because it will help you. Case in point...

I downloaded a free big idea swipe file from a guru recently and when I couldn't really decide which of my current projects I'd dive into, it came in handy. The evil me found a distractor/avoider activity to not work and feed my obsession...

Hey Steve, why not go through the swipe file of these multi-million dollar promo big ideas and see if there are words used consistently.

Great idea evil me I said, *even if my peeps find it weird... it's a safe space, after all...*

So here you go, common words used in some massively successful promos - this list is a great place to start for YOUR ideas:

Secret (mentioned 8 different times)

Money/wealth (or some variant of, 9 times)

How (4)

Now (3)

Discovered (3)

New (3)

Massive (2)

The more things change the more they stay the same. None of those words would be new to you. Here are some others that showed up regularly...

Blueprint, Legally, Extra, Urgent, Revealed, Transform, Loophole, Simple, Opportunity...

Cool stuff, right? And one or two of these words inserted strategically in your next headline may make a huge difference. Afterall, small hinges swing BIG doors.

Embarrassing word obsession confession endeth. Have a great day.

Worst call ever?

Are you 100% CERTAIN your staff are doing what you pay them to do? Why I ask is I received a spam-type telemarketing call. It "sounded" legit, but only because it was so bad.

Here's what I mean…

Phone rings.

Me: Hello (nondescript voice less it be a spammy voice recognition hacker on the other end).

Telemarketer (in nice gentle female Aussie accent): Hi, is that Steve?

Me: Who's asking?

Telemarketer: Look, this is just a marketing call. You're not interested in investing, are you?

Me: Not right now.

Telemarketer: Ok. No problems. Thanks for your time. Have a good day.

Me: stunned silence

You see either it was the WORST EVER telemarketing call or a new phone scam type thingy. Let's assume it was the first one.

OMG… talk about seeding yourself for failure…

Look, this is just a marketing call. You're not interested in investing, are you?

100% true story. I kid you not. Is there a weaker sales lead-in, in the history of sales than this?

The call cost some business owner plenty in terms of the phone charges, the telemarketer's time, setting it all up and on it goes. And it had NO hope of ever succeeding. They should be fired immediately.

So my challenge and question today…

Do you know, 100%, what your staff are doing and how they "turn up" to each sales interaction? Let's hope they are just a little better than my "you're not interested in investing are you?" experience.

On motivation

V exing is one word to describe the human trait of motivation. It's a bit like sunshine…

Sometimes you have it. Sometimes you don't. Sure the flakey world of social media would have you believe that everyone all day every day is out there "crushing it".

Pfff.

Chatting to a client in Mexico one morning and he asked me about motivation, so thought I'd share some thoughts with you too.

I'm not pretending to have "the" answer, more to prompt you to think…

I want to preface this too with the acknowledgement it's easier to be more flexible when you are a freelancer or work for yourself. In many professions you have to show up regardless of how you feel.

That said, it's an interesting topic is "motivation".

My client commented that sometimes he just couldn't be bothered and really had to force himself to work. My response…

"Maybe it's during those times you're motivated to rest and re-charge, not work. Maybe it's your body or the Universe or some other intelligence that's wanting you to slow down, at least for a while."

There was silence on the other end followed by a "Hmmm… yeah…" as he mulled it over.

One thing I have come to realise is that my best ideas come to me when I'm still… or at least not rushed and deadline focused. And so I'd encourage you, the next time you don't feel "motivated", to question what the next best action is for you…

Is it to finish work early and rest?

Is it to halve your to do list and find some stillness in the new time you have?

Is it to change task and focus on a new project?

There's no one answer.

What I will say is if you grind and grind the only thing you'll be "crushing" is your energy and creativity and your effectiveness.

Leave you to ponder "motivation" and how it shows up in your life…

Headline refresher

When critiquing copy one thing that stands out is the headline. A theme commonly runs through much of what I see...

The absence of a clear "BEST BENEFIT" of the product or service. Yep, we must always remember one of my favourite headline acronyms WIIFM (What's In It For Me).

If this isn't clear, chances are the headline misses the mark. Where I think many who aren't A-list type copywriters go wrong is they see a headline idea from someone who is and try and swipe it for their market.

Two quick examples. First, from Gary Halbert:

"5687 Ira Road, Bath, Ohio 44210"

Yep, just a postal address.

And from the great Dan Kennedy:

"We are looking for Authors who Want to Write Children's Stories".

Yes, it uses the word "we" and seems more about the business than the prospect. Both cases the headline worked a treat. And in both cases they are "pretty horrible" when it comes to following headline "rules". Results, though, is what counts and these two were big winners. But adapt for your market?

Understand the research that went into both ideas and the skill and genius of the writers behind both.

But writing "out there" headlines when you are a copy newbie is a bit like running a marathon after you learn to walk.

Leave that stuff to marathon runners!

Boring... 3 ways to avoid it

B oring = no sale.

How then do you create un-boring sales messages? Glad you asked, coz this same question comes up when consulting to prospects and clients, how to avoid boring copy.

Not mine. Theirs. Steady on...

You see always in my mind is that line by the great Joe Sugarman, *"If it ain't in the product, it ain't in the copy"*. Meaning fancy copy won't sell a crappy product.

That said, here are 3 ways to un-boring your copy...

#1 - Get specific. Facts make people curious. Do your research (like if you were selling anti-man flu meds find evidence to prove man flu is real... coz all men know it is... So you'd say, "Studies show men XYZ...")

#2 - Tell stories. We love them. They are hard wired into our DNA. Like this client the other day who made a huge error and lost big $$$ because his copy was plain boring. What happened next shocked him... (see, you were drawn in, even just a little)

#3 - Write to a timer. When you write to the clock that sense of urgency comes through in your copy (won't delve into woo woo about words having "vibrations" here but it's true)

Even if you think there's nothing earth shattering about what you sell, it doesn't mean your sales message has to be boring.

Get excited and let this vibe come through your words.

A one-legged man can't run

I really hate these types of questions… You know the ones that look for the magic bullet answer. Take for example this from a prospect who asked, in my view, *what the key to business success is.*

How long's a piece of string?

Channelling the show *Air Crash Investigation,* my response was along the lines of, *just like no one single thing brings down an aeroplane, no one thing makes it fly.*

Which is like your business.

Reckon you can however, if you're looking to simplify it, build your success around two key PRINCIPLES. And, just like a one-legged man can't run fast, nor can your business if you don't have…

A **great product and service** backed by **great marketing** to tell your targeted prospects about it.

Take away one and your business doesn't last long. Or, like the one-legged man, doesn't run fast.

I believe these two areas are where you need to devote most of your energy… getting better at what you do… plus… getting better at telling others about the great things you do to help people.

Great marketing backed by poor products or service only goes so far… like the already mentioned proverbial chocolate coated turd… easy enough to sell because it looks good on the outside… but when they try it out, it's still, well, a turd.

The smell spreads.

And the inverse applies… a great product or service that's a secret doesn't sell well.

Get 'em BOTH right and you give your business and fighting chance.

Breaking religious habits

We are creatures of habit. Sometimes though, long developed habits no longer serve us.

Case in point…

Even though I've heard it many times over the years I never acted on it…

But…

About 7 years ago I gave up my religious-like habit of watching the news. For as long as I can remember, every evening I'd watch 1 or 2 news programs. Every morning I'd read the paper.

Why did I do this? I enjoy current affairs and events and like to keep up with what's going on.

I think, too, it gets back to old patterns…

Dad did the same. So it was kind of ingrained in me.

But…

Thankfully, I've broken the habit.

Now? I maybe catch 1 TV news every 2 weeks and the paper maybe 2 or 3 times a month at most. Usually less.

Results?

Happier. More time. And a realisation that as "fun" as it was to "know" everything, "knowing" had absolutely ZERO influence on the outcome of it. And often things just plain pissed me off. So why get mad and send that negative energy out for NO RESULT.

So I stopped. My challenge to you today is…

What "thing" are you doing or thinking just out of habit that no longer serves you? Time to jettison something for a lighter and freer view of the world???

Mistake

D o you make this mistake in your marketing…

Sell what you do…

NOT…

What your clients really get?

You must sell the RESULT…

Not the THING.

Most focus on the thing and lose. Focus on the result they get, this gives you the best chance of winning.

Lesson over my padawan - have a great day.

You, totally biased?

A re you prejudiced, in a marketing sense?

By this I mean…

You favour one media over another. It's Facebook for you or it's nothing (because "everyone" is doing it)? Or are you a bandit for email? Or you only run offline ads?

Reason I ask, and the purpose of today's message, is to get you to think about your marketing mix.

Why? Well, here's an interesting piece of data…

According to a report in the US-based *Response Magazine*, Google, Facebook and Microsoft spent almost 70% of their ad budget on TV.

What the?

The online kings of the world went offline? And you haven't lived unless you've received direct mail from Google offering you a PPC deal.

I could quote other figures from the mag (like Google devoting $260 million to TV ads, most of it lead gen, not branding) but you get the point.

Never rely too heavily on ONE media.

The big boys don't… and they got big for a reason.

Need to diversify? One is a very dangerous number… which is why I favour a multi-channel approach.

Knowing when to do it

Words, you've heard me say over and over again, are important.

Quick example...

The debate over learn Vs discover. As in "Here's what you're about to learn". Or discover. I usually use discover.

Why?

It implies speed. Ease. Hey presto.

On the contrary, learn reminds us of school. It implies long and slow. And feels like work.

No one wants that, right?

But there are exceptions.

Take the work I did for a client in the higher education space. Now in this market, the reason for their existence is "learning" so I used "learn" and not "discover".

In this space, discover sounds like hype.

And there's no way the client wants to come across like this.

Lesson: know the principles that work... but... be flexible with them to adapt to different markets.

Is branding dead?

Age old argument isn't it...

"Get your name out there" Vs "Make them an offer"?

Ad agencies preach the former and look down on the latter as crass and salesy. The counter argument often is...

Do you want to look good or make money? Direct response advocates usually then up the ante with...

No one really cares about your corporate colours or logo, they just want their problem solved. True.

Here's some food for thought... why not combine both.

Case in point:

Got a letter from a big company explaining their new look. How their vibrant colours reflect their new approach and other, frankly boring to yours truly with "me me me" stuff from the company no one cares about.

Why waste a golden chance like this?

If you're going to the trouble and expense of snail mail, to announce new logos and colours to a world that doesn't really care, why not make them an offer at the same time?.

As in...

We're writing to you to let you know about our fresh new look which benefits YOU our valued customer in X, Y and Z ways. To help us celebrate this major change we're offering you <insert something new/cool/special>.

Now...

The "branding" has been announced AND... An opportunity to grow your influence has not been missed. Best of both worlds really. Only trouble is, most companies do not do this. So always have your thinking cap on. How can you market your business and solve more problems of your customers?

Branding is ok but...

No sales = no business.

Yet another "best headline formula"

G ot this question from a student one day…

"Go on then, tell me what's the best headline formula?"

Little bit like asking a batter in cricket, what's the best shot to play. Depends on the pitch conditions. The bowler you're facing. Stage of the match. And more.

Everyone, it seems, always wants a simple answer to a complex problem. And it gets even murkier…

There is no "formula" for selecting my headlines…

I generally go by how it "feels" or lands on me.

What? Yup… it's a feeling thing. That said, to help you get your head around it some more here are 2 formulas to play around with…

HEADLINE FORMULA#1

Headline with WIIFM (what's in it for me) which then goes to the opening paragraph -- bang straight into it.

Or…

HEADLINE FORMULA #2

Prehead calling out who it's for, attention grabbing headline with WIIFM then a subhead which explains the WIIFM.

Fairly straight forward, right?

Which one works best?

See cricket analogy I just told you about!

Your dumb ideas can pay off

How resourceful are you? Because these days, it's NOT lack of opportunity that determines success. It's more about how we respond to the opportunities on offer, and there are plenty. In fact, it's easy to argue, there has never been a better (or easier?) time to make money. Even with apparently "dumb" ideas. And yep, it's often as simple as taking an old idea and putting a new twist to it.

Don't believe me? Check this out…

Exhibit A - CAW

CAW was the birthday gift to one of Jenny's work colleagues… Crystal Activated Water. It's a water bottle with a crystal in the base. Old concepts of crystal healing combined with old concept of a water bottle. They have several different crystals depending on the needs of the buyer… smoky quartz, clear quartz, obsidian etc. And like any good business there is a whole raft of spin-off crystal products.

Exhibit B - Goat Yoga

Not a misprint. In the US (where else?) there is an Arizona based business that runs yoga classes with specially trained yoga goats. The goats can be rented out along with their alpacas. Yoga is ancient. Animal therapy is not new. So combine the two and you have "goat yoga". Apparently, their income is $250,000 per year (*source: No BS Marketing Letter June 2019*).

Exhibit C - Sunshine Coast Craft Beer Tours

Driving home one day I passed a new-looking minivan with said name prominent. Here on the Sunshine Coast, we're known for some of the world's best beaches, great weather (when it's not raining) and beautiful hinterland. And apparently, craft beers. Now, I'm not a fan of craft beer, so am not in the "scene" but there's clearly enough locals who brew to create a tour company business… again nothing new… tourism + beer. Wine tours have been around forever. Now there's a craft brewery tour right on my doorstep.

So yep, opportunity, based on "dumb" ideas, is everywhere. Start with the old and add a new twist.

And if you think your idea is dumb, just remember, in a meeting somewhere at some point, someone thought that making a movie out of talking blocks of plastic was a good idea… Netflix is advertising the release of the *Lego II* movie… animated cubes of plastic… so dumb, they've made TWO movies out of it… old idea with a new twist…

Leave you to ponder today how you can add a new twist to an old idea and increase your market share.

I made women cry

P icture this... 53 people packed into a wedge-shaped section of a popular local watering hole... a hushed silence...

The sun had reduced itself to a golden glow in the western sky and guests had had a few cold looseners...

The speeches had to happen by 6pm which was when the live music started. The occasion was wife Jenny's 50th birthday party. There I was, mic in hand. Just over 3 minutes later, most of the women and some of the men in attendance were wiping away tears.

True story. They cried. And so did Jenny.

Here's why...

Instead of giving a traditional speech that wandered on and on about how nice the wife was, what a good mother she'd been to the 4 kids and so on...

I totally changed the mood of the room and it even shocked my kids (they were in that late teen phase when dad definitely isn't the coolest dude they know).

What did I do?

Well, flashback to 1989 when we were courting (how long since you heard that expression!!), I wrote Jenny a poem called, *I Thought Of You Today*. Naturally she loved it then. And it had stayed buried for 30 years until the birthday Saturday when I segued into it with...

It's difficult to sum up someone's life and do justice to it, so thought I'd read a famous poem.

And then I launched into it. A couple of stunned silent minutes later, my "close" was...

Those words are as true today as they were in 1989 when I wrote them for her. Happy birthday my love.

Silence and tears. The lesson here...

Well-chosen words delivered with emotion move people. Never underestimate this. Business, influence, and even life success are shaped by what we say and how we say it.

The multi-tasking myth

A re you good at multi-tasking? Take pride in juggling many balls at once? Able to leap tall buildings in a single bound while getting the kids' lunches, sending an email, and "engaging" on Facebook?

If you answered YES, then stop a moment and think about this...

That's right...

Cease your multi-tasking for a moment. Yep, log out of Facebook. Close that Google page. C'mon, I know you're doing it. Just stop for a second.

Here's why...

Chances are, if you rate yourself as a good "multi-tasker" you also feel there's never enough hours in the day. Yes, even with all of today's apps and tech tools available...

Multi-tasking HURTS your productivity.

According to a recent study by consultants Activate, people choose engagement with technology over work or sleep. Mobile access to everything all at once seems to be causing an overlap which reduces our focus and productivity. Dr JoAnn Deak, a noted author, educator and psychologist says the brain is only able to focus deeply on one task at a time.

And not only that...

Trying to do too many things at once causes the brain to lose the capacity for deep thinking altogether. Which is why dedicated, UNINTERRUPTED time on your most important tasks every day is gold.

And the key to your productivity.

And certainly the way forward for your business.

Features and benefits issue solved

W hen you collate your sales argument, you need to articulate the features and benefits of your product or solution. There is a third level you need to be aware of.

To be clear...

A **feature** is what the product or service has or does eg extra wide tyres, a live Q&A session (as part of a training)

A **benefit** is how the feature impacts on their life, what result it brings eg from the examples just given the benefits are... a smooth ride, an end to confusion.

A feature is not a selling point.

A benefit is however because it articulates what it does for the client, the result they get.

There is a third level here... the **emotional benefits**. You must go deeper than features and benefits and uncover what feelings the product or solution gives the buyer.

Why? Well, you've no doubt heard the saying we buy on emotion and justify with logic. So if we all buy on emotion, makes sense for our copy to "sell" here.

Continuing with our two examples, the deeper emotional benefits are increased safety from the bigger tyre footprint, so you worry less taking the family for a drive (or if it's a sports car you get to make the other drivers jealous)... and in the second example, your skills and confidence grow so you move ahead with certainty.

Always dig deeper to find not just the benefit, but the deeper emotional payoff the benefit brings.

The speed of knowing

L ove this quote by O.B. Smith…

"Confidence and enthusiasm are the greatest sales producers in any economy".

Reason I love it so is that it's deeper than you think. You see in sales, people pick up and "feel" where the seller "is". Call it their vibrations if you like. We all have a speed of knowing which is faster than the speed of thought. And if you pick up on a weak salesperson you feel it before you think it.

Think back to your last encounters with a good salesperson and a bad one…

You knew you wanted to engage or run away quicker than you thought it. Same in copy.

You need to be confident.

The reader picks up on the confidence and enthusiasm in the writer. Sure it probably takes a little longer than face to face…

But it's the same process.

Here's the kicker…

YOU CAN'T MANUFACTURE CONFIDENCE.

You are either confident in who you are and what you sell or you're not. Which causes issues when it comes to closing. The big question for today: are you secure enough in your writing skills to convey your message with CONFIDENCE?

Think this is an area which requires some work?

It is for most people, so it's a great thing you are investing in yourself by reading resources like this one. EVERY little thing you do over months and years contributes to your growing skillset which boosts your confidence and by extension influence in the marketplace.

Business is a contact sport

Ever get totally pissed off with your business? To the point where you think getting a job would be a whole lot easier (and safer)? If you answered yes, you're not weird. You're not the only idiot in the room. And you're not the only one who's had some bumps and bruises.

Business IS a contact sport.

I was at a business meeting/workshop once and the final speaker got up and told his story. He started from nothing. Joined with a partner and built something. Then he got a golden opportunity at a world-wide sporting event to promo his product (which ended up making no money). He moved to Australia. Started another business with another partner.

They did extremely well until the GFC, when the business partner enacted a long forgotten clause in their agreement (*"Don't worry mate, I'd NEVER do that to you"*) which said something along the lines of, if sales drop below X, the business partner had the right to ask the speaker to exit the business.

The *"I'd never do that to you"* partner who kept the business after the speaker was forced to exit sold it a few years later for close to $40 million US. The speaker said he got nothing.

The speaker went on to say he'd had several "exit and retire plans by X date" and NOT ONE had come to fruition. At each turn and fall he's picked himself up, tended the bruises, dusted himself off and got back in the game. And he was on the verge of winning major government contracts in 4 states which will more than triple the business.

Good luck to him.

Point is…

At any stage he could have chucked it all in. But he didn't. He kept going. Gee it was refreshing to hear a real-life-warts-and-all story of the ups and downs of business… not the social media snapshot of one-off success.

As you head into your day, if you're feeling a little jaded…

That's normal. You play a contact sport in business. You'll get some bruises.

Little known pro writer tip

B lank screen and a flicking cursor... buh-boom, buh-boom, bah-boom... can induce terror in anyone who writes.

The much talked about writer's block is a workplace health hazard for some.

It's rare that this affliction strikes me down. Would love to say it's because I'm pure genius and exist in some kind of elevated, rarefied state...

Alas, that's far from the truth.

The reason I rarely suffer writer's block is because I do my research. But also this...

I've developed over the years a well organised writer's mind.

Here's just one example...

I've trained my subconscious to be on the lookout for "entry points"... those places where I can START a story or any piece of copy... email... sales message... ad and more.

What this means is that everything I consume - others' emails, blogs, ads, sales letters, conversations, life experiences, TV and more - is potential fodder for my writing.

It's not a stress-filled effort. It's a background effort.

Example:

The day after the passing of Judith Durham, lead singer of The Seekers, I sent an email to my list with the subject line "The carnival is over" which was the title of arguably their greatest hit. That song has always felt melancholic to me... about endings/goodbyes/time over...And so Durham's passing provided an "entry point" for the message about finite time and living our best life.

So yeah...

The little-known writer's tip is to have your subconscious radar up for "entry points" for stories.

Along with great research, it's another powerful but subtle way for you to never stare at a blank screen.

Put your subconscious to work... it rarely lets you down.

Best headline this year

At least by the definition given by the great Gene Schwartz in his book *Breakthrough Advertising:*

"Your headline has only one job - to stop your prospect and compel him to read the second sentence of your ad."

And boy, did this one stop me in my tracks. Quick backstory…

When mum was alive, I'd visit her in the nursing home. Often I'd pick up one of her *Take 5* or *That's Life* magazines and do the crossword with her. It kept her mind sharp. At least when she could hear the question. Frankly, I think most on her floor did the crossword with us because she was as deaf as a post and the clues were read out to her 2, 3 or 4 times… the last one yelled at her. But she did pretty well, average success rate of about 70% of all words and we'd get the crossword finished in about 30 minutes. So it was fun and kept her "active".

Anyways one day just before Christmas I picked up one mag, scanned the cover, and was stopped by this gem:

Tina's turkey tryst: I bonked the butcher to bag a big bird

Notice the alliteration… the triple t and the 4 b's which gives it great rhythm. Being a student of the art, I just had to flick to the story and read it (no other reason, I swear). The story copy wasn't quite as good, the headline being: **Turkey with BENEFITS** and the cute subhead **No matter how hard I tried I couldn't tell him to get stuffed.**

And the story unfolded of how "Tina" was dating a butcher but wanted to dump him before Christmas but kept the relationship going just so he'd supply her with a good turkey for the festive season.

Side note, to break up the copy in a magazine, like we would do with bullets in sales copy, they had a coloured "cut out" quote: **"I'd lay there like a slab of steak from his shop"**. Let you interpret that one.

Point is, the headline stopped me dead. It did its job. I read the article. So yep, it pays to put time into this part of your copy, if you want success. Your headline must stop them and make them do something they don't want to… read the next sentence in the article.

And just to prove that "Tina" wasn't a total cow, and that all good stories have a happy ending, this one finished with…

"Now, one year later, we are expecting our first bub and I couldn't be happier". Yes, seriously.

But that headline… **I bonked the butcher to bag a big bird** still makes me chuckle.

The power of discomfort

There's nothing better is there, than feeling like you've got it all under control. Things are ticking along. No major dramas. Things are good. Aaah… made it.

Or is there?

You see one of the things I commit to at the start of every year is more discomfort. No, I'm not revealing some deep dark masochistic side. What I have found by observation and study is that, as "good" as it is, there is danger in comfort. We get lazy. We get sloppy. We drift along. And we are never prepared for the hit that may be coming.

And then there's that saying, if you aren't growing, you're dying.

This is not one of those social media type rants to urge to get out there and "crush it" but to get you thinking about areas of comfort in your life and where these may not be serving you. What do you need to do more of? Or less of? Or start? Or eliminate? And it goes for any area of your life where you feel the danger sign that is comfort. In business, what are your areas of comfort that may not serve you? Do you need to send that new offer? Shoot that video you've avoided? Create that new campaign? Move the staff member on? Hire the new staff member? Speak to the copywriter?

What about your health? Something niggling away at you but you're just a little comfortable right now to do anything about it?

For me…

We started yoga. I haven't done yoga since I was in the Amazon in 2018 but for some reason felt it was the right to do it again (yep, would have been easier just to put it off).

I'm doing more speaking gigs. Plus got a few things brewing including live trainings and some podcast invites… easier and more comfortable to say no, but it's time to get uncomfortable.

Here's the other part of this…

Don't let your brain tell you you're not ready. You're never ready. No one ever is. Everyone could always use more preparation. More study. More feedback. More trial runs. Those are places of comfort. Growth is minimal. Out on the edge or in the arena in the thick of it, that's where growth occurs. Where in your life are you "comfortable"? Is it time to ditch the comfort and challenge yourself more?

Food for thought today: get uncomfortable, your future self will thank you.

Neat writing hack

Sounds a bit woo-woo I know, which explains why you don't often hear this talked about. But here goes…

Your words have a vibration.

Your reader will "feel" it before they rationalise it with a tangible thought. Another word for vibration is energy. How do you give your copy energy? Will give you 4 ways in a sec (slow down my eager padawan).

First, you must know WHY vibration or energy of words is important. Answer from ye ole Jedi word master…

Energetic copy gets read AND acted on. Flat or lifeless copy does not. Here is your Fast Lesson on 4 Ways to Give Your Copy Energy…

Energy in Copy Method #1 - You

Yep, that's right… YOU have to have energy, be "up" for it otherwise your lethargy comes across. True. So do whatever it takes to get yourself ready to write… sleep well the night before. Play your favourite pump up music.

Energy in Copy Method #2 - Your words

Make them active and fun… passive writing is boring.

Energy in Copy Method #3 - Emotional works

Use plenty of emotion and emotive words… nasty, embarrassed, cheated and so on.

Energy in Copy Method #4 - Your stories

Show don't tell. Take the reader with you. There is a definite skill to this, which is why I always spend time on the story whenever I teach copy.

Lesson endeth.

Harry the door-to-door salesman

I t was 1pm in my writing cave and I was under the pump. Big deadline looming. I'd just got up from my desk to grab a bite for lunch. There was a knock at the front gate. Lucky I was on a break because I ignore interruptions like this if I'm in writing mode. Anyway it was a fresh faced early 20 something door to door salesman named Harry selling auto servicing.

The offer was something like, pay just $169 today and you get a whole year's FREE labour on your car services. I let him go with his spiel. I'm interested in the sales process, so it was fun. One thing he did really well was put in my hands the flyer outlining all you get. But it was a flyer with a twist. Bulldog clipped to the right-hand side was a stack of already completed tear off sections, about 25 in all so it was heavy on the right side, you couldn't miss it. The effect?

Twofold: get the product in the customer's hands means you are one step closer to the sale AND…

Social proof. The stack of already completed forms was important social proof. Ticks to Harry. But… One big error (will tell you in a sec).

Being curious I started to ask him about the process. He works 5 days a week, 8 in the morning till about 7 at night. Commission only. Long days. Lots of leg work. But boy is he getting a crackin' business education. His close rate? 5 new customers a day is a good day for him. Turns out he was very new to this gig, it was his first week. Good on him. We talked for about 10 minutes. He was super keen when I told him I could help him close more and up his average. He got out his phone straight away.

No pictures mate, I'm not dressed for this. He started making notes in his phone. Gave him 3 or 4 pointers. A big one he liked…

He hadn't worked hard enough to show the VALUE of his offer. Pay $169 today and you save, over 12 months, $1,114 in labour costs… He had missed this vital ingredient of the value proposition. He loved the advice, thanked me profusely and walked off with a spring in his step.

Harry called by again about 10 days later. He just wanted to say hi and tell me his results since he'd made the change to his sales script… He was now closing an average of 6 people, an increase of 1.

Yep, just 1 but it had been only a week or so. Add that up over a week, a month a year of door to door and well it's not bad for a few minutes chat. He thanked me again and moved off that spring in his step again…

Question is, what NEW things are you doing (other than being smart enough to read this book!!!) to discover those small things which create big wins?

No one likes entering a dark room

What do you instinctively do when you walk into a dark room? Reach for the light switch, right?

Apart from the practicalities, here is a simple truth about us humans… we don't like entering a situation where we are unsure, or where something could go wrong, and we might get "hurt".

And it's the same in marketing…

Prospects won't enter a dark room. It confuses and even scares them. Plus it makes it easy for them to say no.

Part of every marketing message must be about "turning the light on" so they know what happens.

It can be something as simple as adding to a sales script telling them what happens next…

When you click the button below you'll be taken to a page to enter your details. It takes literally just 30 seconds to complete.

Or it can be as complex as…

Here are the 9 steps we go through with you to build your new home (and then you outline each step in the building process from inquiry to handover).

Of course the media and the point in the buying process dictate the level of detail you need.

Just remember, **no one likes walking into a dark room.**

So if you want to boost response, make sure you turn the light on for them by telling them what happens next. In doing so you remove a friction point from the sales process which makes it easier for them to say yes.

Just relax, baby

J ust relax, baby...

So went the words of the Eddie Cochran song circa 1950s...

Just relax, baby let's don't fight

Everything's gonna be all right

And while it might be about relationships (or more specifically bedding your partner) there is a business lesson here...

Forcing ideas to come to you... under stress, rarely works. As hard as it may be in the heat of the moment, relaxation is the key to success. Not just in writing. Or business. But in sport and just about every area of life.

In his excellent book *Psycho-Cybernetics* Dr Maxwell Maltz says, "It has been amply demonstrated that attempting to use effort or willpower... has an adverse, rather than beneficial, effect."

Relax, don't force it...

If you haven't read *Psycho-Cybernetics*, regarded by many as the seminal work in the personal development field, suggest you get it. Written sometime in the 50s, the book was resurrected by Dan Kennedy before Matt Furey took it over. The latest version has commentary from Matt, like on page 93...

Best ideas without effort.

Not without thought mind you... but without focussed effort.

Try it out.

Just relax, baby and let the ideas flow.

How to use language to boost proof

We've already seen how important proof is to your sales message. Here's another way to ramp up the proof elements... language.

Be specific.

A number is much more believable than a general statement.

Some examples...

Light and easy to carry is nice but...

Weighs just 1.2 kilograms really gives it meaning.

Large storage area tells a story, but...

34% more space is specific and quantifiable.

Well established suggests longevity and therefore safety. But...

Now in our 14th year is clear and definite.

Fast acting is good, but...

Removes stains in just 60 seconds or less is even sexier.

See the difference?

Get specific if you want a bump in conversions.

Key to great copy

What separates ordinary copy from great copy?

Tough question to answer.

Sure it's about the big idea behind the promotion.

The eye-catching headline.

Words that read fast.

Strong offer and clear call to action.

Those are the "mechanical" things.

The real answer though is the "feeling" the reader gets.

Because great copy, from the reader's perspective, is like a great talk you hear...

When they read it, **it feels to them like time has stopped** and the only thing that matters is the next word they read.

And yes, that is BIG.

When you achieve that in your copy you're well on your way to a greater influence on the world.

Crisis or opportunity – you get to choose

" *We're going under and I can't make it, good luck hope it goes well.* "

Was a rather forlorn email I received from a subscriber about a week before one of my live trainings she had booked into. She was at a crisis point and was letting me know she and her 2 staff members could no longer make it. I thanked her for her courtesy and refunded her booking fee as per the guarantee. And I also sent her a list of 4 suggestions she take immediate action with.

To keep her situation private, I won't go into details, but this did get me thinking about business and life's big moments…

Are they a crisis or an opportunity? The Chinese word for crisis is made up of 2 symbols which mean "danger" and "opportunity".

And …

Interestingly the English word crisis comes from the Greek krisis which means "choice".

When you're in the middle of one of these big moments in business or life, it often doesn't seem like a choice does it… but I guess it really is. At least from the point of view of how we THINK about it…

Do we look for the gift in the situation and trust in our own ability to work through it? Or do we choose to go the other way…

Get down in the dumps which starts a negative spiral?

Famed Depression era businessman Henry Kaiser, who made a fortune out of turning around catastrophic situations and building businesses which put thousands of people in work, was asked on his deathbed about some guiding principles in his life.

His response: Problems are simply opportunities in work clothes.

Crisis = choice.

I truly believe there is balance and a choice of response in EVERY situation… even ones we don't like what's happened… if only we get out of our heads and see it.

Tastes like chicken

So what does buffalo taste like?

A bit like beef but stronger.

Ah… ok.

What about crocodile?

A bit like chicken, just a little more stringy.

Righto.

Now even without tasting buffalo or croc, you have an understanding of their flavours. It's now "easier" to make a decision. If you like beef or chicken, it's now "safe" to give them a go.

This copywriting "click" called "tastes like chicken" (for obvious reasons) is a powerful persuasive device.

It's best used to explain a complex concept or something unknown to the reader. You frame the unknown in terms of what they know.

Remember, confused people do nothing.

So tastes like chicken is important in a complex sale.

Boost believability

These days, there's a lot of shouting going on in marketing. The "million-dollar promise" has been done to death. Even big bold claims can become boring if overdone. How then can you be more authentic in this sea of shouting.

Try what I call "the drop". This is when you include something "average" or "ordinary" to make the message more believable and attainable.

Just one example… a chunk of copy might read…

Want proof. Well, three recent clients report results like:

Mary with a spike in sales of $95,000 in just 6 weeks

John from Perth says he made $102,000 in 4 months

And Cory from Cairns boosted his sales by $75,000 in 9 weeks

Yes, you too can do the same…

Ok, it's a rough example for a small business market. But notice how they are all big numbers? They seem way out there… potentially difficult, too difficult and unrealistic for some or even many to achieve.

Look at what happens when you include "the drop"

Want proof. Well, three recent clients report results like:

Mary with a spike in sales of $95,000 in just 6 weeks

Bill from Brisbane made an extra $15,000 in 4 weeks

And Cory from Cairns boosted his sales by $75,000 in 9 weeks

Yes, you too can do the same…

See how this dials the hype back… "drops" the expectations so it's more reachable for a segment of the market? It also sends a message that not everyone scores big, but this doesn't mean they don't get results.

If you're having trouble getting them to believe, include "the drop" in your next sales message and see how you go.

Last thing…

You can only ever use real proof… choose a smaller win from your bank of client successes.

Note: the above are examples only created for illustration purposes… but "the drop" is an effective way to keep results within reach of a broader audience.

Choice = power

Want to feel personally powerful?

Understand this important truth...

There are TWO and only 2 things you can really control in your day.

Best part is you have a choice about both.

What are they?

First, what you do with your time - the work/people/tasks you do...

And second...

How you FEEL about the work/people/tasks you do.

That's it.

And yep, you get to choose BOTH.

So why waste what precious time you have doing crappy things and feeling crappy about those crappy things?

Choose to feel good about what you do and you change your results.

A couple of mentors I have are really big on this because it is a "secret" to personal power and happiness.

Internet trolls are great

When you hear the words "internet troll" if you're anything like me the words *GET A LIFE* immediately spring to mind.

But not so fast.

Believe it or not, we can (and need to) learn a thing or two about those poor souls who criticise, bring down, and defame others online.

No, I'm not advocating you do this.

What I am saying is, if you really want to connect to and empathise with your target market you need to take a leaf out of the trolls' book and spend time online.

Check out forums your market hangs out on.

Go to the Facebook groups they frequent.

Give Reddit a good going over.

If they're on LinkedIn, check that out too.

Why?

Well, when you become a "troll for good" you get to know your market and the WORDS they use. In these groups you'll see certain language patterns coming through. And you'll get to know them at a much deeper level.

More:

Everyone talks about research but really, like I've already said, no one teaches it. This one little snippet, if you act on it, will make a world of difference to your copy.

When you use their language you connect more.

And your response skyrockets because they feel you're one of them.

Hate seeing the distress

R eally hate it when I see business owners in distress. Like "Greg". We were in a consult and he was lamenting lack of conversions. You see employees don't get it (I know, used to be one). All they (mostly) worry about is doing their job, paying their bills, and getting to the weekend so they can have fun. Ok, sure, that's over-simplified, point is their mindset is different.

Because for the business owner the buck stops right here. And unless you've been that guy or girl, you don't know the feeling… where you lay awake at night wondering where the next sale is coming from… or how you'll make payroll this week. It's why I get a real kick out of helping business owners out of their distress… they are the hardy souls who put it all on the line to run their own race. And that alone is a trait I love. Here are just three quick examples (read them for the marketing lessons) of how I've helped business owners lately:

For "Greg"… like I said he was pretty upset because his ads were not converting. The ads were "ok" but lacked that little bit of pizzazz… so I gave him several headline options to test, one of which was a version of the classic…

How to Achieve X Without Y… the key word here is "without" because it taps into the sloth in all humans… we all want fast and easy with little work… his market especially. "Greg" went away and tested this and other new headlines and came back smiling.

Then there is my client in the higher education space with a headline that was the business name. They are small competing with some big fish. So apart from anything else, it was poor positioning. We fixed that. The headline/subhead combo now appeals to the market's pain points and positions the business as the logical alternative.

And then my client in the corporate space… the industry they are selling into has taken a media-generated beating over a few dodgy providers which has tarred the whole industry.

So what did I do? Sniffed an opportunity.

The conversations going on in the minds of industry CEOs is all about the stress of dealing with this increased scrutiny. Just so happens my client has a solution to protect them. So we wrote to CEOs offering to meet with them to discuss how we can help.

Here we are leveraging the conversations already in the mind of the target audience. So yep, easing peeps' "distress" is what I love to do. For them the value comes because I bring fresh eyes to their business and help them see things, they may not see themselves.

Speed of the read hack

We want our sales message to be read FAST.

One way to do this is to vary your sentence lengths. I do have a bias towards short crisp sentences.

When we talk, we generally use a variety of sentences…

Some are short and quick.

Others more long-winded when we are trying to convey more information, or a strong emotion. Just vary them. (See… shorter, longer, shorter).

WARNING: too many short sentences together can be "bumpy" ie your copy has no rhythm and flow.

So make sure, despite what length your sentences are, your copy always reads fast and smooth.

But do so with a bias towards shorter, easier to read sentences that flow.

Respond effectively to "no"

Y ou'll never close 100% of prospects. And when they say "no" it does NOT mean no, never ever. People buy in their own time, not in yours.

I've never seen a "formula" for when to give up on a sale.

Some marketers recommend you focus on the now or soon buyers because at a certain point the law of diminishing returns kicks in.

Others tell the story, with great pride, of how they made 103 calls to a prospect before they got a yes.

What to do then? Every business owner every day is faced with the pursue or move on decision.

Here's the thing…

According to direct mail legend Dick Benson a person who buys twice from you is TWICE as likely to buy again compared to a one-time buyer.

The message…

One and done never works.

If you want to grow your influence by building your business, get the same buyer to buy from you more than once. Because when they do, it increases your chances of future sales.

What to do then…

- Map out your sales process
- Develop a marketing funnel so you can see holes in your sales system
- And plug them pronto to turn each customer into a multiple buyer

Look for where you can upsell. Where you can add a second offer. Where you can get them to buy at least twice to take advantage of the "twice buyer syndrome" Dick Benson revealed.

Pick the winning headline

Q uick contest to click your marketing mind into gear today (and a little twist to get you thinking even deeper). Here we go, which headline was more successful?

Exhibit A: **"The 4 Hour Work Week"**

Or

Exhibit B: **"How to Get Rich Slowly"**

Got your answer? Ok, good. Hands down, Exhibit A would be better, right? Way better. Quick analysis:

Exhibit A is Tim Ferris' famous book. Great title and really taps into human sloth and our ever-present desire for quick fast and easy.

So it should "win", yes? Not so fast.

Exhibit B is, surprisingly, from the guy most consider the greatest living copywriter, Gary Bencivenga.

Who wants to get rich slowly? Can't possibly work can it? But…

And apparently Gary had to dig his heals in to have the company run the headline… But this one also kicked butt and was the control for an ad that ran for a long time. No I don't have exact figures, but the answer to the "which won" question is "both".

Two BIG points here…

It's all about market awareness - WHO you're targeting, what's gone before you and what's worked and not worked.

And…

Don't assume you "think" you know what will work best. You must test it.

Turn every customer into 2

U psells work, it's a fact.

You've been asked MANY times, "You want fries with that?" for a reason.

That one simple 5-word sentence has resulted in billions of $$$ worth of sales!

Here's why…

According to a study by Marketing Metrics, you have a 60% to 70% probability of selling to an existing customer, compared to just a 5% to 20% chance of selling to a new prospect.

So yep, there's a reason the Golden Arches folk ask you that question… and Amazon uses "people who bought your book also bought…" and show you about 8 more to choose from.

Be clear about this…

The person most likely to buy is one who has just bought.

AND…

The time the person is most likely to buy again is while they are buying or immediately after buying.

Do you upsell enough?

Why gossip is the BEST thing ever...

What do you feel when you see two people whispering? And what about if they are whispering and then look over at you?

And...

What if they then suddenly stop?

Or worst of all... laugh.

How does that make you feel? Horrible, right? You just have to know what they are saying.

It burns at you... eats away... you just have to know.

And this force is one of the greatest tools in copy, and more specifically your headline.

Curiosity.

It's the same if you're walking along and you see a group of people standing there looking up into the sky pointing, what do you do?

Stop and look up. Why?

Curiosity. Us humans are hyper curious beings.

So it makes sense to leverage this, especially in your headlines... you want to make people curious to read on. You need to have curiosity with the benefit for them based on the market's emotions.

Curiosity may have killed the cat but it's your path to conversions and influence!

Use it wherever you can.

Why I hate fake tans

H ere are the top 3 reasons I hate fake tans. No, it's not that they go all yellow. It's not that they are, well, fake. It's not that they even cost money.

Quick backstory and marketing lesson: August and September are BIG social months in our house. All 3 girls and 1 of the boys under our roof have birthdays... plus it's our wedding anniversary. So there are several things on the go... and, let's say a desire to look good for said occasions. Which requires some tanning, apparently.

I'm not a fan. Three reasons why...

#1 - It smells funny - #2 - It smells funny – And #3 - It smells funny

You see, being an empath, I have a heightened sense of smell (a big nose helps too... proof: I'm almost always the first to whiff cigarette smoke, some perfumes are way too strong, and well, that fake tan smell).

To my great displeasure recently a box of the stuff arrived at our doorstep, but it did provide marketing fodder. The company packaged it up nicely and included two marketing pieces. Not bad.

The first was an attractive postcard (which missed the mark, more on this in a sec). The second was a full colour catalogue with all their products, quality before/after pix and a cool little story about the company revealing their organic/eco credentials.

To the postcard and where they missed the mark...

FRONT:

Congratulations on being you! Don't be too hard on yourself, you deserve love and care! (with a nice sunset beach scene from Currumbin on the Gold Coast).

BACK:

Hi Beautiful, Thank you for your order! You're going to love our Aussie Made Organic Goodies! We love seeing photos from our tribe so tag @biz name in your photos. Shine bright! Blessings xx <name and business name>

Nice connecting copy. What's missing I hear you ask??? An incentive... a reason to look at the catalogue... a special offer.

I've spoken about this in a couple of the recent entries: the best time to sell someone again is when they buy or receive their purchase... they are excited and more likely to buy. Something as simple as ***"Take 20% off all items in the enclosed catalogue - make sure you use the discount code on the last page to claim your special price"*** or similar. That's just one example. There are many other ways to encourage the buyer to open and respond to the catalogue. Reckon they are leaving big $$$ on the table here... small hinges swing big doors...

The #1 Mistake to avoid

This cuts across all demographics, all industries, all businesses. The biggest mistake people make is underestimating the difficulty of the task of selling. You need to really understand this because it's not so much about you, it's about them out there who you're trying to sell to.

Consider this… what did you get up this morning and think about? If you're anything like most people, it was stuff like…

Gee I hope the traffic's okay, I've got to get there on time.

I've got to set things up at work.

Hope <child> goes ok at school today.

And on it goes.

Key thing…

At some point, you thought of the immediate problems in your day. That's what was on your mind. We think about our own problems. Not buying something from someone. And the thing is, as business owners, what we try and do is show up and overcome all that stuff going on in people's heads and sell them something.

Look, it doesn't matter if we arrive dressed nicely, and if we've got a good brand and all those sorts of things. They won't buy YOUR stuff because they've got THEIR stuff going on. It's ALWAYS a challenge to cut through that busy-ness in people's lives and I think even more so today, you know with social media and all sorts of distractions.

So hear this good and proper…

NEVER UNDERESTIMATE THE DIFFICULTY OF THE TASK OF SELLING.

When you do, you are ALWAYS disappointed. Always.

Use templates... beware of templates...

Templates can be a GREAT short cut. But also a trap. 2 KEY POINTS: all copy is situational, meaning it may not work in another market in another time, so you need to test it... AND... importantly, there is usually NEVER one simple solution.

Take for example headlines.

I love what I call the emergency poncho of headlines, the already spoken about **"How to Get X Without Doing Y"** because it taps into the human trait of sloth. We all have a lazy streak... who doesn't want success without the hard work? It's why Gold Lotto is so popular! Which is why this template can work.

But... it may not work all the time in every situation in every market.

Here's a QUICK TIP TO BOOST HEADLINE PUNCH...

Use Proven Power Words. Statistics have shown that certain words in your headline – and in your copy – get you better results. Here are a few examples:

Amazing - Secret - Suddenly - Now - Quick - Easy - Free - You – Discover - Announcing - Revolutionary - Breakthrough - Improvement - Introducing - Miracle and on it goes.

Remember, templates are great but not a silver bullet.

Don't surrender to this thought

This is really destructive to your success and it's also complete and utter bullshit. But if I'm being totally honest with myself, in the past, I've succumbed to this "woe is me thinking".

Flashback to recent discussions with a business owner. She dropped this nugget…

"It's ok for you and guys like you but I'm just not a natural business owner".

No idea who "guys like me" are but in my humble (and correct) opinion, this is an excuse for the results you have right now. Period.

Here is the TRUTH…

There is no such thing as a natural business owner.

No one comes with a natural or God-given set of business tools they open up to magically produce business excellence and success. Thinking "they" do, and "you" don't is a cop out.

Heck, I was in a school for 40 odd years… not a business environment. And I've done "ok" over the last decade or so. Natural? Nope. Magic set of tools? I was never gifted them.

REALITY CHECK…

Business owners work hard. They test. They think. They fail. They learn. They solve problems.

And just about everyone in business today also evolves… from the skill of what they do to mastery of it… and then from operator of a skill to owner of the whole show. People don't simply get better at business because they want to. They get better because they get better. So don't ever let your mind wander with destructive thoughts about success.

In her book *Reclaim the Magic* Lee Milteer says every one of us is gifted each day with 5 kinds of energy… physical, mental, spiritual, emotional, and financial…

Which is why you must guard your thoughts against gremlins like "I'm not a natural business owner"… all they do is rob you of focus and energy.

Magic words

Write ONLY to those people who are prepared to give you money... NOT to everyone!

Every market has its own "Magic Words" or Phrases which, when used, help you connect to your prospects (remember... "Boobies Make Me Happy").

Also, I mentioned in entry #51 John Carlton's Famous...

Amazing Secret Discovered by One-Legged Golfer Adds 50 Yards To Your Drives, Eliminates Hooks and Slices And Can Slash Up To 10 Strokes From Your Game Almost Overnight!

One of the reasons it was so successful was because it contains words specific to the golfing market... drives, hooks, slices, strokes. Water polo players for example would turn the page.

My headline that did so well for a webinar in the real estate investing niche...

"The Once-in-a-Lifetime Real Estate Deal"

Here's a rare and exclusive chance to invest in cashflow positive freehold properties in one of Australia's most sought after CBDs - anyone earning $60K pa or more can get started now!

Contains "magic words" for the real estate investing niche... invest, cashflow positive properties, CBD.

Use the "magic words" of your market to attract and bond prospects to you.

Box of fruit

The WORST marketing piece of the year candidate has emerged. It was a postcard which was a serious waste of money and a "worthy" candidate. If marketing dross offends, look away now…

Side A:

Full colour photo of a box of fruit, with several boxes of vegetables behind like you'd see at a local store. Four words of copy only and both down the bottom… bottom left corner had the biz name (one word); bottom right corner the "headline", the glorious "Spring has arrived".

Like I said, look away now. Sigh.

Side B:

Top right quadrant had the copy:

"Spring is traditionally a time of renewal and change while also being when the property market becomes more competitive. With buyer activity heating up, our team is ready to help you get the best possible result on your property. Call us today to ensure this is your best Spring yet." Then right down the bottom, 2 people's names, emails and mobile numbers.

Lots of white space.

Sigh. Again.

Ok, I get the attempt at "entering the conversation in our minds" ie Spring is here but beyond that there is almost NOTHING here that constitutes even "average" copy/ marketing/strategy. This is not the first (and won't be the last) of this nonsense to emerge from the real estate niche (and it's why my good mate Glenn Twiddle has pulled all his hair out fighting against this industry standard gunk).

Follow the fundamentals of copywriting, don't throw them out the window like this postcard has done. It's a total waste of time and money. And a good example of the danger of being "creative".

Lead magnets – quick refresher

Need some ideas for a lead magnet? Here's a quick refresher (if you haven't used a lead magnet before it's something of value you offer to your market in exchange for their contact information).

Lead magnets can be a:

- ✓ Checklist
- ✓ Free lesson
- ✓ Template
- ✓ Free sample
- ✓ Short training
- ✓ Consumer Guide
- ✓ Industry Report
- ✓ Resource guide
- ✓ Free upgrade and on it goes

Keys to these:

It needs an enticing title based on the emotions of the market and solving a problem they have.

It needs an offer/call to action as a next step for the prospect.

It can be anything from a single page to a longer piece.

There is a school of thought these days that lead magnets are better off being small, something that can be consumed in 5 minutes or less. Test this.

What they think about you

How confident are you that how you show up for your customers is how THEY see you? Two quick examples to sow you what I mean.

And no, it's not an apples-to-apples comparison but it's still instructive.

Example #1 – my busted coffee machine

Disaster struck one morning. The Nespresso machine started spurting water and coffee from holes it shouldn't have. No way was I going back to instant, no way! Quick call to their hotline… They courier a loan machine to you while they check out and/or repair the old one and courier it back. Nice and easy and close to painless.

Example #2 – me being nice for Mother's Day

Rang a local cleaning company to do a house clean on a Friday in prep for Mother's Day on Sunday. Eldest was coming home etc so nice thought, right? (Ok, it's close to husband of the year stuff I agree but modesty prevents me accepting the award). Anyways, the company, which was recommended, had a mobile phone number on the website. Hmmm. Reservations aside, I rang it. Voice message was a version of… *Our office hours are 8:30 till 5pm Mon-Fri please leave a message and we'll get back to you.* I left a message. 5:45pm the phone rings but I can't take the call because I'm in a meeting. I ring back the next day. Same voice message. I leave another message. 24 hours later, nothing. One more go the following day (yes, totally deserving hubby of year award, the trouble I've gone to, gee whiz, what a guy…).

This time I got a live voice, yay. Business owner said, in response to my can you clean our house on the X date inquiry, and to paraphrase: *I'm out of the office right now, will have to check availability, will get back to you.* I heard nothing more. No, it's not a fair comparison… one's a BIG company that hired George Clooney… the other a mum and dad type operation. But…

They just lost this job… and any future jobs… and any recommendation from me. No points for guessing how I NOW see these two businesses.

EVERY interaction you have with another human… written, spoken, non-verbal… is a SALES TRANSACTION, even when no money changes hands.

How DO they see you? Hopefully more like I now see Nespresso and not how I see the cleaners.

Cool "no cost" research tool

During your research, if you want to see what's working in your market now...

Who the big players are...

What things interest people...

And even what key phrases hook your prospects in... then check this out... like I said, it's "cool" and "free".

Teased you enough?

Ok, here you go...

It's called "Vid Tao"

https://vidtao.com/

You need to sign up for a free account.

After that the world of You Tube video is your oyster.

How is this useful?

Well, say you sell software in the writing space and a competitor is Grammarly...

Go to VidTao, type "Grammarly" into their search bar and you can see how many views all of the Grammarly Youtube ads have had.

If something has had more than, say, 500,000 views... then this ad's a winner.

You can watch the ad. Hear the key words they use.

Plus, you get access to data on higher level stuff like trends in your market and...

Specific stuff like what type of ads are working.

That's half the research battle... being able to see quickly and easily what's going on in your market.

Here's the link again if you want to check it out: https://vidtao.com/

Enjoy!

My embarrassing Netflix confession

O k, I admit it. When we first got Netflix, I was kind of hooked on it. Mostly the movies. Reckon I watched more in the first 3 months than the previous 3 years. It's a little difficult to admit it… maybe a little embarrassing… because…

Instead of telling stories of punching out winning promos one after the other… Of how disciplined I am and what a fine example to you I am… like many do on Facebook… I admit it. I'm watching movies. Usually with a bowl of popcorn in hand. Often. Maybe too often - sorry family, will join you in 15 minutes!

Sure, the work still got done and to a high standard… with sexy results for my clients.

But…

Aaaah… the movies… love' them!

Recent fav was *Walt Before Mickey*. Which tells the story of Walt Disney's early years before he skyrocketed to fame on the back of Mickey Mouse. Wow.

What Mr Disney went through. It's one heck of a persistence story every entrepreneur should see. He got into BIG financial trouble, closed a business, and moved cities. He endured false friends, disloyal staff and an investor who set out to screw him (and succeeded).

But he had a dream. He never gave up. And truth be known he got out here and hustled. There, I said it. If you're having a crappy day and want a bit of inspiration to pull your downtrodden butt out of the self-pity mire (we've all been in)…

Then watch this movie.

To be clear, it's not a great movie. It is a great persistence story. And well worth the 90 odd minutes it goes for.

Word hacks explained

Should we really cut back on adverbs and adjectives?

Yes. Class is in, sit up and pay attention…

Adverb = word that describes a verb, usually ends in 'ly' eg I ran quickly.

And often unnecessary because it weakens the message.

Sample:

The XYZ product will solve your problem quickly.

Vs

XYZ gives you fast results.

Which reads quicker? Which is shorter? Which is easier to read? Which is more active?

So yep, avoid adverbs if you can.

Next…

Adjective = word that describes a noun eg he is such a lazy dog.

Not "wrong" but too many adjectives can lessen the power of a message.

So yep, writing hack for today… test your copy with fewer adverbs and adjectives.

It can make the message stronger and easier to read.

Copywriting Click – The Story of Two People

O ne of the most famous and successful sales letters of all time is the Wall St Journal Letter (just Google it for a copy). It was based on an old ad from the Civil War era. With this Click you create a story that compares two people with the same background and same opportunities but only one is successful… the person who used your product or service.

It's another powerful way to demonstrate the RESULT your product gives. Example:

Two beginning writers with similar backgrounds met at a copywriting event. Both were enthusiastic, skilled, and full of great intentions about building a successful business.

They left the event promising each other they'd stay in touch. Life got busy and they never did.

Quite by chance they met three years later.

One of the writers had struggled all this time. He was never fully booked and charged below industry rates, just to get himself some work. He'd even contemplated giving up writing and returning to a job.

The other writer? His career went completely the other way. He was one of the speakers at the event and told the story from stage how he'd booked five jobs in the last week, the smallest of which was $25,000.

Over a few quiet drinks after the event the two caught up again and were chatting about their careers.

"I'm so happy for you man," said the struggling copywriter.

"Thanks brother," said the speaker.

"Tell me something," the struggling writer said next, "How did you get to where you are so fast?"

It wasn't desire. It wasn't skill level. It wasn't even luck.

The difference was revealed by the superstar copywriter, "This one book changed everything for me man, you got to get yourself a copy, it's called The Influential Marketer by Steve Plummer."

See? This is just a quick example, but it shows the structure of the Wall St Journal letter.

Ok, look it's my book so allow me to have a little fun, will ya? Just remember, the story of two similar people, where one makes it (because of your product or service) and the other doesn't is time-tested.

Give it a go.

Drop you with one punch...

I'm 71 and I could drop you with one punch!

So growled veteran boxing trainer Rob to me one day in the gym. Talk about a pattern interrupt...

There I was in the gym working "hard" when in comes Rob with a local iron woman he's been training for years.

Want to join us? He said with a weird smile I immediately mistook for a sadistic grin. Turned out my instincts were in fact right...

Old school Rob sure as heck gave me a training "pattern interrupt". Haven't worked that hard or sweated that much since I was about 23.

But gee it was good.

The hard work I put in under Rob's torture tutelage meant I could do way more in the gym the next time I went. So yes, we all benefit from a shake-up.

Interesting point:

You're strong in the legs, strong in the shoulders but weak here. Thump to my solar plexus. Ouch. Was how the master coach described me... all based on about 5 minutes of watching.

You run or something do ya? (No idea how he knew). So yep, for me more ab work was needed.

Give me 6 weeks with ya and I'll give you a 6 pack your missus will rub her hands all over!

Gotta love old school. So yeah, a pattern interrupt works at all levels...

How can you apply it today?

Is everyone really doing it?

*O*h *God, you've got to be on Tik Tok , everyone is there, it's like the biggest marketplace today.*

So said a prospect of mine in a conversation recently. Really? I mean really? A word of caution.

Me gets a little twitchy when I hear the words "everyone is doing X". As in you should be too. For starters, there is ageless wisdom that says, "the masses are almost always wrong". Plus, good old Tik Tok's a media, not a marketplace. So let's deal in facts.

Again I'm not saying Tik Tok and other social media are NOT effective. Know of lots of businesses built through it… to generate leads, entertain and educate, build groups to get people into a funnel and eventually sell them. As a media its generated millions upon millions for businesses of all shapes and sizes. That said, it's NOT for every business. Every campaign. Every situation.

Take my client in the higher education space. We are NOT using Facebook or Tik Tok or Insta. Their prospects do NOT shop for their services on social media.

It's a close, relationship-driven, and tight market that requires a different, more targeted, and personalised approach. The socials would be a waste of time and money.

Not so if the client was a gym or personal trainer or the like.

So be discerning with how you spend your marketing coin. It can be tough with so many instant experts popping up these days with their latest shiny object.

And because "everyone" is doing something, doesn't mean you "should".

What to focus on in your message

What should you focus on in your copy? Many things of course is the obvious answer, but this came up while critiquing a client's first effort recently. Like many who know enough to be dangerous, this copy "almost" did the job.

But…

It focused too much on features and not enough on benefits. Which is a common trap.

To help the client, and you too, here is a list of 5 essential benefits to highlight in your copy…

- Increased time, money, power/control
- Reduced risk/exposure
- Increased security/safety/protection
- Make you more attractive
- More knowledge to give you a better chance at above 4 appeals

If you talk too much about your program, product or service and not so much about one or more of these appeals, chances are your sales message is "weaker" than you want.

Last point…

All of these must then lead to a strong offer so the prospect is left with the feeling of:

"I'd be nuts, right now, to say no".

Did your last piece of copy do this?

The importance of rituals

Y our life is ruled by rituals. Take for example Christmas/New Year festivities. The coin toss at the start of a cricket match is another. And you can name any and all religious traditions for more. In her excellent book *Reclaim the Magic* author Lee Milteer says the main purpose of rituals is to focus your intent and energy on your objective.

She also is adamant: "Ritual must be focused on want you want to create, not on what you want to get rid of; this is a very important distinction." And so I thought I'd let you in on my "first day at work" rituals used at the start of a new work year. Mine go like this…

I write something that's going to be published (to get back in the groove)… an email to my list is an example.

I read the first 3 chapters of *Breakthrough Advertising* by Gene Schwartz.

To me this is a great "re-set" and "re-focus" tool for my many upcoming writing projects… Chapter 1 talks about the force that makes advertising work, Chapter 2 about the prospect's state of awareness and Chapter 3 is an important reminder about the sophistication of the market you sell to at any one time. There's a good chance too I'll flick through Chapter 4 because it reveals 38 ways to strengthen a headline. Re-set… re-focus…

Next I go to my goals for the year and re-visit these.

I'll also, to get my head back in the game, revisit important notes taken at one of the mastermind groups I'm in, especially those that set up success in the New Year.

And the last thing I do is ensure I have a "new" sales call booked… note, as the old year closed out, I made sure sales calls were booked for this first week back… I'm talking here about a NEW sales opportunity. That process begins day 1. Even if I don't have the call this first day or week, I want my mind focused firmly on "new opportunity".

We hear a lot about it in sports today… momentum… how a team can get on a roll and the losing team must do something to break the momentum of the winning team. So my first day back is all about setting that momentum in train.

Case in point…

I recall dinner with friends one January and the guy had returned to work. He reported the first 2 days were "tough" where he never got anything meaningful done. He admitted day 3 was when he found his groove again. Why wait? Work has started… My rituals, worked out over several years, set me up to hit the ground running because as entrepreneurs, we ain't got time to "ease into" work… we got a business to run!

Go ahead, get stuck in, there's work to be done. Rituals help.

Breaking news: proven headline words

C heck this out... Breaking news from a copywriting blogger I stumbled upon (my bad, should have noted their name down - apology in advance). According to the blogger, here are the top headline words to use online these days "because you've only got 3 seconds" to get their attention:

You

Results

Health

Guarantee

Discover

Love

Proven

Safety

New

Now

Free

Great, right? Anything "new"? Hardly. For years I've been teaching business owners and beginning writers to use as a headline starting point the most used words in the top 100 most successful (offline) headlines of all time...

You

Your

How

New

Who

Money

Now

People

Want

Why

Note the cross over. When training copy students, after these top 10 proven headline words I also give students about 30 other "power" words to use. And no surprises... the "power" words appear in the list of "new" headline words. This is not a criticism of the blogger. They've given solid advice with that list of words. But here's the thing...

Just because the media has changed, doesn't mean you sell to a robot... there's still a human with all the same needs, wants, desires and fears reading your message. So stick to proven before you get fancy... even when trying a new media.

When not to pile on the value

I t was a complete flop.

Flashback a few years when I was working for the big boys as their "hired gun" copywriter...

We ran several really big competitions for themselves and clients... we're talking chance to win big prizes... $100,000... $250,000... a $500,000 investment home... the list goes on.

You get the idea. Big wow factor to get attention and lots of entries. GREAT list builder. The cool thing about these big promos is they are relatively cheap to run.

It does highlight, even when you get the copy part right, a promo can still flop.

Case in point: they ran a huge value competition offering a luxury cruise to horse owners was tested as a lead generator. It bombed big time...

I wasn't a fan of the idea but lost the argument.

Why did it not work?

Main reason: a horse owner was never going to leave their beloved alone in the paddock for 10 days to take the cruise... too much of a hassle to organise feeding, supervision etc... so they didn't enter.

What if they'd tried "win free feed for a year"? Now that may have got horse owners' attention.

The message is clear: be strategic and think through all marketing efforts. Just because you can, just because it worked for "them", doesn't make it a sure or good thing for your business. When you really know who you sell to and what floats their boat, you have a much better chance of succeeding.

And sometimes, even when you get this right, it can still bomb.

That's marketing.

Learn the lessons and take another swing.

They almost always miss this, do you?

This is so easy to say but harder to do. Which is probably the reason many do it so poorly. What am I talking about?

Showing up differently in the marketplace.

This gets down to two fundamentals…

What you say (your copy, your sales messages).

How they see you (your marketing assets like your website, lead gen, shock and awe pack, and so forth).

Take for instance the IT services niche I've done a reasonable chunk of work in. So many of the marketing messages are product focused… a version of…

Great IT solutions at a good price.

Sorry, your business (IT solutions) is NOT different. And the market you are selling to, other businesses, is NOT different. They still buy on emotions (which "may" be different to consumers, but emotions nonetheless) and justify with logic.

My challenge to you…

Do you show up like NOBODY else in your niche… or like EVERYONE else?

Here's an important truth: people often pay for WHO you are rather than WHAT you do.

The WHAT is really a commodity eg you can get a website done on Airtasker for $100 or pay a top-notch web guy or girl $30k plus. Whatever it is you do, they can almost always find someone who does it cheaper.

Therefore, the unique YOU is vital to your messaging…

Do you show up differently to everyone else? Does the YOU leverage your point of difference in your market…Or do you fade into the grey of quality sameness out there?

When things are tight, do you do this?

Here's a fast and easy way to generate cash in your business. Because at some point, everyone faces this. And no, this is not a magic pill... But a strategy you can deploy rather quickly (and frankly should use often). This comes from a discussion with a client recently about ways to get more moolah in the door. You see they bemoaned the expense and time of getting new customers.

And they are right. You have to attract/lead generate. Build trust. Convert. It takes time, effort, and resources. So why not tap the unbanked money in your existing customer base? It's relatively easy and much cheaper than chasing new all the time. So I suggested a reactivation campaign targeting customers who've not bought from them in 6 months or more.

This required these jobs...

- Go to the database and identify those who've not bought and create a sub list (it might be 50, 100 or even 10, depending on the type of business you run)
- Choose the media to reach them in (is it phone call, email, post card, direct mail, SMS or other)
- Create a special offer (eg 30% off if you come back in before X date, buy one get one free this week only and on it goes)
- Craft your "reason why" sales message
- Deploy

The message can be as simple as...

Hi <name>,

Have you moved or been away lately?

Reason I ask is we haven't seen you recently and we miss you!

We'd love to see you back. So just <whatever the mechanism is eg bring in this postcard> and save 25% off your next purchase with <biz name>! It's our way of saying we miss you and welcome back. Just hurry, this special offers expires on <date> and we'd hate you to miss out.

Sign off

Ok, that's quick and rough but you get the idea. And it really can be as simple as that... leverage your past efforts of building trust with your tribe and invite "lost" customers back with an incentive. Some baulk at this... the cost... seems needy... I'm cutting my margins... and on it goes. But think of life-time customer value. This is quick and easy to do, and it can move the needle in your sales very quickly.

Your job today: make a list of 10 or 20 or 50 (or pick a number) of customers who've not bought from you in a while. Then reach out to them like I've shown you just now... not all will buy... but you might be surprised by the response you get.

Use numbers in copy

Two ways you'll get push back on this…

From a guru (or fan boy/girl of a guru) who says otherwise… and your English teacher at school who commanded, "Any number under a hundred should be written out in full". Yes Miss.

Just remember, we have a sale to make. So do what works, not what's "correct" or what "they" say you should, unless you have tested it.

Especially in headlines, but in copy in general, **there are 2 VERY powerful reasons why you MUST use numbers:**

1. A number goes into the brain 3 times faster than the same words; and

2. It takes less space, so it aids the speed of the read.

To be clear, it's ALWAYS – 52% of people… NOT fifty-two percent of people or even 52 per cent of people.

Or The 7 Ways to Improve Your Headlines… not The Seven Ways to Improve Your Headlines.

Skim read that again and see for yourself how powerful the number is!!

Use numbers!

NOTE: some advocate numerals under 10 should be written out in full… six not 6 and everything over 10 is ok as numerals… 19 not nineteen.

For me it's a situation specific choice. But as this book proves, I have a bias towards the numeral.

These 3 copy levers to pull

Your crash course to boost conversions starts… now…

Having worked as a deputy principal in high schools and 20 years teaching teenagers, plus my time as one of Australia's leading boxing writers and my decade + in the trenches writing winning promotions for some of Australia's biggest marketers and companies, including an ASX listed top 200 company which retained my services for more than 18 months, has left me with a unique skillset and view on what it takes to create success.

Yes, it's been a hell of a ride but one my clients leverage all the time. For example, I've just returned from Brisbane to help one of my clients plan sales training for their team.

Cut. What have I done there?

It's lever #1. Tell your story. It happens too often in copy I critique there's no sense of history and therefore connection to the present and why you're here. People need to know about you. They need to continually be reminded of why they chose you to do business with. Your story does this. They chose you for a reason, there is a connection there… tell your story, often. It's true we get sick of telling it long before people get sick of hearing it. So make sure you pull lever #1.

And… Notice it doesn't have to be pages… I told my story just then in a couple of sentences.

Lever #2?

No story here… just a straight telling… make headlines newsworthy. People thrive on new and interesting stuff, so always look for a new angle. You don't want to be "just"… as in just another product or discount of a product.

"New real estate investment opportunity yields 11% pa or more guaranteed" is better than **"House and land packages start at $450,000"**.

See the difference? One has curiosity. The other has been done before, to death. So lever #2… always look for a newsworthy angle.

Lever #3 is clarity… as in NO CONFUSION… make all instructions in your call to action straightforward. Be clear what you want them to do and tell them in as few words as possible. It can be a fragile time for them, so you need to make it easy for them.

Crash course endeth.

Hook 'em!

L et's talk angles or hook for ads…

That new or different twist that stops a reader and compels them to look deeper.

To be clear there is no right or wrong, it's about trying different things.

Let's get your creative juices started with these 5 examples of ad hooks…

- Good thing is actually bad (eg Is kale healthy for you?)
- Credibility + says this (eg Naturopath: Do this 3 times a week to XYZ)
- The new trend (eg Why Aussie Homeowners are ditching [some popular thing])
- Contrarian (eg What this [popular thing] does to your [desired result])
- Fast results (eg When you do this thing daily, THIS happens)

Try them out and see how your ads perform

Sticky

T he numbers are big. At least they appear so on the surface…

- 14,102,102 files scanned and secured
- 847,271 file reputations monitored
- 164 downloads analysed

They come from my "Monthly Protection Report" from my anti-virus software.

There was a bunch of other numbers there I won't bore you with other than to make the point about…

"STICKABILITY".

You see once the sale is made in any business, but especially long-term or ongoing relationships, there is a need to "keep selling them".

One way is monthly "see the work we've done for you" reports like this.

And I share this with you today to prompt thinking around the principle of "stickiness" or "stickability" and…

How you can do this better in your business.

If I'm honest…

Times when deals have dropped off or ended sooner than they may have, this is one area I've been lacking in.

I haven't "re-sold" them… or at least reminded them of the value they received… enough times.

So over to you to see how and where in your business you can leverage "stickability".

Confuse 'em, you lose 'em

Each marketing piece should have 1 purpose and 1 purpose only.

Seer this into your mind: CONFUSED PEOPLE DO NOTHING.

So…

Is your message clear?

Are YOU clear about why you are writing?

Is what you want them to do clear and easy?

Is the value they get clear?

Is the pain of NOT acting spelled out?

Have you turned the light on and told them what happens, so they don't feel like they are walking into a dark room?

Lack of clarity is huge and responsible for many a lost sale.

Have someone read your copy. If they raise questions, chances are your market will too.

Clarity, clarity, clarity.

The alcoholic relative no one ever spoke about

H e used to scare the hell out me. As a kid playing in the yard, the old man next door would sit on his front steps, cigarette in one of those black plastic filters hanging from the corner of his mouth and call out…

"Steve! Young Steve. Come here for a minute."

I'd tentatively navigate my way around the hedge that separated our houses, butterflies in stomach.

You see old Bluey, as he was known in the neighbourhood, was an alcoholic. The yelling matches, accompanied by loud bangs he'd have with his wife when she got sick of him on the sauce AGAIN, frightened me. He'd usually call me over when he dropped his lighter under the stairs. My good deed getting it for him was always rewarded with a shiny 20 cent coin, a small fortune in those days (hey, c'mon, it was the early 70s).

Not sure about you but when I was growing up it seemed relatively common…

More than one family I knew had an alcoholic father, uncle, older brother, sometimes mother. We all "knew". We were often scared by it. But no one ever spoke openly about it. It was like some family secret too painful to mention, at least openly. Yet most understood why said father/uncle/brother/mother was rarely seen at social functions…

What's this got to do with business? Thought you'd never ask, my padawan. You see the story is very similar to your customers…

They will have some unspoken fear, an "alcoholic uncle" always in the background that eats away at them, which they rarely mention. But it's there. And if you can find out what it is and offer a solution for that very deep, very real, unspoken fear…

Then you can connect better than your competitors. You can convert better than your competitors. And you can virtually put yourself in a category of "1" which is the best, most influential place to be.

Quick copy tip [38 second read]

This tip boosts response, big time.

And yes, it gets back to, ahem, size.

In almost every case - "almost" - long copy produces a better response than short copy. It's a "known" fact in direct response circles. Ok, opt-in pages is an exception, granted. Native ads too. Ok, ok...

There is one other place where "short" is better than "long".

The first paragraph.

More often than not, a short punchy opening of 3 to 7 words helps the reader "get into" your message fast.

They often make a decision to read on based on what that first sentence says... and yes, it gets back to the age-old mantra of the job of the headline is to get them to read the first sentence... the job of the first sentence is to get them to read the next sentence and so on.

Thought for today...

Pay closer attention to your opening sentence in every message you send.

Notice my lead sentence is only 6 words... designed to make you read on to find out what the tip is coz there's a payoff for you... better response.

Can you shorten your openings for greater impact?

Secret to headline glory revealed

Recently I wrote a 2-word headline that produced a $71,000 sale for a client who sells sheds to farmers. It wasn't the first iteration of the headline. So where did the headline come from? As in how did I come up with it.

Truth:

I didn't.

The two words came from the mouth of my client. One success secret for me is this…

Always have a pen and paper ready when speaking to a client…

AND…

Have your marketing radar "up" and actively listen to what they say.

Because they will drop, without knowing it, key words and phrases that are "out of the ordinary" but roll off the tongue like everyone uses them. And because these key phrases "just come out" in conversation, they can be easily missed.

You need to be alert for them. You need to write them down.

I estimate from a page of notes over, say a 30-minute consult, you get maybe 2 or 3 useful phrases this way… natural, in their own words, that roll off the tongue.

And if you can use these in your sales copy you get instant emotional connection, because they are words and phrases the market uses, almost without knowing.

So yeah, radar up is key. Don't get mentally lazy, you never know what you might miss.

The mother of all mistakes + fun resource to fix it

This powerful sales tool is often missed, so here's a quick reminder.

The error is... drum roll please...

To NOT include one of the most powerful sales forces in your headline...

CURIOSITY.

Here's why rookies often miss it... Yes, and I'm big on this in any trainings I run, your headline must answer WIIFM (what's in it for me). But many leave it at that. Often this isn't enough. You need a strong curiosity factor that teases your prospect to want to find out more. Remember John Carlton's famous "one-legged golfer" headline...

So remember, curiosity is a POWERFUL sales force. People want to know the answers to secrets. The curiosity factor compels them to read on or open the email. Want more ideas?

Here's a cool and fun little resource I stumbled across to help give you inspiration. There's some real curiosity inducing crackers like...

"Horny roo stalks NT women" – what the, I've gotta find out more!! Or ...

"Man nearly killed by croc pee" – how the... Or even...

"Man arrested after cops spot suspiciously small package in his undies" – ok, Tiny, I need the answer!!

You get the idea.

For inspiration just Google "NT News" and click on "images". There are hundreds of pics of the front page with these types of high curiosity headlines ("Man stabbed with fish" and "Horny ghost haunts house" etc). And it's a lot of fun.

Word of caution: use these for inspiration only. Cute, clever headlines rarely work in direct response marketing.

So use resources like this when you need inspiration to crank up the curiosity factor. Just one idea can change the game.

TMS

H ere's a quick clarifier and way to keep your message simple and easily understood.

TMS

Hey?

Simple…

What do you offer that's different and provides a compelling reason to say yes?

If you need help crafting your message around this, give the TMS acronym a go…

T = Transformation… in other words, what does your thing do?

M = Mechanism… or how does it do it?

S = Speed… naturally how fast it does it (at least compared to others in your space)

Pretty simple, right?

And you can build a solid sales argument around these 3 pillars.

Ok then, over to you to go forth and TMS.

Cracker writing tip from Hemingway

Here's a gift about writing from the great Ernest Hemingway. He said…

"THE FIRST DRAFT OF ANYTHING IS SHIT."

Not much to add to that really.

So when you write, write.

When you edit, edit.

Don't mix the two.

And don't despair if you hate what you see first time round… channel the great man… and fix it up AFTER the first draft.

The other trap to fall into is to compare your first draft to a piece of copy that's reportedly brought in millions of dollars in sales. Rest assured the winning copy you're comparing yours to did NOT look like that at the first draft stage.

But it's easy to do an apples to oranges "mine's crap, yours is great" comparison in the moment which can seriously dent your confidence.

Heed Mr Hemingway's words.

How to create flow

A powerful way to create flow in your copy is to add connectors. These are the short 2 to 5-word phrases that break up longer sentences. As their name suggests, these phrases join ideas together so the copy flows better

Here's what I mean...

That sentence is an example by the way!

Here are 5 more...

1. Listen up...

2. Let me say that again...

3. Let's face it...

4. Want proof?

5. Yes, it's true...

These promote a fast read and keep your copy conversational.

Frantic text from a child late at night

When the phone pings late at night and you see it's from one of your kids, your heart skips a beat. Mind you, what's now considered "late" is getting, well, earlier and earlier...

Anyways, flashback to a Saturday night and eldest, Eliza, shoots through a message via WhatsApp (yep, I'm out there). She gushed about the meet and greet she was at, including photo op with Julia Michaels. My response:

Who's Julia Michaels?

Apparently an up and coming singer who was performing at Brisbane's Tivoli. Eliza and her friends had paid extra for the after gig meet and greet... chat with the performer, get a few selfies etc. Tickets to the gig were in the vicinity of $80... for the meet and greet, $120. Which is a nice little marketing lesson/reminder...

In every market there exists a group of people who want and are willing to pay for a PREMIUM service.

If you don't have a premium offer, truth is, you are leaving cash on the table. Think about it like this...

In the concert space, they do the work to get the bums on seats, so it makes sense to EASILY boost their coffers by offering a premium to people who are already sold, already there, already excited.

More:

The music industry is a good one to study. For example, every big concert now leverages FOMO (fear of missing out) where a small number of tickets is released in "pre-sale". This gets fans excited, gets them activated, and for those who don't get one of the limited pre-sale tickets, gets them motivated for when the tickets go on sale proper. It always pays to have your "radar up" to see what goes on in other industries, so you can adapt them for your own.

From music... pre-sale and upsell/premium offer are just two.

Sometimes, it's little reminders like this, acted on by you, that can move the needle in your sales VERY fast. And no, I don't think I'll ever quite get used to late night messages from my kids, even if they contain (unintended) marketing lessons!

Make it easy for them

It's important to make the sale as easy as possible for your prospects. Any friction in your process reduces response because it becomes too hard.

I've lost count of the number of times I've bought something online only for there to be some glitch. When the glitch was pointed out and fixed, I had every intention of buying but never did... I got busy or lost interest... the friction made the sale hard.

Apart from ironing out technical glitches, another way to make it easy for prospects and customers is to give them multiple means of contact.

Never assume. Always test.

I remember several years ago a client in the property investment space ran lead generation ads every second Tuesday in a major daily metropolitan newspaper. They offered a free investor's guide.

To get a copy, prospects were given the choice of going to a website to fill out a form to request a copy, ring a recorded message and leave details or fill out a coupon in the ad and mail it to the business.

They tested this. When they ran the ad WITHOUT the coupon their response went down by something like 29%. Yes wow.

Now for the life of me I could never work out why someone would bother to find a pair of scissors cut out a small coupon, find a pen, write their details in the small spaces, find an envelope, lick a stamp, go to the post office, and mail the thing. Why would you do that? Answer? Who cares. They did.

So never assume or put your own biases onto your marketing. Let the people you are selling to decide. Give them multiple means of contact and let them choose which one suits them.

Your response rates will say "thank you".

How to "Apple" your message

A re the benefits of what you sell clear to your reader?

I mean 100% crystal clear?

Or do you focus on features?

Quick example…

Apple's original iPod ads listed the features of…

"Storage for 1GB of MP3s"

Response was so-so.

The change up?

"1,000 Songs in Your Pocket"

Which compels you more?

No contest, right?

So do you sell more of the features?

Maybe it's time to "Apple your message" and sell the benefits?

PS Even global giants don't get it right all the time, and nor should you expect to.

The gift in it

F ailure hurts. You aren't human if you don't get "that" feeling in your gut when...

A relationship sours.

A business deal you were about to close falls over.

A client engagement doesn't work out even though it appeared perfect at the start.

Or a campaign you've put months into doesn't get the results you thought it would.

It sucks.

But here's the thing...

In amongst all that hurt, turmoil, confusion and negative energy, there will be a gift in there, if you look.

A learning. A closing of a door to open up a new one. A better opportunity you wouldn't have had the time or energy to see.

Life and business is full of ups and downs. Even nature has her seasons. So when it's a down time or 'winter' season in your business, look for the gift, there's always one there.

Oh yes, and make sure you take time to acknowledge and celebrate your successes. Onward!

Final word

And so, we come to the end, theoretically 366 days after you started this book. The reality though is you have probably finished it sooner, which is great. It also means, this is more of a beginning than an end, a start of "greater influence" for you in business or marketing or copywriting.

If you've integrated the messages here, you are a different person to the one who opened the book for the first time. Your thinking will have shifted. Your skills will have improved. And the way you look at business and the world of marketing will have expanded. So yes, this is a new start.

It's my wish that you get out there and implement what you've learned because there is no greater force for good on the planet than free enterprise in the hands of the right people.

Thank you for your presence here. May you take your new knowledge and use it to shine your light on the world and amplify your influence and impact.

Best wishes for the journey ahead.

Steve

Free & Helpful resources

I f you'd like more help to grow your influence and sales go to

www.theinfluentialmarketer.org/resources

When you enter your email address you'll get access to the vault of resources at no charge:

- **"The One Thing" to generate Deal Flow:** if you've ever been stuck for how to reach out to prospects – or – you feel your business is in a flat spot then access this 11-point weekly action list that gets you back on track fast

- **My comprehensive 42-point Copywriting Critique Checklist:** what to look for when you review your written messages… broken into key parts… Headline – Offer – Proof – Copy. Just one or two things identified and tweaked could be the difference between success and failure

- **How to close more sales recorded training:** discover the 7 ways to present price so you show up in the market the right way and move more people to a "yes". Duration: 44.08 minutes

- **The "10 Read Throughs" that turn average content into high quality and high converting messages:** more than the "mechanics" of writing, when used in conjunction with the 42-point checklist, it elevates your thinking and communication skills to a new level

- **How good is your headline?** Free online sites that help you test your headlines – an invaluable resource for anyone who writes plus they are simple and easy to use

- **Copywriting Deep Dive:** an interview where Steve appeared on the same show as Gary V, Richard Branson, Arnold Schwarzenegger, Eric Thomas, and others! Duration 25.41 minutes

Plus more! The page is added to regularly.

Acknowledgements

I 'd like to thank the following people who've helped me over the years, either via personal connection and mentoring, advice and support, books and trainings, or some other way, I'm forever indebted to you for passing on your skills and knowledge. There's a saying that success is about standing on the shoulders of giants. And for me, this has certainly been the case, so I'd like to acknowledge the role these "giants" have played in my success:.

Mal Emery, Dan Kennedy, Bret Thomson, Gary Halbert, Gary Bencivenga, Pete Godfrey, Shaune Clarke, John Dwyer, Frank Kern, Ben Settle, Bob Bly, Michael Masterson, Oren Klaff, Kelvin Parker, Simon Bowen, George Bakrnchev, Colin Cooper, Russell Brunson, Adam & SJ, Donna Sutor, Jay Abraham, Brian Kurtz, Cam Roberts, Glenn Twiddle…

… and if I've left you off the list, humblest apologies, it's an accident not a deliberate 'forgetting'.

About The Author

Steve Plummer
Marketing Strategist, Copywriter,
Coach, Author, Speaker

S teve is a master in the art of marketing strategy and sales language. He has consulted to and written promotions for just about every type of business from start-ups to major national speaker tours and even the corporate world where an ASX listed top 200 company retained his services for more than 18 months.

He has devised strategy and written copy that has produced sales collectively in the 10s of millions of dollars.

Steve's energy and wisdom makes him a prized guest on podcasts, Facebook lives, workshops and seminars.

A former high school Head of Faculty and Deputy Principal, Steve is widely regarded as a gifted and intuitive teacher who loves nothing more than mentoring others in groups large or small, to bring out their brilliance and genius. He also regularly runs training courses teaching the art of sales language (aka copywriting).

Steve lives on the beautiful Sunshine Coast with his wife Jenny, four young-adult children (when they are home) and a gentle little white ball of fluff named Tilly. When not writing or working with clients he can be found at the beach bodysurfing, fishing or walking. He spends the rest of his downtime reading, writing poetry, and exploring the spiritual side of life.

More information at: www.symmetrymarketing.com.au